Théroigne de Méricourt

Théroigne de Méricourt.
From a painting in the Musée Carnavalet

Théroigne de Méricourt
Woman of the French Revolution

ILLUSTRATED

Frank Hamel

LEONAUR

Théroigne de Méricourt
Woman of the French Revolution
by Frank Hamel

ILLUSTRATED

First published under the title
A Woman of the Revolution, Théroigne De Méricourt

Leonaur is an imprint of Oakpast Ltd

Copyright in this form © 2021 Oakpast Ltd

ISBN: 978-1-78282-892-1 (hardcover)
ISBN: 978-1-78282-893-8 (softcover)

http://www.leonaur.com

Publisher's Notes

Contents

Preface

In writing the biography of a "Woman of the Revolution" I found myself face to face with a great difficulty. It was either necessary to presume a more thorough knowledge of the events of 1789-93 on the part of my readers than is general, or make constant digressions from the main theme of my story as it proceeded. Inequalities have resulted from a vain endeavour to avoid these pitfalls. Inequalities, however, are to be expected when stirring incidents taking place against a background fraught with huge possibilities are viewed through the eyes of a single figure of the crowd. That figure is of a woman who has more claim to recognition for her personal characteristics than for her performance of outstanding actions either noble or valorous.

One of Théroigne's chief charms lies in her elusiveness. While she has remained practically unknown to English readers, the French have never lost interest in the doings of a woman of whom they knew little that was authentic and in whom their curiosity was aroused by the imaginative accounts of Lamartine, Lairtullier, and Lamothe-Langon, on the one hand, and the coarse satires of the royalist pamphlets and journals on the other.

Before the publication of Théroigne's *Confessions* in 1892 by M. Strobl-Ravelsberg, all that had been written concerning her early life was little better than conjecture. But since that date several biographers, amongst them M. Marcellin Pellet, M. le Vicomte de Reiset, and notably M. Leopold Lacour (whose work is very valuable), have all done much to drag forth from the mists of obscurity and tradition the history of a woman who was neither a fiend in human form, as she has frequently been depicted, nor yet a *houri* of transcendent charms and beauty. The latter misconception is speedily dispelled by one account of her appearance, which credits her with "a wrinkled little face, a mischievous expression which suited her down to the ground, and one of those turned-up noses which may affect the fate of nations." The implication of her wickedness also falls away in the light of the remarks of one of her enemies, who summed up her attitude by saying:

> It is difficult to draw the line between sentiment and policy in her case. She is capable of anything when she wishes to be pleasant and useful to those who engage her affections. Her extreme simplicity goes as far as abandonment. . . . She is made for love and close intimacy.

The dramatic possibilities of Théroigne's life were turned to account in 1902 by M. Paul Hervieu, the title-role of his drama being interpreted by Mme Sarah Bernhardt. The stage version led to a discussion of its heroine and brought to light the fact that the real Théroigne was a striking figure, passionate, eloquent, determined, fearless, and loyal; a lover of liberty, the people's friend, and an advocate of her sisters' cause. It has been said of her that she was not a heroine in the best sense, that her faults were too glaring, her standard of morality too low, that she had little nobility, and only enough purity of purpose to redeem her obvious shortcomings to some extent.

But she possessed adaptability and resource, and better still versatility. From village maiden and humble *vachère*, who wandered in the green meadows or washed linen on the river banks, she became courtesan and *virtuosa*, adorned with fine robes and resplendent in diamonds. Then, impelled by the rush of events, she turned patriot and reformer, lavishing the remains of her wealth on the altar of her adopted country. She followed with unabated interest the work of the National Assembly, she became an orator of the streets and a partisan of the Girondins. The common people, soldiers, deputies, even nobles and princes were influenced by her personality. She was carried away by the same fanaticism that led many to the scaffold, but her fate was even more terrible than theirs, for she became lost in mania. Brilliant at the beginning of her career, she was caught in a tangle of unbridled passions and drawn into a whirl of terror and bloodshed.

Thus, it was said of her that she typified the spirit of the Revolution. Perhaps truth is strained in this search for an effective symbol. But side by side with the legendary Théroigne who stalks through the moving scenes of the late eighties and early nineties like a demon possessed, slaying and leading others to slaughter, plotting against the life of Marie-Antoinette, and suffering at the hands of the enraged Jacobins women, is the no less interesting and far more realistic figure of the Théroigne of the streets, in her neat riding-dress and feathered cap, deftly handling her pike and haranguing the mob from the tribunes of the clubs, joining in the *fêtes* of Liberty and raising the voice that had been trained for the concert-hall in the inspiring revolutionary hymns. This Théroigne, with her captivating ways of cajoling, bribing, and threatening by turns, is the one to know and to love. The work she did for the people's cause was not valueless because it was sometimes misdirected, and the enthusiasm with which she inspired the crowd was not to be despised because, through no fault of her own, the liberty she and others worked for degenerated into licence.

Frank Hamel.

London, 1911

CHAPTER 1

The Peasant

A journey by post-chaise through the Ardennes was at all seasons a laborious undertaking in the eighteenth century. Only the most determined travellers cared to attempt it when the hilly forest roads were rendered almost impassable by snow and ice. In the February of 1791 two purposeful gentlemen were making their way in wintry weather towards the frontiers of Luxemburg. They were French *émi-grés*, although nothing in their appearance proclaimed this fact. They preferred to be on Austrian soil. On the evening of the fifteenth of the month they reached Liège, but the urgency of their expedition made it impossible for them to halt, in spite of fatigue and hunger, and they pushed on half a league farther to the little village of La Boverie.

Their mission demanded secrecy. Leaving the carriage, they proceeded on foot to the straggling cottages which, together with the little church and a single inn, composed the village. The inn was their destination; it bore the sign of the "White Cross." Midnight had already struck, but the travellers did approach the house until the night-watchman had gone his rounds and all was silent. Then they knocked at the door.

"Who is there?" inquired someone within.

"Open in the name of his Imperial Majesty," was the command.

A frightened innkeeper admitted the strangers.

"You have a lady staying here? Show us to her room without delay."

The innkeeper's hesitation vanished at a threat. Unceremoniously the strangers entered the apartment he indicated. Within all was silent save for the regular breathing of a woman asleep.

The noise had not awakened her, but when a torch was brought in the light made her open her eyes. Seeing two strange men in her room, she sat up in bed and asked them to account for their presence there.

"I do not know you, gentlemen," she began. "What do you want with me? It is odious to disturb people at this time of night."

One of the intruders answered courteously enough: "I am commissioned by the emperor, *mademoiselle*, to remove you to a place of safety. Dress yourself and follow us."

The young woman was not satisfied with this reply. She asked for more particulars.

"You have enemies, *mademoiselle*. Your life is in danger. Your whereabouts have been traced. Those are coming who would capture you. You must flee, and at once. We will protect you."

"You! By what right do *you* constitute yourselves my protectors?"

"By the right of friendship, pretty one. By the right of nationality. Being Austrians, we desire to guard you against your enemies the French aristocrats."

In the meantime, the speaker's companion made a thorough search of the room. Clothes, books, letters—all the occupant's personal belongings, in short—were heaped together ready for removal.

Helpless and bewildered, the young woman could do nothing to prevent this ruthless handling of her property. Her mild protests were unheeded. She was told that her papers, if they were left behind, would lead to her capture.

When she was dressed and had eaten some food, which was hurriedly put before her, she was taken to the carriage.

"But of what could my worst enemies accuse me?" she asked when told to take her place in the vehicle.

"Of a very serious crime—of being implicated in a plot to kill the Queen of France."

"It is a lie. I know nothing about it. All I know is that the people hate the queen."

"Why?"

"For one thing, she is Austrian—a foreigner. She does not understand the people's needs. Besides, the Austrians—" and then, remembering her companions had claimed to be of that nationality, she lapsed discreetly into silence.

A passing suspicion grew into a certainty. Her companions' offhand manners had already given her food for reflection, and she realised very soon that her supposed friends were nothing of the kind. They were her captors, and in calling themselves Austrians they had misrepresented the truth.

In due course the ill-assorted travellers reached Coblenz, where Metternich, the famous father of a more famous son, was then staying. This Austrian minister had French sympathies and was disposed to be friendly to the little colony of *émigrés* settled in that town.

The day after their arrival the two men asked for an audience with the minister, and informed him of what they had done.

"I congratulate you, gentlemen," replied Metternich when he heard their story, "but your work is not yet finished. You must conduct the prisoner to Freiburg in Breisgau."

These instructions were obeyed. They were followed by others, stating that the captive was to be conveyed to the fortress of Kufstein. On March 17th, under the name of Mme Théobald, she was received there by the governor himself. She had lost her last chance of escape.

Two months passed. Then one day a carriage drawn by four horses dashed up to the prison gates and out stepped an examining magistrate.

"How is Mme Théobald?" was his first question.

"She is only fairly well," was the reply.

Before long the newcomer was taken to the prisoner's cell. He was surprised by her charm and youthful appearance. The purpose of his visit was to hear her life-history from her own lips. With a wave of the hand he dismissed the jailer who had accompanied him, and was left alone with the prisoner.

Fixing his steady gaze upon her, he said, "You are Mlle Théroigne de Méricourt, are you not?"

"Yes, I am she," replied the prisoner simply.

★★★★★★

The story she told, supplemented from other sources, some more, some less reliable, was full of strange vicissitudes, of ups and downs in fortune, of struggles and of aspirations—the story of a waif and stray of lowly birth, who was carried by forces stronger than herself amidst scenes of bloodshed and horror into which were drawn at the same time the very highest in the land of France.

Born on August 13th, 1762, at Marcourt on the Ourthe, in the province of Luxemburg, some forty miles from Liége, Anne-Josèphe was the daughter of Pierre Terwaine or Terwagne and his wife Elisabeth Lahaye. Terwagne became the more euphonious Théroigne in French, and Anne-Josèphe added de Méricourt from the name of the village where she was born—a name, she said, for which she had never

13

had cause to blush. Some biographers have called her Lambertine, but there appears to be no authority for this appellation, nor was it a recognised nickname.

Anne-Josèphe was the eldest of the family and was born a year after the marriage of her parents. She had two brothers; Pierre-Joseph, born on December 25th, 1764, and Joseph on September 28th, 1767. Three months later Mme Terwagne died, and, after being a widower for six years, her husband married again and reared a second family of nine children, the eldest of whom was born in 1774.

Terwagne was a well-to-do peasant, but he engaged in lawsuits and unsuccessful speculations, and his affairs became so much involved that he had to mortgage or sell his land.

When Anne-Josèphe was left motherless she went to stay with an aunt at Liège. There she was sent to a convent school, and learnt to sew. She made her first communion about this time. After she had been at school for a year her aunt married, and refused to pay any more school fees. She made her niece work in the house, and turned her into a domestic drudge. Presently she was set to mind the children. Anne-Josèphe fled from Liège back to her father's house, only to find that her new stepmother treated her no better than her aunt had done. Then she and her two brothers fled from the paternal roof

The elder of the boys went to Germany, and stayed with relatives of the name of Campinados. This name is worth noting, because Mlle Théroigne admitted that she presently assumed it herself. Her younger brother accompanied her to Xhoris, in the principality of Stavelot, now in the province of Liège, to stay with connections of her father's. Here, too, her lines seemed to have fallen in unpleasant places. She was now thirteen years old, and was forced to work very hard, harder almost than her strength allowed; nor did she find compensation in the affection of her relatives. Feeling life to be unendurable, she returned to her aunt's house at Liège, but was treated there no better than before.

Once more it became necessary to make a fresh start. In the face of her aunt's protests, and sacrificing all her childish possessions, Théroigne escaped from the conditions she found insupportable and went to Sougné, in the province of Limburg, where she learnt to herd cows. In this humble calling she spent a year, when, actuated once more by the uncontrollable restlessness which seems to have been one of her chief characteristics, she went back to Liège and took a situation as a seamstress. Still dissatisfied, she begged hospitality of another aunt of the name of Calment, at Xhoris.

But no sooner had she arrived there than she became acquainted with a strange lady, who apparently took a fancy to her, and asked her to accompany her to Antwerp and take charge of her little daughter. Her new employer, however, did not wish to pay Théroigne's expenses from Xhoris to Antwerp. Théroigne appealed to her Aunt Clamend, who sided with the girl's grandmother in advising her not to travel so far with a lady about whom she knew nothing.

Théroigne insisted, and won the day, her aunt finally contributing towards the travelling expenses. Some weeks later Mlle Théroigne's new mistress abandoned her at the inn where they had been staying in Antwerp, and she might have been left destitute had it not been for an English lady at the same place, a certain Mme Colbert, who interested herself in the girl's forlorn position and engaged her as a companion and governess to her children.

Théroigne was now sixteen. She had more charm than actual beauty. She was well grown, but not tall, with bright eyes and chestnut-coloured hair, rosy cheeks, and a wonderful vivacity that seemed inexhaustible. Never for a moment was she dull or inactive. When she was happy, she blossomed like a flower on which the sun shines. There was a sparkle in her eyes, alertness in every change of expression, and life in every gesture. She often hummed at her work, and she spoke at this time in the language of the Walloon peasants, which, crude as it may be, sounded like music when uttered by her tuneful voice.

There was harmony and a sense of completeness about Théroigne which made it difficult to remember that she was only an uneducated girl of the lower classes. Concerning the extent of her knowledge at this period it is difficult to discover anything definite. The most that can be said is that she possessed an insatiable love of learning. She had been for a short while in a convent school, but the fact that she had moved from place to place in her youth made it impossible that she should have had much opportunity of study.

Her letters, even of later years, are not the letters of a well-taught individual; but many of the best-trained women of that day disclosed the same faults in writing. She confessed that when a young woman she was very ignorant, and could hardly read or write; but this admission was made under examination in prison, when it was to her advantage to feign to be illiterate. The appointment of governess which she claimed to have filled is no guide as to her own attainments, as her teaching, if it existed at all, was probably most elementary. But anyone who knew the value of education as Théroigne did—for she continually exhorted her brothers to make the most of their chances, even at the cost of working all night long—was bound to make the best of her many opportunities of acquiring information. She was soon to travel, to live in luxury in several of the capitals of Europe, to study operatic singing, to consort with well-informed men, to acquire books and music, and to gather experience from the wide field of human struggles and human sorrows; so that, taking into account a natural aptitude for assimilating knowledge, Théroigne cannot be regarded as ignorant or stupid, although she was by no means brilliant intellectually.

Her benefactress, Mme Colbert, was the first to discover her genuine musical talent, and to turn it to account by allowing her to train her voice. For four years Théroigne remained in the household of this lady, who treated her kindly. During that period, they stayed at Ghent, Malines, and Brussels, and from there they travelled to London. All this time Théroigne's relatives had no idea of her whereabouts, and she gave as an excuse for not writing to tell them her ignorance of this ordinary accomplishment. But the truth was probably a little more complex. We have only Théroigne's own word to go upon as to the way in which the years of her early womanhood were spent. She did not wish to divulge anything that happened to her, for very obvious reasons.

In London a foretaste of romance came into her life. A rich young Englishman who visited Mme Colbert's house began paying court to her in a manner she felt to be honest and, at the same time, delicate. He was good-looking, persuasive, apparently in earnest, and he uttered words of passionate love to this charming untutored girl of twenty. Realising the difference in their positions, Mme de Colbert, who took a motherly interest in Théroigne, warned her to be on her guard, and finally, when the young man insisted on continuing his importunities, she forbade him the house. But he never ceased to write passionate love-letters to the object of his adoration—Théroigne does not say that she was unable to read these—and he walked up and down outside the house for hours in the hope of catching a glimpse of the woman who had fascinated him. Théroigne followed the wise counsels which had been given her, and sent back his letters with a message that he must write to her no more. She confessed artlessly that it would have hurt her terribly if he had obeyed. For a whole year his attentions in no way relaxed, and his constancy inspired in her a love as keen as his own.

One evening Mme Colbert was out. The young man made his

way into the house, and with passionate insistence begged Théroigne to elope with him. At first, she protested, but he would not take her refusals, and continued to make advances which she found it difficult to repel. She was on the point of screaming for help, when he put his hand over her mouth to silence her, and carried her off by main force to the carriage which he had waiting. Théroigne spoils this dramatic account of her abduction by adding that his promises sounded sincere, and her affection for him stifled her prudence. She was not an entirely unwilling victim therefore. Her chief sentiment appears to have been a feeling of regret at leaving her protectress in this unexpected and seemingly ungrateful manner.

The eloping couple, according to Théroigne's account, went to live upon the young man's estate near London, where they were to have been married. Her abductor was not of age, and how he came to have an estate of his own is not explained. At any rate, he was expecting soon to be in possession of a considerable fortune. He thought the wise course to take was to wait until he had inherited his money before entering into a marriage with a penniless bride of no family without his parents' consent, feeling certain that such a step would meet with their entire disapproval. Théroigne admits in her rather confused narrative that, had she wished it, she was sure he would have married her then and there in spite of everything. She preferred to wait, so that he should not risk the loss of his fortune.

When at length they were in possession of the money it brought them no happiness. Théroigne's lover turned out to be a spendthrift. He took her to Paris, and there lavished his money on luxury and vice. Théroigne did her best to check this taste for excess, but was unable to arrest his downward career. Feeling certain that it was impossible to hope for her lover's reform as long as he remained among his boon companions in Paris, she did everything she could to persuade him to return to England. At last he agreed to this plan.

"If," says Mlle Théroigne naively, "I had married my lover when we were back in England, we might very easily have remained happy until this day." But vice had eaten into his heart. He no longer cared for the simple joys of the country. He returned to London, and left his mistress behind. She, feeling assured that it would not be for her happiness to bind her life irretrievably to that of this dissolute young man, decided to flee from him. This she did, not without much grief, for she still loved him. It was the year 1787.

Her lover had behaved very generously to her. She was now in possession of a sum of two hundred thousand *livres*. She placed forty or fifty thousand *livres*, according to her own statement, out at interest in the hands of a friend.

There is probably a great deal of truth in this version of Théroigne's lapse from the path of strict virtue, yet it must be accepted with caution. Was the young Englishman of wealth and position her first lover? He was not her only lover. Another story which bears as little guarantee of scrupulous accuracy as Théroigne's was told by the Baron de Mengin-Salabert, who arrived at Kufstein in possession of a detailed report of her past life made out in connection with the procedure of the *Châtelet* as to her doings on the famous 5th and 6th of October, 1789.

The little one, when about thirteen years of age, had herded cows, said the clean-shaven, powdered baron, who had been a priest until the Revolution had deprived him of his living and sent him to dwell in the Low Countries. Growing weary of her humble station, and feeling within her the power to rise to a very different sphere of life, she determined to go out into the world and seek her fortune. Her first venture was in domestic service at Liège, and this position was not likely to extinguish the fire of her ambition. Quite to the contrary, declared the facetious baron—who enjoyed his joke more than was altogether consistent with one who had belonged to the priesthood—after being a servant she felt herself more than ever capable of playing the role of mistress, and, with this end in view, she made the acquaintance of a young lawyer in the town, who speedily succumbed to her fascination. But growing weary of the arrangement before long, she looked forward to fresh adventures, and in this chance favoured her.

One day when she was washing linen on the banks of the Meuse she began to sing. A romantic chronicler gives some charming details of her appearance. She was wearing a short, striped skirt, and the cambric handkerchief that was pinned across her shoulders left her beautiful white neck and arms bare; no ugly cap hid the luxuriant tresses of her hair, which were loosely tied together with a ribbon. Her eyes shone, and her teeth were like pearls. She was quite alone. Her voice was peculiarly attractive. She gave utterance to a melody which had all the charm of a siren's song. As the last notes died away, she became aware of a listener. Standing behind her was a young Englishman "with a form like Antinous and the head of Adonis." Fascinated and enchanted, the newcomer was not long in remarking that so sweet a maiden was wasted on the menial occupation of washing, and he proposed that she should leave her task and accompany him to Spa.

According to the baron's account, Théroigne showed no coyness, nor did she scruple to leave one protector for another. A promise that her musical abilities should be developed was sufficient to make her throw caution to the winds. After Spa, the Englishman took her to London, and fulfilled his word by giving her a music-master.

She went on the concert-platform and became a successful performer. Abandoned by her lover, continues the baron, she lived alone, and after three or four years spent in London went to Italy.

But here the baron went too fast. His zeal had outstripped his knowledge. He might have dwelt more carefully on the identity of Théroigne's music-master. He knew, apparently, nothing of the visit to Paris.

Théroigne had said very little about the stay there, speaking more fully of her return to London. One indiscreet word she had let fall, however, referring to a certain individual with whom she had had financial dealings in the French capital.

The second journey to London had been arranged so unexpectedly that she had not had time to sell her furniture or to rearrange her investments. She says:

> We left suddenly, to my great contentment, but to the regret of my friends, especially the one who managed my income for me, and who desired to keep me in Paris.

Questions as to this individual being forthcoming, she was obliged to confess, a little reluctantly, that the gentleman had paid her attentions which had not altogether escaped her notice, but because he was elderly she believed that his years precluded any possibility of a warmer affection for her than might safely have been indulged in by an uncle. She had accepted his "more than sympathy" with gratitude and a sense of absolute security. He had shown his affection in a manner suitable to his years and to her position and tastes. He had given her good advice, he had had a say in the matter of her household arrangements, and he wished to teach her French. Nothing could have been more innocent. "From time to time," she adds, in that childlike spirit which is so charming, "I found presents lying on my toilet-table, valuable presents, without my being able to guess how they came to be there, or who was the anonymous donor."

At the moment of leaving Paris she discovered all. The old gentleman was the author of these mysterious gifts.

She did not fail to impress upon her examiners the surprise that she had felt when she knew the truth. She declares:

> He reproached me with my coldness, I confess I thought it very ridiculous that he dared to speak to me in the way he did. The whole thing offended me, and I forced him to take back all his presents. If I had known to whom to send them in the first instance, certainly I should not have kept them for a single moment.

But here Théroigne would have done better to spare her indignation and her hearers' blushes. She implies that there were so many possible sources from which the presents might have come, that to trace their origin would have been no easy task. She continues in her *Confessions*:

> In spite of my honesty, he was not to be deterred from writing to me in England and later to Italy—(letters which she considered most unsuitable)—They wounded me to the last degree, and I made him aware of it. Since then I have had to complain of this man on various grounds. . . .

All the time she knew that several of the letters were in evidence against her. Her judges, after reading them, were obliged to state that her relations with their writer, the Marquis de Persan, were not to be dismissed as lightly as she would have liked them to be.

A deed was in existence concerning the fifty thousand *livres* she was supposed to have placed in the care of the marquis at an interest of ten *per cent*. It was dated April 21st, 1786, and worded as follows:

> Anne Nicolas Doublet de Persan, Chevalier, Marquis de Persan, Comte de Dun and de Pateau, acknowledges his liability to Demoiselle Anne-Josèphe; Théroigne, minor, living in the Rue de Bourbon-Villeneuve, to the extent of an annuity for life of five thousand *livres* exempt from all tax or deduction, payable in two sums, at an interval of six months, this arrangement being made in return for the fifty thousand *livres* which the said Marquis de Persan acknowledges and confesses to have received from the said Demoiselle Théroigne. He is at liberty to liquidate the debt by returning the said sum to her.

Was this document genuine, or, which is more probable, was it a method invented by her protector to save a young woman's reputa-

THÉROIGNE DE MÉRICOURT.

From a painting attributed to Greuze.

tion and at the same; time ensure her a good income? Théroigne kept up; the fiction for several years. She declared she had amassed her little fortune in England and only invested it in Paris. It had been her intention, she said, to return to her father's house under an assumed name, explaining that she was a widow whose husband had left her well provided for. She was prevented from carrying out this scheme by the untimely death of her father, as will presently appear. Her affairs were in the hands of two bankers. One in London, a Mr. Hammersley (she spelt it Hammerslys), was probably a partner in Messrs. Ransom, Morland & Hammersley, of 57, Pall Mall, a firm connected with musical interests who received subscriptions for operas and concerts at that time. The other was a well-known Paris banker, Perregaux (whose name oddly enough is mixed up with the story of the queen's necklace), to whom she wrote voluminous letters, many of them preserved.

Whence her income was really derived it is difficult to be certain, but that she had plenty of money at this period of her life and enjoyed spending it may be regarded as convincing. Both in London and in the Rue de Bourbon-Villeneuve, Paris, she led a life of ease and pleasure; frequenting the opera, supping at restaurants, making a stir wherever she went on account of her youth and beauty, her sparkling eyes and her dazzling diamonds, her pretence of modesty, which revealed, when once dispelled, a happy confidence and a yielding familiarity. She was fresh and lithe and charming, and her reserve melted like snow before the sun of wealth and kindness. Her musical talents were undeniable and they won success both in London and Paris.

It was said that she sacrificed everything for notoriety, for triumph on the concert-platform; that she exercised lavishly her power to gather laurels and inspire violent passions; that she desired to illumine all the gatherings she honoured by her presence as though she herself were their centre, their brilliant sun. Her grace, her originality, the play of her mobile features, her coquetry, taste, and elocution were gifts which ensured the achievement of her aims. Comte Thomas d'Espinchal in his *Journal de Voyages et de Faits relatifs à la Revolution* wrote:

> Persons who like myself used to frequent the theatres and public places of entertainment before 1789, can remember that only a few years previously there often appeared at the Opera, and particularly frequently at the Concert Spirituel, alone in a large box a fair unknown who called herself Mme Campinados, covered with diamonds, having her own carriage, coming

from a foreign country, wearing the air of *une fille entretenue*, but giving no account of the resources at her disposal. This was the same person who, after the Revolution, appeared under the name of Mlle Théroigne de Méricourt.

D'Espinchal, who accused her wrongfully of many excesses and even atrocities, described her as little, not very pretty, and wearing already a somewhat dissipated air, although, he said, she did not then show signs of the ferocious character she exhibited later.

If it were indeed to M. de Persan that Théroigne owed her livelihood, the means by which she obtained her musical training, her luxuries and diamonds, it can only be admitted that she appears in the worst light possible, for she neither loved him, nor did she apparently show the least gratitude to him for all he gave her. The marquis was a personage. Born in 1728, he had become a Councillor of the Parlement of Paris at the age of twenty, and *Maître des Requêtes* in 1754. He married a Mlle Aymeret de Gazeau; and at the time he knew Théroigne, when he was himself nearly sixty years old, he had a son over thirty. He was only distantly connected with Mme Doublet de Persan of *salon* fame, although inaccurate biographers made him out to be her son.

During the continuance of the strange relationship between marquis and peasant-maid—that is to say, for three or four years—there was a constant struggle for the supremacy of the love of the former over the "demon of music" possessed by the latter. But Théroigne was to win the day, and de Persan was left disconsolate and disillusioned. Probably their liaison began in 1785, perhaps in 1784, and before 1787 her affections, if she ever indulged in any towards him, had wandered elsewhere, and the connection was finally broken in the following year. His letters are full of reproaches, and he condemns her for not having kept to her bargain—such a bargain as any courtesan might have made.

You are right in saying that all things here are a matter of exchange, but it is necessary that it should be a fair exchange. You know that my attachment to you will last for ever, and you say in response that the feelings you have for me will be as my behaviour merits. There is no equality about this. When you apparently gave yourself to me, I endeavoured to obtain for you all that you could desire; even going beyond my means to do so. What have I had in return? Often harshness, and never a continuance of the affections which alone give happiness. Have I found this sweet gentleness, this abandonment, this confidence that a man who loves has a right to expect from the woman who is attached to him?

Another time he writes to her:

You will not doubt that it will be a pleasure to me to see you, especially if you will treat me as a cherished lover. But if you put on airs I shall be miserable.

At the end of October 1787, about a month later, he reproaches her anew.

What have I done, dear one, that you should write to me with the coldness which is apparent from your last two letters? I answered you with sentiments of the most sincere attachment. I have always counted on your affection, and I hope that you do not mean to give me cause for grief; to me who have never caused you grief. Have I not always done whatever you wanted? You desire to part from me? You wish to exploit your talent and woo a fortune? Your mind must be wandering! I brought you to a better way of thinking, and you agreed with me when I had a talk with you some time ago. You made me pay a year's more annuity than I owed you, so that you might be furnished with all you required. Nevertheless, I did it.

Grant me a year to pay off the remainder. You might very easily do me this favour. I will pay you every six months, including the interest, and your income as well. Send me a receipt for the half-year as a sign that you agree. It seems to me that I merit this mark of friendship.

As you say you desire to part from me, I expect you to deal me this blow, although I can hardly believe that you will wound me so deeply, for I confess to you that if I saw you exploit your talents and go on the stage you would be destroying the good opinion I have formed of you. I should not think it worthy of you. I sacrificed everything to hinder you from making this mistake in connection with David two years ago. You do not do your true friends justice. If you have decided not to return to France, sell me your furniture. I ask this as a privilege. You will at all events find it ready for you if you return. . . .

This reference to Giacomo David or Davide, the great Italian tenor usually known as "David *le père*," is significant. He was probably the first who inspired Théroigne with a wish to break away from her amorous old protector, the Marquis de Persan.

Born at Presezzo, near Bergamo, in 1750, David was thirty-five when Théroigne met him in Paris in 1785, whither he had come to take part in the concerts *spirituel* which were then at the height of their popularity. These concerts, which had become quite a musical institution in France, dated from the early years of the reign of Louis XV. They were held in the Salle des Suisses of the Tuileries on the occasion of religious festivals when the Opera House was closed; that is to say, not more than twenty-four times in the year. Foreign artists usually met with a courteous and often an enthusiastic reception there. Among the most illustrious who sang in Paris at this period were Cafarelli, Farinelli, Raff, Mme Mara, and Davide.

The first appearance of the last-named was not an unqualified success, owing, it was said, to the fact that the Parisian public was not then accustomed to the florid Italian style. But at least he won one devout admirer. Possessed by the dangerous demon of music already referred to, Théroigne was suddenly seized by the desire to follow Davide to Italy and to sing with him there. Probably the musician, flattered as he may have felt by the girl's evident adoration, was too discreet to take advantage of it.

It is fairly obvious that if he had been a willing partner to any such arrangement, no powers of persuasion exercised by de Persan would have been sufficient to prevent the hot-headed Théroigne's "mistake," even at the cost he mentions of "sacrificing everything." It is far more likely that Davide's domestic ties were too binding to permit him to enter into any compromising connection with a woman, however beautiful. He was rewarded for his discretion in the person of his talented son Giovanni, who earned for his father and teacher the title by which he was known to posterity.

The danger from an attachment to Davide once averted, de Persan expected to recover his former influence over his mistress. In this he was mistaken. Her submission was not to be of long duration. Self-willed, impulsive, whole-hearted in whatever she set out to do, already at the mercy of states of exaltation which were to increase when fed by the excitement of the Revolution, Théroigne soon broke loose and followed the musical tendencies which at that moment called to her more strongly than any other passion.

She describes her return to England, but as regards her life there all is conjecture. In his letters M. de Persan upbraids her for her callous disregard of his wishes that she should remain in France. Was she with a lover, as she declares in her *Confessions*, or was she alone? Was she secretly married? Why should she have concealed the fact? She never admitted having had a daughter, although two receipts were brought forward at her examination in prison which referred to expenses connected with the death of a little girl of the name of Françoise-Louise, otherwise called Mlle Septenville, the daughter of Mlle Anne-Josèphe Théroigne, or Campinados. The documents are dated respectively April 18th and 19th, 1788, and refer to sums of sixty-seven *livres* for a doctor of the name of Cervenon at Paris, and three hundred and sixty *livres* for board and other expenses connected with illness to one called Kertzen. Not a word is there as to the child's age, nor a clue as to its father.

One thing at least is certain with regard to her visit to England. She thought of increasing her means by singing at concerts, and in trying to find the best music-master in London she fell into the clutches of the notorious Tenducci, with whom she was presently to sign a curious agreement.

Tenducci's career in the United Kingdom had been chequered by strange adventures. He was born in 1736, at Siena, and in his youth, steps had been taken to render his voice of a peculiar quality and timbre—a custom which was usual among opera-singers in Italy of that date, and which survived in the choir of the Sistine Chapel until the middle of the last century. About 1760 Tenducci left Italy for England, where he speedily gained a vast reputation as a singer at Covent Garden and elsewhere. He was associated with the celebrated Dr. Arne, and took part with Peretti and Miss Brent in this composer's opera, *Artaxerxes*. In 1764 Walpole heard Tenducci in London, and described him as "a moderate tenor." Not long after this the singer went to Ireland, where he disgraced himself by abducting a young heiress.

Villiers tells the story, more or less accurately, in his *Souvenirs d'un Déporté*; Tenducci, the Italian singer, proud of his successes at the concerts *spirituel* in Paris, came to London, and from thence went to Ireland, where, in spite of his hideous face, this new Abelard managed to please a young heiress and elope with her. This event, which made a great deal of noise, was the occasion for a lawsuit which for many years kept all England interested and amused, and almost ended in the hanging of Tenducci. The laws of the country making no reference to the condition of the singer, the judges were greatly embarrassed. Tenducci maintained that no law prevented him from contracting a legitimate marriage. Everything was arranged, however. The young Irishwoman was returned to her family a virgin, and Tenducci was set free from prison to go back to the stage.

The other side of the story appears in a document printed in 1768 by Mrs. Dora Tenducci, which she entitles *A true and genuine narrative of Mr. and Mrs. Tenducci in a letter to a friend at Bath, giving a full account from their marriage in Ireland to the present time.* This pamphlet appears to be a true account of the persecutions which attended the rash elopement. Tenducci was seized and cast into prison at Cork, Dora was captured and kept in confinement by relatives who brutally ill-treated her. It appears that the lovers had met frequently at a friend's house near Dublin, that Dora's love of music had been the cause of the original friendship, that her parents had invited the tenor to their house, and that he had given her lessons in singing without taking any fees.

This point was of technical importance in the case, for it was endeavoured to prove against Tenducci that he had abducted a pupil. The defence was that the young lady had married him entirely of her own free will. In the *Public Advertiser* for September 16th, 1766, a note occurs in the Irish news to the effect that:

> Mr. Tenducci desires, by a letter from his confinement, as an act of justice, to contradict the mention of his having been a tutor to the young lady whom he married.

The tenor went so far as to state that he never was entertained as a singing- or music-master by any person or persons since he had performed in the kingdom, had never taught the art of singing, and consequently had never had a pupil. Nor was he received by the friends of the young lady—whose name he would not mention but with the utmost respect—on any such footing.

The persecution of the young wedded couple went on for a year. Tenducci was a spendthrift and continually in debt, which fact greatly aggravated the audacity of his attempt to carry off an heiress. At length Dora's father ceased to oppose the match. The young wife's narrative, which had ended in August 1767, received an additional note by September that a remarriage had taken place and that she was allowed to remain with her husband in a chosen retreat.

Another version of this curious episode is to be found in the *Morning Post* for June 16th, 1781, under the title of "Authentic Anecdotes of the celebrated Tenducci." The journal states that:

> About fourteen years ago this remarkable character visited

Ireland, and from his acknowledged capacity in the science of music, added to a natural pleasantry in his disposition, which suited the temper of the natives, he soon became a favourite. The females of *Ierne* are not proof against those tender sensations created by 'concord of sweet sounds'; and Tenducci was so unfortunate as to be the object of a lady's affections, who was beautiful in person, elegant in her manners, a perfect proficient in music, and descended from an ancestry both antient and respectable. After some tender, *stolen* interviews on the subject of *Almighty Love*, an honourable union was agreed upon, and Cupid conducted the fair native of Hibernia to a neighbouring priest, who joined her in wedlock to this *son of Romulus*. It is thought the pages of romantic love do not furnish such another instance of persecution as Tenducci suffered in Ireland, in consequence of this connexion; but it had no other effect upon the fond couple, at that time, than to unite them still stronger in a mutual affection.

After many fruitless efforts made by the family for the purpose of separating them, it was agreed that they should leave the kingdom and *warble* their *woodnotes* in some foreign land for a subsistence. The first place these celebrated fugitives visited after their departure was the capital of Caledonia; here they were received with open arms. Tenducci was remarkable for singing the Scotch music, which, it is acknowledged, reaches the heart with greater force than the compositions of any other nation; and his *bride* was little inferior to him, either in the excellence of her voice, or the elegance of her taste. They continued here for some time, until he was called to London in consequence of an engagement at the Opera. On the expiration of his agreement with the managers, they changed the scene, and visited Italy, mutually participating in all the enjoyments of domestic blandishment. But alas, who can command a life of happiness? The lady, as she advanced in years, had acquired an experience destructive of her peace; she found herself uneasy, and would sit and sigh 'the live long night away.'

Tenducci grew *fatigued* in his turn, and a separation ensued: she returned to England, and shortly after an application was made to the Conclave at Doctors' Commons for a *divorce*, which was obtained to the satisfaction of both parties. On the completion of this business,

Tenducci again visited Britain; and so devoted, says our correspondent, is he to Scotland, that he goes every summer to Edinburgh; no foreigner, we are informed, was ever so hospitably received in that country as Tenducci; and if we are not very much deceived, few people entertain a more grateful sense of past obligations than this disciple of *Calliope*."

Tenducci appears on the scene again some twenty years later in his connection with Théroigne, who, it is to be hoped, knew nothing of the manner of man he was. It is in her favour, perhaps, that he deceived her as he had done many other women. Villiers continues in his account:

> In spite of his age (which was now over fifty) . . . his ugliness, and his still more hideous character, . . . Tenducci doted on our illustrious Comtesse de Campinados. She brought him back to Paris in 1788, and as she then had many diamonds, much silver plate, and a quantity of gold, he took possession of her, refused to leave her, travelled with her to Italy, devoured all her possessions, and died at the end of a year.
>
> Mme Théroigne de Méricourt, having nothing else left, returned to Paris, where, as is well known, she became the *coryphaeus* of Robespierre's *tricoteuses*.

Here mistake is heaped on mistake. Tenducci did not die until the following century, and Théroigne, who was not absolutely ruined by the musician, never joined the furies of the guillotine.

The truth, as far as it can be ascertained, was as follows. In 1785, whilst Théroigne was still presumably under the protection of the Marquis de Persan, though ready to leave him for the first musician or foreigner with musical abilities who presented himself, Tenducci was at the height of his reputation as a teacher, if not as a soloist, in London. In the *Morning Herald* and *Daily Advertiser* for July 2nd of that year, it may be seen that he had under his care "a pupil who promises to become the greatest singer that ever was in this country." This was not Théroigne, but a sister-in-law to the famous Professor Cramer. The journal continues:

> Under so able a hand, we do not doubt that her future fame is assured, particularly when we remember the improvement he has made in the voice of the present first opera woman—so powerful a rival will perhaps bring down the insolence of the supercilious Mara, as well as add honours to Tenducci.

Mme Mara was at the height of her wonderful powers, and, like other famous opera-singers, was inclined to be capricious at times.

Théroigne, then, aflame with her desire to sing before the public, had discovered a musician with a splendid reputation as a producer of *virtuose* available as a teacher. Hideous, repulsive, and a deformity as he must surely have appeared to her, all physical drawbacks were forgotten in her ambition and a passionate devotion to music. She had admittedly taken up her plan of singing in order to earn money. "The more," she adds, with one of her sudden scruples, which appear oddly out of place when viewed in the light of many of her actions, "because in England prejudices against singers hardly exist, or have very little importance. The position is not regarded unfavourably, especially if one limits oneself to singing at concerts."

Tenducci's usual charge for lessons was half a guinea each, but Théroigne, feeling unable to afford so large a sum, offered him eight shillings, and consented to have her lessons at odd hours whenever it suited her master. Moreover, this price was not to be paid until she had earned it by singing at concerts. Tenducci seemed content with this arrangement, and took her to a lawyer, who drew up an agreement between master and pupil. It was not surprising that Théroigne, in spite of her apparent astuteness, was imposed upon by the unscrupulous musician. For one thing, she knew little English and less Italian. she says in her *Confessions*:

> There was not a single person who could have advised me. I had no experience. I was acting in good faith, but was dealing with a scamp who had a very different contract drawn up to the one he described to me. It did not contain any of the things we had agreed upon. Everything he substituted was to my disadvantage. It was a false agreement in all the clauses, and I had the imprudence to sign it without having it read over to me and explained. Amongst other things there was a clause relating to a forfeit of a thousand *louis* if I failed to carry out my part of the contract, and other conditions which utterly revolted me when at length I had the deed read and explained to me for the first time in Italy. A statement was even inserted that I should sing at the theatre, which was simply a lie, as it would have been easy for me to prove.

In the contract Théroigne was described by three different names, which led to considerable confusion. First of all she appears as Anna

Gioseppa le Comte, an appellation which she said had been given her by Tenducci; secondly as Anna Gioseppa Campinados, which was her grandmother's name, and which she adopted "by a fantasy which appeared to her quite innocent"; and, strangely enough, the third time she is described as Anna Gioseppa Théroigne Spinster. This manner of describing her absolutely nonplussed her examiners at Kufstein. Not recognising the English word "spinster," and receiving no help from Théroigne (who had either never known its meaning, had forgotten, or was resolved for purposes of her own not to explain that it meant she was unmarried), they attempted to trace the existence of a possible Mr. Spinster who might have been, had he existed, the father of her child.

"What does the name conceal," inquired her interlocutor in prison—"a secret?"

"You have no right to ask me that question," replied Théroigne angrily; "my private life concerns no one."

He still pondered. Spinster of the 73rd regiment in England. Who was he? A husband? A lover? He would never know. "We cannot force your confession," he said.

This curious mistake has since been made by other chroniclers, whose exhaustive research on this point has likewise proved fruitless.

Having signed the contract drawn up in favour of the unscrupulous and grotesque musician, she also agreed to travel with him to Italy, accompanied by her two brothers and a half-brother. She tells in her *Confessions* the story of the manner in which their journey came about.

Having no distrust, and still acting from good faith, moreover, feeling assured that the contents of the contract were according to the arrangement I had proposed, I quietly prepared to return to my country to offer money to my father, afterwards meaning to go to Paris and sell the furniture which I had left there. My music-master, whose involved affairs, as I discovered later, made it necessary for him to flee from London, knew I had money. Being cunning as well as a rogue, he foresaw, not without reason, that my father, pleased to have me with him again, might wish to keep me and my money, and that I might be compelled to renounce my career as a singer. My master prepared to come with me for this reason, under pretext that business was calling him to Paris. In reality he hoped to obtain the forfeit of a thousand *louis*, and to return to London alone to pay his debts.

Here Théroigne credits Tenducci with too much honesty.

Not knowing the real motives which forced him to leave England, I accepted his offer, with the intention of doing him a good turn, and for the sake of continuing my lessons.

In order not to lose time I carried a small pianoforte in my carriage. This procured for me the pleasure of singing as often as I wished, even whilst travelling. So, we set out.

When approaching the Ardennes and near the village of Jupille, I was suddenly informed of bad news. My father was dead. I thought I too should die of grief. It appeared they had written to me at London, but the letter reached England after my departure.

I had therefore to modify my plans. After having given a little money to my stepmother, I took my brothers with me and went to Paris. There I placed in the public funds forty thousand *livres* at eight *per cent.*, to give me an income of three thousand two hundred *livres*. In the meantime, my master, installed with us at Paris for the purpose of attending to his supposed affairs, found himself very much embarrassed. The death of my father had spoilt his plans, and he dared not return to England, as he had nothing wherewith to satisfy his creditors.

He tried therefore to persuade me to leave for Italy. He represented all the advantages which would accrue in the way of education for my brothers. He insisted above all on the facilities I should have in that country for perfecting myself as a musician. One of my brothers who had also a taste for music would be in a good school, and so forth.

In short, I decided to take the journey to Italy, I, my three brothers, and my master. Tenducci promised to reimburse me for the expenses of the journey. In the interest of my brothers, in the interest of my art, I thought I was doing the right thing in undertaking this fatal journey.

The actual date at which this ill-assorted couple left London is difficult to determine. In April 1787 Tenducci appears to have been still teaching in the English capital, as on May 3rd of that year one of his pupils was singing "for the first time on any stage" at the Theatre Royal, Covent Garden. With regard to his indebtedness, the declaration of his bankruptcy is to be found in the *London Gazette* of Febru-

JÉRÔME PÉTION

ary 12-16th, 1788, in which he is described as Ferdinando Tenducci, now or late of Dean Street, Soho, music-seller, dealer, and chapman. He was cited to surrender himself to the Commissioners on February 21st and 28th, and on March 29th. This is all the evidence from which the date of departure may be conjectured, but it is safe to assume that it was somewhere between May 1787 and February 1788. Nor can the length of their stay in Paris be definitely fixed.

A letter written by the Marquis de Persan shortly after Théroigne had left for Italy throws some light on her movements. From it Théroigne would appear to have shown him but scant consideration, nay, hardly bare courtesy. He complained that he was not allowed the privilege of seeing her alone for more than a few moments, after all that he had done for her. It was with difficulty she had obtained his acquiescence to her visit to London, and she far outstayed the limit he had fixed for the journey. On her return to Paris she had broken entirely away from his influence. There is one significant passage in the letter. "You were always duped," he says, "by all the Italians and foreigners with whom you made friends." This statement throws a light on Théroigne's revolutionary career. She was led far too easily by her companions. De Persan's letter reveals his bitter disappointment in her.

My sentiments towards you will never change, can you say that you have anything to complain of in me? It is true that I could not come to see you before you left. Two reasons prevented me. Business was the first, the second was that I knew I had very little influence on your manner of thinking. When you left for England, it was only to be for two months. You remained there for six. On your return to France I saw you still had the same passion for music. You were bound by relations with a *virtuoso* in whose company you intended to go to Spain. From Paris you went to your own country. After that you were taken by a desire to go to Italy. Can I find in that the slightest mark of friendship and gratitude for me? With difficulty I saw you alone for a quarter of an hour. I foresaw what would happen with your master. You always treated me badly, though I never did aught but good to you, and you were always duped by all the Italians and foreigners with whom you made friends.

You were right to give me particulars about yourself and your family. No one will ever take a greater interest in them than I. If you believed that I neglected you, it is necessary for you to let me know as soon as your season at Genoa ends. You will have proved by then how the one who has sworn to love you for ever will have carried out his bargain. What did you tell me when you went to England? That it would not interrupt our friendship; yet when you return to France, I know that you have entered into an engagement for five years. Did you ever keep a single promise that you gave me? Tell me, which of us two has a right to complain of the other? Yes, *chère amie*, you have treated both my heart and my purse very badly.

Adieu, dear one. Count on the feelings with which you have inspired me, and which, in spite of the wrong you have done me, will only end with the life of him who will love and honour you always.

De Persan.

P.S.—I see with pleasure the progress you have made in your studies, because you write French far better than you did. It is strange that you should grow perfect in this language whilst you are in Italy. I fear the demon of music which possesses you. It has not helped you at all so far.

The marquis was a shrewd man of the world and perhaps no one understood Théroigne better than he at this period. He foresaw that her impetuosity might be the cause of her undoing. It was apparent in everything she undertook; in her music, her friendships, her revolutionary activities. She advanced blindly, without pause or forethought, and she dashed herself against the obstacles which appeared in her path without calculating the danger she ran of injuring her own powers and leaving the obstruction exactly where it stood before. Of stuff like this, martyrs are made!

She had not been in Genoa for long before she realised that Tenducci was utterly unscrupulous. She broke away from him as soon as she could.

She explains in her *Confessions*:

My master threw off his mask. He told me I should have to carry out all the clauses of our agreement. He endeavoured to force me to sing at the theatre of this town. I felt it was an outrage. I took the advice of honourable people. I wrote to my friends. I consulted my lawyers. All of them assured me that under the circumstances my contract was absolutely null and void. During these proceedings my master spread calumnies about me everywhere. But people knew him as well as me. My friends sent me infamous letters which he had written about me and which I produced against him. The man I had loved even sent me, by an express from London, information about my professor with an extract from bankruptcy proceedings, accompanied by the advice of an English lawyer.

I obtained justice. I was at last free of him, but I lost the expenses of the voyage and two hundred *louis* which I had advanced on the lessons he had still to give me. The disdain that people have for singers in Italy and the unpleasantness I had experienced disgusted me with a musical career, as much for myself as for my brother. The latter, who had been sent by me to Naples when my lawsuit took place at Genoa, was recalled; I did not wish him to continue his studies. Being rather more accustomed to economy, I thought we had enough to live on.

Had she but realised it, the price she had paid for being rid of so dangerous a companion as Tenducci was a cheap one.

When she had been there about a year the stay at Genoa began to weary her, and she thought of going to Rome. What she did in Genoa can only be surmised. The lawsuit, the fact that she had trusted her master only to be deceived, the mere idea of being connected with the stage against her will gave her a feeling of distaste for the life she had been leading. It must be confessed that her scruples concerning the continuation of a musical career appear so inconsistent with her ambitions and general attitude towards life that a suspicion creeps in as to whether she has been misjudged in other respects. It is impossible not to call in question her sincerity, if not her uprightness. Perhaps her friendship with the Marquis Durazzo had something to do with this question of her future, or perhaps after her quarrel with Tenducci she found the avenues to musical success closed to her. Some of the experience she had gained was all to her advantage.

In the course of study, a classical singer acquires general information which is useful in other walks of life.

Théroigne's financial position was now becoming insecure. She found it difficult to obtain the supplies from de Persan which she had come to regard as her chief resource. She borrowed money from Durazzo and from Perregaux, and tried to establish a correspondence between these two, who were both of them financiers. She wrote to the latter concerning the former:

I should be charmed to be the means of making the letters of so delightful a gentleman acceptable to you. Command my services. I expect to make some stay in this lovely town.

On March 9th, 1789, she wrote from Genoa to thank Perregaux for the trouble he had taken to obtain payment for her from M. de Persan, and enclosed all the necessary papers to make such formalities easier in the future, as another six months' income was already due. Her letter is simple and businesslike, although somewhat discursive, as her letters to her Paris banker always were. He seems to have been as easily wound round her little finger as most of her other friends, and she never hesitates to ask for his financial help both on behalf of herself and her brothers, although, in his case, she was never lacking in gratitude. She continues:

I am much obliged to you, *monsieur*, for the kindness you have shown in permitting me to draw upon you whilst I was waiting to be paid. I beg you to send a draft of a hundred *louis* to your correspondent at Genoa, with an order to pay M. Durazzo and to give me the rest, so that I can meet the expenses of my voyage to Rome; and, at the same time, it would be convenient if you had the kindness to send me a letter for your correspondent at Rome, to whom you can give my money when I am paid.

As regards my diamonds, I will send them to you when I reach Rome, and you can keep them until my talents permit me to return to England.

If you will be so kind as to send me letters of recommendation for Rome and Naples, where I hope to go when I have stayed in Rome some time, I should be extremely obliged. I shall write also to M. Hammerslys. He has already recommended me to his correspondent at Genoa. I owe him a great deal for all the marks of esteem which he has given me. I had the honour yesterday to dine with your friend the English Consul, who, for your sake, has shown me a great deal of politeness whilst I have been at Genoa.

I beg your pardon for bothering you with so many things. But I have something else to ask of you. I believe that you can render me a service. This would be all the more agreeable to me since I shall not have to have recourse to my supposed friends again. I came to Italy to sing and to study. I brought with me my three brothers—one of them is studying painting, and the two others a commercial life. As I am obliged to travel, I wished to establish the eldest at Liège, where we have relatives who are in business. I have need of three thousand *livres*, or three thousand five hundred *livres*, in order to purchase a managership for my eldest brother, so that the income derived from it will be enough for his needs while he is studying in an office.

Nevertheless, I have reflected that if I should die you would lose your money. I wish to render this service to my brother, and I am rather embarrassed about it. If only you would advance the sum for a year, you should receive half of it back every six months, with the interest, and you would be entirely repaid in a year, counting from next month. If you will do that for me, I assure you I should be extremely obliged. I would have asked Mr. Hammerslys instead, but as my income is from France, I thought it would be simpler to make the proposition to you. I beg you to give me an answer to this by return of courier, as I shall not decide upon any other course until I know what you think about it.

Your servant,

Anne-Josèphe Théroigne.

Please address your answer to the English Consul's, your correspondent at Genoa.

Impulsive as ever, she changed her mind almost immediately after despatching the letter and, instead of awaiting a reply, sent her brother to Paris with a second appeal dated March 22nd.

I beg you to give ten *louis* to my brother who will hand you this letter, he is the one of whom I spoke to you who is going to Liège. You will then have the kindness to send three thousand *livres* to Liège, not to include the ten *louis* which you will give him for his journey.

Please send the money to your correspondent as I have already advised, with orders that it is only to be used for the purchase of this appointment, and that he will have the kindness to pay the same in my brother's name, for fear that they would make him pay more than the business was worth, or counsel him to invest his money less solidly. I have no other fears on his behalf, for the young man is very sensible, and I hope that, considering his good carriage and manners, you will be persuaded to take an interest in him. It is true that I have no real claim to so much service and good-nature on your part.

You hardly know me, and I can only ask for the generosity of a kindly heart from you. So that I hope my brother will awaken your interest on his own behalf, and that you will do your best in order that he may be well recommended at Liège. You will therefore please give him a letter of recommendation. He has need of nothing beyond advice and protection, because he will be established at Liège as soon as his talents and faculties enable him to start in business. That is why I beg you to give him a letter to your correspondent in order that the latter may take him into his office and teach him. I ask no more of you than this.

She informed Perregaux that she was leaving for Rome and asked him to address his reply to the Poste Restante of that town.

Her concern for the happiness of her brothers is one of Théroigne's noble traits. They were hardly ever out of her thoughts, and whenever she had any money, she willingly shared it with them.

Her younger brother, who was to be a painter, was to begin his studies at Rome. Théroigne did not make a protracted stay in the Eternal City. The stir and movement of the Revolution in France could not long remain hidden. Reports of the doings in Paris reached her ears and excited her latent curiosity. As soon as her brother was settled in lodgings, she left Rome and made her way back to France. What happened to her half-brother at this juncture does not appear. He was called Pierrot and eventually he became a soldier.

When she was back in Paris Théroigne wrote to Perregaux to thank him for the care he had taken of her books and for his thoughtfulness in returning them to her as soon as she gave him a permanent address. Then followed the usual request for a favour on behalf of her brother Joseph.

I hope, *monsieur*, that you have not forgotten my request and that you have sent a letter of recommendation on behalf of my brother at Rome. If by any chance you have not yet done so, I beg you to recollect this matter and to ask your correspondent to watch over his progress and over his person whilst he is staying *en pension*, in order that we may be able to judge what sort of an education they are giving him. I shall be extremely obliged to you.

With Théroigne it was a case of "Love me, love my brothers."

CHAPTER 2

The Patriot

These first rumours of the Revolution which reached her at Rome produced a great impression upon Théroigne. "When I learnt that a National Assembly was in process of formation and would be open to everyone, I was enraptured by the idea," she says in her *Confessions*. In that hour the patriot was born. In that hour the aspirant singer, the adventuress in search of culture, fine raiment, and jewels, died in her. She forgot that she was not French by nationality, she forgot that she had been spending a life of luxury and ease in Paris; she remembered only that she had been a peasant, that her sympathies were with the French people, and that in a struggle for liberty she must take their part.

Her natural love of life and movement, her thirst for knowledge and experience, her need of a definite form of expression for her energies, made it inevitable that she should be drawn into the whirlpool where these qualities might be utilised and satisfied. But as yet no thought of such activity had entered her mind; she was simply the student, and desired to understand more of the political crisis which was shaking the country to its very foundations. Hence her interest in the National Assembly and her desire to be present at its sittings, and to learn something of the constitutional measures brought up there for debate.

Fascinated by the prospect of witnessing the grand and extraordinary spectacle which she believed was about to unfold before the gaze of an astonished and applauding world, she had hurriedly put her affairs in order so that she might be able to depart for France without delay. It was the 11th of May, 1789, when she reached the capital, full of curiosity and expectation, a woman whose heart beat wholly for the people, and who was willing to devote her untiring powers to their services.

At first, she felt strangely bewildered after her return, not in the least realising the meaning of what was going on around her. Paris was changed as well as herself. There was a murmur of expectancy, an undercurrent of discontent she could not fathom. The French were no longer the happy, busy, gay people she had known. They gathered into knots and groups at the street corners, in the wine-shops, and in the public gardens. They scowled and muttered threats, they spoke loudly and gesticulated wildly, or they whispered ominously, which was the most dangerous of all. They spat, they swore, they stamped, and flourished the newspapers they were reading, full of a tremendous purpose at which Théroigne could only guess.

She looked for old friends who could explain matters to her, but it was not easy to find anyone who had leisure enough to repeat to her eager ears all that had taken place in the past few months, with which they were already perfectly familiar. It was not the time for retrospect; the hour of the forward march had struck. In her doubt she turned to the papers for enlightenment; and the reason of the people's agitation, which at first was dim to her comprehension, grew gradually clearer.

The people were perishing, unable to pay the price of bread, unable to find work; or if at work, then wretchedly under-paid, over-taxed, burdened with dues, an oppressed multitude, "a vast herd scattered far beyond the visible horizon, everywhere ill-used, starved, and fleeced."

Women, hearing the price of food was dearer, gave vent to shrieks of rage, men cursed their own impotence—both compelled to these forms of expression by fear of actual starvation. Women and men stood for hours in the queues outside the bakers' shops, fighting for the sour, earthy lumps of dough which did duty for the staff of life. Women robbed the grain markets, men attacked loaded carts on the main roads, supposing their burden to be grain. The determination of these plunderers was extraordinary; nothing seemed to tire or repulse them. Violence produced violence. It was not easy to stay the hand of the desperate workmen who were fighting grimly for a bare existence.

Théroigne recognised no place for herself in this general hubbub, and remained quietly waiting in her lodgings at the Hôtel de Toulouse. She tried to occupy herself with the music which had hitherto been her greatest solace. She hoped that if strife were to come, as it seemed it must, she too might share the people's struggle and help them, if only with her voice, to regain their freedom. The fever that was in the air was creeping into her blood. Insidious, slow but sure, the poison of class-hatred was spreading more and more, and threatening an outbreak between the antagonistic forces which must result eventually in bloodshed. How, then, should Théroigne remain immune from this infection? She says significantly:

> The general stir and excitement affected me very soon, I had no understanding of the unacknowledged rights of the people, but I naturally loved liberty. An instinct, a keen feeling which I could not define, made me approve of the Revolution without in the least knowing why, for I had but little instruction.

Presently she learnt, fragment by fragment, at the sittings of the National Assembly, and from talks with some of the deputies, the needs of the people, the evils they desired to remedy, and the means that were proposed in order to bring about these longed-for results.

When Théroigne arrived in Paris the first riot of importance had already taken place at the factory of the paper-maker Réveillon, the employer who was accused of believing fifteen *sous* a day enough for any journeyman. Théroigne might have learnt something there of the starvation wages of the people and their sufferings. She was too late also for the opening of the States General at Versailles on May 5th, and only heard afterwards of the terrible disappointment of the populace when it was found that the government had made no definite proposals of reform, and that Necker, in the opinion of the black-robed deputies of the *Tiers-état*, had utterly failed to grasp the situation.

What had they not hoped from his speech! Being ordered to confer on the subject of their legislative powers with commissioners of the other two orders, those of the third, among whom were Garat, Thouret, Volney, Barnave, and le Chapelier, debated for a fortnight to no purpose, as Target, Mounier, and Rabaut de Saint-Etienne had to confess in consultation with their colleagues. On June 10th they decided on the bold step of inviting the nobility and clergy to join them. All to no purpose. Then they declared themselves ready to form a separate entity. On June 17th, on the motion of Siéyès, the deputies of the *Tiers-état* constituted themselves the National Assembly, the legislative body which should be open to all, and to the sittings of which Théroigne was looking forward with an eagerness which seems strange in one who had lived her previous life.

Théroigne's interest in the Revolution was not allowed to slacken for want of events to feed it during the first few weeks of her return to Paris. On June 4th the *dauphin* died, and the queen was plunged in grief It was left to the friends of the Comte d'Artois, her brother-in-law, to complain of the people's insolence in taking matters into their own hands, and to attempt to discipline the rebellious *Tiers-état* by announcing that there should be no royal session, which, owing to the closing of the Salle des Menus, brought about the celebrated oath of the tennis-court. On June 23rd the postponed session took place, and the *Tiers-état*, inspired to the step by the stirring words of Mirabeau, defied the Crown. A few days later the nobles and the clergy, at the king's request, accepted the invitation previously offered, and the union of the three orders was complete. The people's parliament had taken definite shape.

Théroigne was not slow to profit by the privileges accorded her of listening to the debates. She says:

> The National Assembly, seemed to me a fine and noble spectacle; I was struck by its majesty. I experienced emotions of an elevated nature there and my soul soared to unknown heights. At first, I did not understand much of all these discussions and deliberations, but gradually a light glowed in me, am I realised clearly the position of the people as opposed to that of the privileged classes. Then my sympathies for the former grew greater, the better informed I became, and were transformed into an ardent love when I was persuaded that justice and right were on the side of the people.

At first, according to her own account, Théroigne was quite content to remain a spectator among the crowds. She walked in the streets and squares, questioning one person and then another, trying to understand their hopes, their fears, and their struggles. The early years of hardship she had endured had never been forgotten, and served now to awaken her quick sympathies with their sufferings. Her independent and resourceful nature rebelled at the thought of oppression for others. Her heart thrilled with compassion. Her mind demanded time for reflection.

One of the busiest spots in Paris at that day was the gardens of the Palais Royal, which had been thrown open to the people by the Duc d'Orléans. This space was surrounded by *cafés*, wine-shops, booksellers', and gambling-hells, all of them places where eager people congregated to hear the news which came through from Versailles in a constant stream, brought by the agents of the duke. In the gardens themselves men spoke treason and women cried revolt. Those who shouted loudest against the existing form of government received the

THE FALL OF THE BASTILLE.

most applause. Self-constituted politicians gave voice to impossible schemes for the regeneration of the social system; they spoke of extinguishing privileges, of establishing numerical sovereignty, of applying the teachings of Rousseau's *Contrat Social*.

A huge audience of the floating population applauded their diatribes, however chimerical or fanatic—failures, for the most part, in the arts or at the bar, unemployed clerks and officials, professional gamblers, touts, loungers, foreigners: all, in short, who had no settled calling. The orators, mounted on chairs or tables, gesticulated more and more wildly, the crowds of agitators swayed and rocked with the strength of their emotions. Closer and closer the people thronged, until they became so tightly packed that, as Arthur Young described the scene, an apple thrown from a balcony on to the moving floor of heads would not have reached the ground.

Those who were in favour of monarchy, aristocracy, law, and order dared not venture into the gardens if they valued unbroken bones and whole skins. They ran the risk of being ducked in the fountains, of having to dodge chairs that were flung at them, or if not chairs then stones, bottles, or other dangerous and unpleasant missiles. And physical activity once aroused, windows were shattered, doors were battered in, pavements torn up, and trees uprooted. Friends, on the other hand, were carried in procession' shoulder high. People were no longer judged by appearance or wealth, but by their attitude towards the new movement. Théroigne realised that in this spot she could learn much. She says:

> At the Palais Royal, where I went to walk nearly every day, I assisted at the dawn of the new era. That which struck me most was the air of goodwill. Egoism seemed to have disappeared from all our hearts. There was no longer a distinction between the classes. We elbowed one another, we chatted as though in the home circle. The rich, at this moment of fermentation, mixed willingly with the poor and deigned to speak to them as though they were their equals. In short, all the countenances appeared to have undergone a change. Each one dared to show forth his character and natural faculties in public. I saw many who, although covered with rags, wore a heroic air. However little sensibility one possessed, it was not possible to witness such a spectacle with indifference.

On July 12th the Palais Royal gardens were the scene of an organised debate. Necker had been dismissed the previous evening, and in the morning, rumour was busily spreading to that effect. The populace hastened to its usual meeting-place. Camille Desmoulins, not yet famous, enthusiast, thinker, and orator, was present in the gardens that Sunday morning. He leapt upon a table and cried, "To arms, to arms!" He moved the crowd by his eloquence; he gave them a green cockade as a symbol of their purpose. They stripped the leaves from the trees and wore them in their hats. And then he led them in procession through the town, wax busts of Necker and the Duc d'Orléans being carried in triumph at the head of the column. The people pillaged and sacked the bakers', the butchers', the wine-shops, and the gunsmiths', and as the evening wore on the rioting became more pronounced and dangerous.

The crowd tried to recruit all who passed, even the peaceable people on pleasure intent, or those returning from some place of entertainment. All who were stopped were forced to answer the invariable question, "On which side are you?" Women rolling along in their carriages found ruffians at their horses' heads, and stepped out into the mud in dainty shoes to cry " *Vive le Tiers-état!*" Dirty ragamuffins, only half clad, approached well-dressed people to beg in the name of the *Tiers-état.*

Théroigne was in the streets accompanied by a servant. An intense curiosity impelled her to see all she could. Armed men passed and repassed, besides many who were in search of weapons. She deliberately stopped some of the soldiers and put the favourite question to them:

Are you for the *Tiers-état*?

The proceeding was not always a safe one. An officer resented the liberty she had taken and threatened to arrest her. She fled, and he followed, until, discovering that she had no one with her but the maid, and appeared to be actuated merely by curiosity, he gave up the pursuit.

On the following morning the crowd was even greater, there were more armed men than before. They had guns, swords, and pikes. The green cockade was to be seen in all their hats. Théroigne followed the practice and adorned herself with the prevailing colour. From her account, it would seem that she had not noticed the green cockade before, in which case she could not have been present at Camille Desmoulins's meeting. Green was the colour of the d'Artois liveries, and was soon discarded for the tricolour. Théroigne followed the change of fashion without delay. She was hardly able to control her excitement, and was as much aware as anyone of the coming struggle.

That day, the 13th, the electors of Paris, chosen by the districts for the purpose of sending deputies to the States General, having refused to disperse, flocked to the Hôtel de Ville. The hours were occupied in forming the National Guard of Paris. At first this body was composed of twelve thousand volunteers, the number being rapidly increased to four times twelve thousand. The duty of the Guard was to maintain order in the streets. They had not been enrolled a moment too soon. On the following day the Bastille fell.

Théroigne had been in the capital one month and three days. She had so far done nothing except to try to grasp the position of the people and understand what was going on. But her chroniclers do not allow that she needed so much time to look about her. They accuse her falsely of being already active in the revolutionary ranks by July. The poetic Lamartine writes:

> From the first gathering of the crowds she appeared in the streets, and devoted her beauty to serve as an ensign to the people. Dressed in a riding-habit of the colour of blood, a plume of feathers in her hat, a sabre at her side, and two pistols in her belt, she hastened to join every insurrection.

The populace thronged about the great prison on the evening of the 13th, The ringleaders interspersed the cries for arms with cries of "To the Bastille." De Launay ordered up the drawbridges; he knew what was threatened. On the morning of the 14th the predominating cry was first for arms. The tocsin rang at daybreak from the tower of every church; shops were closed and barricaded. A report spread that there were arms in plenty at the Hôtel des Invalides. Patriots rushed tumultuously towards this possible source. Théroigne, says the incorrigible romancier, Lairtullier, was at their head. Pauline d'Aumez and Louise Bourgeoise, as determined Republicans as herself, followed her lead.

The governor, worthy Sombreuil, denied admittance to the rabble, assuring anyone who would listen that he must first send to Versailles for orders. Turning a deaf ear to all such expostulation, the crowd invaded the halls, rooms, vaults, and gardens, seized cannon and musketry, which they dragged and carried to the Hôtel de Ville. In the shortest possible space of time not a musket or a sabre remained visible to human eye at the Invalides. The unscrupulous Lairtullier continues:

> Théroigne was everywhere. She gave the orders, they were

47

obeyed; she had detachments of men placed at the barriers, she seized the dispatches which the Court were sending from Versailles to Paris—in short, she organised the undisciplined masses who were newly armed.

Truly a valiant Théroigne, literally inspired, not unlike the Maid of Orleans, for she knew nothing of soldiering. Lamartine calls her a name that does not suit her—the impure Joan of Arc of the public streets.

Encouraged by their success in obtaining arms, the people were ready for action. They joined the large crowd already besieging the Bastille. Cries of "Let us storm the prison!" were added to the already existing babel. The little garrison summoned the assailants to retire. It is an oft-told tale—a well-known tale. Those attacking persisted. Two men mounted the roof of the guard-house and broke the chain of the bridge with axes. Down came the bridge with a rattle and clatter; no less quickly the rabble were on it and across it, making for the next bridge over the second moat. A discharge of musketry brought them to a stand. But the mob was desperate; the firing continued for four, five hours. De Launay had half a mind to put a lighted match to the powder magazine, and take decisive measures by blowing up the fortress. Was it the garrison opposed him, or did he fail for want of resolution?

Instead, all of a sudden, came the word of surrender. The Bastille had fallen. The rush of the crowd, the seizure of de Launay, the infinite danger of a young woman thought to be his daughter, the escape of the Swiss, the triumphant rescue of the seven dazed prisoners, the bloodshed which neither Hulin's nor Elie's word could hinder; all these things are familiar to every one: yet even reliable historians have over-coloured a picture which had more than enough of the dramatic element in it, without their aid. De Goncourt, writing of Théroigne, gives a stroke of unsurpassed imaginative genius.

> She leapt with joy, she was carried away by the crowd, gunpowder blackened her, blood stained her. Beat the drums, sound the tocsins, let the people march on. She ran furious, brandishing death and destruction. She armed herself at the Invalides. *She took a tower at the Bastille!*

Such a feat is too marvellous to be passed over in silence. Dusaulx, (*De l'Insurrection parisienne et de la prise de la Bastille*), places her in the rank of the conquerors, and many have followed him. Lamartine bestowed upon her the *sabre d'honneur*, adding that it was voted to her on the breach by the victors.

Lamothe-Langon, an even more picturesque liar than Lairtullier, heaps detail on detail regarding her presence at the Bastille on the unforgotten 14th. She showed herself first in the hottest fire, urged on her brother patriots, encouraged them when they weakened, brought them back to the charge if panic terror turned them momentarily aside. Words he attributes to her are:

> I still seem to be in the midst of that famous day. I hear the sharp whistle of the balls, the thunder of the artillery, the clamours of the multitude, the cries of the wounded, the despair of the mothers and wives whose sons and husbands had perished in this holy cause. All remains vividly present to me, both in my mind and in my heart. Glorious moment, intoxicating day! How quickly you passed!

Having forced a capitulation, the people penetrated into the last refuge of despotism; the cowardly defenders who had turned the guns upon them had the impudent audacity to receive them with apparent joy, and dared to mingle with the cries of "Long live the people!" cries of "Long live the King!"

"Where is the governor?" demanded Théroigne.

They pointed him out to her.

"Assassin of the people!" she cried; "you will be conducted to the Hôtel de Ville, there to render your account." She made a signal. They gave him no time to reply. They threw themselves upon him; they dragged him towards the Place de la Grève.

So, he died. But Théroigne did not stay to see the end; she hastened to help others to free the prisoners. When the search was over, the captives freed, Théroigne exclaimed:

> What, citizens! shall we leave this fortress standing to menace us anew with its fatal tyranny? No; we must raze it to the ground. We must leave the spot now occupied by its walls free to the air that will disperse the despotic miasma it has exhaled.

This speech was received with the acclamations it deserved, and, placing her in an armchair which had escaped destruction when the Governor's house was burnt, they crowned her with laurels and carried her in triumph to the Hôtel de Ville, the crowd waving aloft branches laden with foliage, and uttering cries of victory.

"It is the triumph of beauty," remarked a voice. It was Lafayette speaking.

Romancists of the class to which Lamothe-Langon belongs are plausible only up to a certain point. Beyond that they are carried away by their own visions. The armchair saved from the flames, and the part played by Lafayette in the scene, are altogether absurd.

Théroigne's own account of the same day is refreshing in its simplicity after the bombast of her chroniclers. She says in her *Confessions*:

> I was at the Palais Royal, when the news came that the Bastille was taken. The populace gave way to a noisy and prolonged pleasure. Many wept for joy, crying that there would be no more Bastille, no more *lettres de cachet*.

It seems very unlikely that she should have invented that natural remark, but simplicity was, of course, her role. Denials were her safe course, since there was no proof against her. Her accuser, the Chevalier Maynard de la Valette, in his notes entitled "*Dires et Aveux de Demoiselle Théroigne*," declares she was present when, after the taking of the Bastille, de Launay was massacred, that she wished to search the cells and release the prisoners. Dressed as a man, her musket on her shoulder, she hurried through the streets of the capital. She saw the scene with her own eyes, he insists; she saw the Prince de Lambesc trample an old man to death under the hoofs of his horse. That was on the 12th. It was her word against her accusers, and Théroigne adhered to her original statement. In spite of several assertions to the contrary, her name does not appear in the lists of the "*citoyens vainqueurs de la Bastille*" contained in the national archives, on which are inscribed those of some six thousand insurrectionists.

Nor, in spite of her supposed exhortation to the people to raze the Bastille to the ground, does she mention a word in her *Confessions* concerning the demolition of the fortress. This work was officially ordered the day after the surrender, and was pursued without interruption until May 15th, 1791. It was directed by the patriot Palloy, who thought only of the glory of his task and not at all of the money it might have brought him. He gave away a number of interesting objects found in the prison, and, later, was reduced to indigence. The materials of the edifice were removed, and some of the stones were employed: in the construction of the upper part of the *Pont de la Concorde*. The site remained open, and various plans were put forward for its disposal. Palloy wished it to be turned into a *Place de la Liberté*, in which a simple but majestic column should stand. Théroigne desired that a palace should be erected there, in which the sittings of the National Assembly were to be held. She made a stirring speech on the subject before the Club des Cordeliers, and, though her motion was carried, the plan fell through.

Some forty years after the surrender of the Bastille the Column of July, which now adorns the *Place*, was commenced, the summit being crowned by a bronze Genius of Liberty. Théroigne described herself as a mere spectator during the demonstrations of July 12th to the 14th, but she admitted taking an active part in the events of the 17th of the month, when Louis XVL paid a visit to Paris to consecrate the triumphs of the Revolution. Dressed in a white riding-habit and a neat round hat, Théroigne marched in the ranks of the soldiers to meet the king. He had taken the sacrament that morning, made his will, said farewell to the weeping and harassed queen, and set forth from Versailles accompanied by some of the *Garde du Corps* and the hundred deputies appointed by the National Assembly to escort him. The new mayor, Bailly, received him at the gate and handed him the keys. As he drove through the streets of Paris the people greeted him with amity. They trusted him to give them food.

At the Hôtel de Ville Louis was met by the electors of Paris. The occasion was a solemn one. The tricolour was everywhere in evidence. The king appeared upon the balcony, a tricolour cockade in his hat, and spoke to the enthusiastic people. Then others spoke, among them Lally-Tollendal, who made a telling speech and became the real hero of the day. To him was deputed the task of reporting what had taken place to the National Assembly. Meanwhile "the Restorer of French Liberty," wearied with his unusual duties, was returning to the palace, still accompanied by the hopeful and now joyous crowd.

Thus, passed Théroigne's first day of active participation in the Revolution. She was interested in the people's attitude when they cheered the king at the Hôtel de Ville. The cries of "*Vive la Nation!*" had been silenced. They were soon to be heard again. A partial tranquillity reigned in Paris, and the highest in the land, d'Artois and Condé amongst them, seized the opportunity to flee from the capital. But the air of security was a treacherous one, liable to disappear at any moment. Instances of minor violence occurred now and again. Petty thieving, cases of knifing, cudgelling, and so forth made the streets unsafe. Marauders grew bold enough to tear off the jewels women were wearing and remove even the silver buckles off their shoes. Ruffians of the lowest type begged, threatened, and robbed those who were better off than themselves.

In the provinces, riots broke out everywhere and blazed throughout the remainder of July, August, and the beginning of September. The tocsin rang in villages and towns, the drums rolled, and cannon were mounted ready for use. Houses were broken into and destroyed. On July 31st the town hall of Strassburg was pillaged. The populace rushed into the building, and forthwith there was "a shower of shutters, sashes, chairs, tables, sofas, books and papers, and then another of tiles, boards, balconies, and fragments of woodwork." The public archives were scattered to the winds. At Maubeuge in July the rioters forced open the prison, demolished the octroi offices and harbour offices, and carried off the custom and excise stores. Havoc succeeded havoc. Furniture was smashed, valuables thrown into the street and trampled on, eatables demolished, houses left empty, ruined, blackened by fire, or hacked about so as to be uninhabitable.

The spirit of revolution spread rapidly through Caen, Rouen, Besançon, and Lyons. At Troyes the rioters demanded that the octroi should be suppressed, since this had been done in the capital. Chateaux were burning and their owners deserting them in fear of their lives. The upheaval was terrifying, and in Paris a murmuring undercurrent testified to the fact that the good impression made upon the people by the king's visit was speedily dying out. Distrust towards the Court, more especially towards the queen, was increasing daily, fed by suggestive articles in new journals calculated to inflame the people, and by the stirring denunciation spoken by orators at hastily improvised gatherings. Meanwhile royalty grasped nothing apparently beyond its own divine right, and the queen, proud Marie-Antoinette, would fain have brushed aside the meaningless signs of a chaos which she could not understand, and which she regarded as an unwarranted annoyance which must and should be speedily removed.

Incidents were not wanting at this hour to fill the heart and stir the imagination of Théroigne. There was Foulon, the old man not unconnected with the story of hay and thistles, hanged to the lantern once, twice, three times before he died and his head struck off to be carried on a pike; Berthier, who was butchered with such gross accompanying details as make description impossible. At these things she shuddered, but turned her attention with great willingness to the exciting meeting in the National Assembly on August 4th, when the reports from the country were read and new decrees adopted.

The Declaration of the Rights of a Man and of a Citizen—words for ever on Théroigne's lips—was passed before the close of August.

She admitted that she felt an irresistible enthusiasm in the doings of the legislative body, and in order the better to assist at the sittings of the Assembly she decided to go and live at Versailles. She arrived there at the commencement of the debates on the Declaration of Rights. She took lodgings in the Rue de Noailles with a widow whose name, when questioned, she could not recollect, although she was able to describe the exact position of the house in the turning off the grand avenue leading to the castle gates. She lived at Versailles all through the summer, and there made the acquaintance of Pétion and of Joseph-Honoré, brother of the Abbe Siéyès. Both these friends visited at her house. The former was a lawyer from Chartres, grizzled though not old, of sturdy build, and with a fine soul for the violin. The love of music they possessed in common was as strong a bond as their love of the people between Théroigne and the future mayor of Paris.

In September the Assembly was making but little progress with its work, and want of confidence in its efficiency became more and more marked. Misery and insecurity increased. The Court persisted in its nonchalant policy. Paris was defied by the bringing in of additional troops. On September 23rd the Regiment of Flanders was marched into Versailles to remain stationed there as a precaution. It was customary in the case of such arrivals to entertain the new-comers, and on October 1st a great banquet was given at Versailles by the officers of the Bodyguard to these battalions. The festivities became the occasion of a royalist demonstration. Tricoloured cockades were torn off and trampled under the feet of the revellers.

White cockades and black ones for the queen were hastily donned in their place, the national toasts supposed to be in usage were forgotten, the company sang lustily: "*O, Richard! ô mon roi!*" Royalist feeling was allowed full expression. The queen openly rejoiced at the prospect of a lightening of her burdens. Were not there people enough who were good, loyal, and true? What if some soldiers had deserted and sided with the populace? What if others wavered? Authority must be re-established. Her 'must' was law, and she believed it would be easily carried out. She had the indiscretion to show her thoughts and to express approval not only of the spirit with which the banquet went, but also because the royalist acclamations continued throughout the whole of the next day and echoed the singing in her heart.

Meanwhile these signs of disaffection to the Revolution, coming to the ears of the people in an exaggerated form, caused immediate alarm and suspicion amongst them. Something must be done to hinder the royalists from giving expression to these undesirable sentiments.

The king should be brought to Paris with as little delay as possible. The people willed it. They had suffered as much as they *would* suffer. It was time to ameliorate the conditions of starvation under which they laboured. Thousands were ready to submit plans to this end, and to direct, control, advise, even lead those who would become responsible for organising them. Hunger had so far invaded the homes of the poor that maddened women were ready to sacrifice life in redressing the horrors which were causing themselves and their children slowly to perish. If there was no bread in Paris, they would fetch it from Versailles, and fetch those too whose duty it was to see they were supplied. Their opportunity came. Michelet says:

> Men made the 14th of July, the 6th of October, was the day of women. Men took the royal Bastille, women took royalty itself.

Because the complaints of man did not receive the attention their urgency demanded, a woman organised a revolt among members of her sex. She ran to the Café de Foy, a meeting-place where agitators swarmed, and there she loudly denounced the royalists. Théroigne was not present. Neither was she in the Halles when a young woman beating a drum gathered her sisters round her and marched them to the Hôtel de Ville. There were hundreds of them, washerwomen, barefooted beggars, street-rovers, seamstresses, flower-girls, scavengers, who followed their leaders into the town hall, and tore or burned all the documents on which they could lay their hands, saying there had been enough scribbling while they were starving—they meant to have more practical help.

Maillard saved them from riot and disaster by offering to lead them to Versailles, and so the march began, cannon clattering, pikes bristling, hair streaming, arms swinging, women's garments fluttering in the breeze. Some men wore women's clothes, but were distinguished by hairy chins and raucous voices. They helped to swell the ranks of those who were to advance against the military, in the hope that soldiers would not fire on women.

That was a tramp to Versailles of hungry desperate human beings, all intent on one purpose, all full of protest—against the queen!

That day Marie-Antoinette visited the *Petit Trianon* for the last time and looked regretfully at the depredations of early autumn among her flowerbeds. She saw nothing symbolic in this decay. No thought of the dissolution with which the monarchy was threatened entered her

THE MARCH OF THE WOMEN TO VERSAILLES.

mind. But a messenger came to fetch her to the palace, and there, as she faced the first angry mob it had ever been her fate to see, she must surely have reflected on the triumphal entry into Paris she had made as *dauphine*, when the people had cried themselves hoarse in praising her and her life had opened full of a roseate promise which had enchanted her.

Years had passed since that time, dangerous years in which the rosy prospect had gradually faded, vanished, and been replaced by black menace. In that hour long ago, she had visited her people to win their love; at this hour in the present the people visited her to refuse hers with scorn. Horrible threats they voiced against her, loud curses and expressions so coarse that it seemed impossible women could have spoken them. In a frenzy they swore to cut her throat, and to scatter her bones to the winds. They were maddened by suffering, these women, and in their madness meant to make "the Austrian" suffer too. In this they were to succeed, before many days had passed, better than they would have believed possible. And Théroigne—where was she?

Carlyle says the brown-locked *demoiselle* with pike and helmet acted gunneress "with haughty eye and serene fair countenance," comparable, some thought, to Joan of Arc, others to Pallas Athene. De Goncourt cries:

> To horse, when the hour of October struck, with red plumes, riding-habit of red silk, this radiant Penthesilea, this Amazon of Rubens, riding-whip in hand, pistols in her girdle, galloping in her triumph, in front of the rabble, smiling, with sleeves rolled to the elbow—it is the beauty of Liège, bringing to Versailles pikes which are asking for heads and women who demand the destruction of the queen.

Lamartine too, not to be behindhand, writes:

> On the days of October she had led the women of Paris to Versailles, on horseback, by the side of the ferocious Jourdan, called 'the man with the long beard.' She had brought back the king to Paris: she had followed without emotion the heads of the *Gardes du Corps*, stuck on pikes as trophies.

But for sheer imagination Lamothe Langon again outrivals all other accounts and describes Théroigne's doings in those early days of October with additional details unheard of elsewhere.

The tocsin woke Théroigne from a stupor. For four days and four nights she had not had a moment's rest. She had been indefatigable, running hither and thither stirring up the people. Mounted on a wagon, seated on a board, she described to the people at every street corner what had happened at the banquet on October 1st. She aroused their anger, excited their fury, demanded vengeance in the name of the national cockade which had been insulted.

The crowd applauded; it pressed round her. She hurried from place to place—from the Palais-Royal to the Hôtel de Ville, to the Tuileries, along the quays, over the bridges, through the boulevards. Everywhere crowds gathered to hear her speak, everywhere she was heard with attention and respect. Mirabeau blamed her enthusiasm, Bailly thought it ill-timed, Lafayette begged her to be less heroic. These were traitors who called themselves moderate patriots! Robespierre, Danton, and Marat applauded her. She was their inspiration.

She had spent the night in the streets. When she awoke from a short nap she saw before her a group of women armed with pistols and cudgels; behind stood men with pikes and halberds. They were waving flags, brandishing their arms, growing impatient. When her eyes opened, she was greeted by the cry of "*Vive Méricourt, la jolie Méricourt! Vivat! Vivat!*"

She stood up, there where she had snatched an hour's sleep under the statue group of Louis XIV. in the Place des Victoires, there, where some kind friend had thrown over her a protecting coverlet, and spoke to the people.

Friends, comrades, citizens, we must not waste time here. At Versailles our cockade was profaned. At Versailles we must demand vengeance. I thank you for your care of me; offer it rather to the country which has more need of it.

A unanimous shout of approval filled the air. The people embraced one another, shook hands and kissed. They crowded round Théroigne to seize her hand and to kiss that too. "Follow me," she cried, "follow me to Versailles." A responsive roar burst from a thousand throats. She went on:

We want bread, let us seek it at Versailles. The people have been insulted. Where? At Versailles. Where shall they be avenged? At Versailles. Where are the tyrants? Who are they? The aristocrats at Versailles. Where are the deputies, our liberators? At Versailles again. It is from there they menace us, there they prepare our punishment, there where our enemies plot to harm us. Let us go to them, let us stop them in their wicked courses, let us judge them, sacrifice them, and when their corpses lie stretched where we have slain, people will see them and cry, 'National justice has passed this way.'

After this moving speech the crowd marched to the Hôtel de Ville. There stood Maillard. At a sign from him, Théroigne, rallying her feminine battalion, started for Versailles. She was at the head of some two or three thousand *citoyennes*, as well as three or four hundred good patriots. On the road they danced, they sang, they joked, they cried "*Vive la Nation!*" and "*Vive Méricourt!*" Thus in due course they reached Versailles. . . .!

But Théroigne, in her *Confessions*, tells a very different story. How could she march with the women to Versailles, when she was already there? It was stupid, she thought, of people to make such statements. She had been staying near the palace the whole summer, and on the evening of October 5th she had seen the draggled procession of the women arrive. They had started at sunrise from Paris, every woman met with on the way being urged into the ranks, which grew and swelled as each mile passed.

At first, they shouldered high their improvised arms and grumbled loudly at starvation. But after trudging weary miles they had no breath left to cry for bread. Rain and mud, hunger and fatigue, sobered the most eager amongst them—at least until there was a chance of practical gain by shouting. Market-women and fishwives, kitchen wenches, thieves, slatterns, and worse, the scum and rabble of the female population of Paris, "ten thousand Judiths," nearing their journey's end started clamouring anew for food, cried "*Vive le Roi!*" and sang "*Henri IV.*" and patriotic songs in tuneless voices.

Maillard had done his work well. He had brought a straggling mob of despairing women within range of royalty and legislation. He took some into the Assembly House, where it was arranged that a deputation should go to the king. Louis XVI. had been brought back hastily from hunting, and, gazing from the palace windows, saw that strange doings were afoot.

Mounier agreed to lead the women into the royal presence, and insisted on a calm and dignified diplomacy. It was no light task he undertook, as appears from his own account:

The women crowded round me, declaring that they wanted to accompany me to the king's palace. I had much trouble to make them understand that only six would be able to see the king, but that did not prevent a large number from swelling the procession.

We were on foot, in the mud, with a heavy rain falling. A considerable crowd of the inhabitants of Versailles lined both sides of the avenue which led to the *château*. The women of Paris formed various groups, mixed with a certain number of men, for the most part dressed in rags and tatters, their appearance ferocious and their gestures menacing. They were armed with muskets, old pikes, hatchets, iron sticks, and large poles. . . . . . A party of armed men approached us to escort the deputation. The strange and numerous *cortège* by which the deputies were assailed was taken for a riotous mob; the Garde du Corps rushed at us and dispersed us in the mud. . . . We rallied and thus advanced to the *château*. We found ranged on the square the *Garde du Corps*, a detachment of dragoons, the Regiment of Flanders, the Swiss Guards, the Invalides, and the militia of Versailles. We were recognised and received with honour. We crossed between the lines and had great difficulty to prevent the crowd from following us. In place of the six women to whom I had promised an entry into the palace, I had to admit a dozen.

Before the palace stretched the wide Place d'Armes, guarded all along the gilded railings. Through the three avenues which diverge into the Place the scum of the crowd frothed and bubbled. The women tempted the soldiers with pence and caresses. They acted with the coarsest motives and stirred up wicked passions. Corruption was at work.

Within the palace council followed council. The king received the deputation gracefully; the queen, so near to danger, so unaware of bodily peril, used her quick brain to think of some way out. What was it to be? Flight? Retirement to a neighbouring town perhaps? At one time the order was given that horses should be harnessed. How to escape from the clamouring mob outside! The rain had ceased, but clouds still rolling up merged into the darkness of early evening. From the palace windows the shining wet stones of the courtyard looked uninviting, and beyond the railing, out there in the road, the wild beasts clamoured for their prey.

One bright spot remained in all that gloom. Lafayette was marching from Paris with his men. The troops still stood at guard, their lines unbroken. Would they have to be withdrawn before he joined them?

On that point the issue of the day might hang.

The main body of women had sought shelter from the downpour anywhere in the neighbourhood of the palace. As it cleared some came forth again and the crowd increased; the murmuring and jostling grew ever more pronounced. Théroigne, who had spent the afternoon at the sitting of the National Assembly, had come out at five o'clock to see the crowd of women, and moved, alert and eager, from group to group, questioning, expostulating, praising their courage, and aching with sympathy for their suffering. Her mother-heart was full of love for them—such mother-love as since her babe had died had had no other outlet. She gave it to the people there and then.

She had left the Assembly Hall before the deputies separated, and her friend Pétion, meeting her later, offered to take her home out of the rain and the mud and away from the sights of misery. But she refused. She preferred to see what was going on. She says in her *Confessions*:

> I went with him to the corner of my street, where he left me. I pushed my way through as far as the barrier. There I saw on one hand the Regiment of Flanders, on the other the Bodyguard and the people armed with guns. Pushing my way along, I met three or four unfortunates who were weeping. They said to me that they had not had a mouthful of bread for three days. I took them near to my lodgings and fetched bread from there which I divided amongst them.

It was this act which led to her undoing. She was accused of bestowing not only bread, but money, and! that for the purpose of corrupting the soldiers.

Carlyle says:

> Already Pallas Athene (in the shape of Demoiselle Théroigne), is busy with Flandre and the dismounted dragoons. She, and such women as are fittest, go through the ranks; speak with an earnest jocosity; clasp rough troopers to their patriot bosom, crush down spontoons and musketoons with soft arms: can a man, that were worthy of the name of man, attack famishing patriot women?

Carlyle gave no credence to the oft-repeated story that Théroigne distributed money as well as bread.

> Money she had not, but brown locks, the figure of a heathen goddess, and an eloquent tongue and heart.

Michelet writes of the soldiers of Flanders, who were asked not to fire:

> Women had cast themselves amongst them, entreating them not to hurt the people. A woman then appeared . . . who seemed not to have walked in the mire with the others, but had doubt-less arrived later.

He is one of the few historians who are correct in not making Théroigne lead the women to Versailles:

> She threw herself at once among the soldiers, (this handsome young woman), a native of Liège, lively and passionate . . . inter-esting, original, and strange, with her riding-habit and hat, and a sabre by her side, speaking and confounding equally French and the *patois* of Liège, and yet eloquent. She was laughable, yet irresistible. Théroigne, impetuous, charming, and terrible, was insensible to every obstacle. She had had amours; but now she felt but one passion (one violent and mortal passion), which cost her more than life: her love for the Revolution. She fol-lowed it with enthusiasm.

Michelet says that Théroigne, having addressed the Regiment of Flanders, gained the men over and disarmed them so completely that they gave away their cartridges like brothers to the National Guard of Versailles. She would have been the first to laugh heartily had she heard of this tribute to her powers. It was also said of her that she spoke to the sentinel near the Orangery Gate and asked him to close it; whether to keep the mob from going in or royalty from coming out (since there was talk of flight), history says not.

Some of the women had taken shelter in the guard-house of the Regiment of Flanders, but the largest number poured into the *Salle des Menus* to rejoin their friends who had remained with Maillard. The galleries were a forest of pikes and iron clubs. The women grew more and more turbulent, the men rather more quiet and subdued. A deter-mined lady of the gutter seized the presidential chair. Others equally determined sprawled over the benches of the deputies, ousting their rightful occupants. They shouted, sang, and gesticulated, giving unso-licited embraces to all they fancied, and scorning those they disliked.

The women of the deputation, returning from the palace, had a story of gracious promises to tell. At their head was a charming spokeswoman, Louison Chabray, slim and fair, who had had the supreme honour of feeling the king's touch upon her arm. But all their enthusiasm was discredited. The mob jeered at their optimism, and threatened them with physical violence. They escaped with some difficulty and returned to do their work again and bring back an undertaking in writing.

When at length Mounier came back into the Assembly Hall, bread was brought in, and the hungry crowd ate and grew good-humoured. "Let us hear our darling mother Mirabeau," cried the eager women. But Mirabeau refused to speak more than a word, and that was to chide them for interrupting the deputies.

Hour after hour the women sat in the house, feeding when they could get food, talking amongst themselves, some singing, some snoring. The drone of the speakers continued. Théroigne had long since gone home. "I did not leave my rooms again," she says, "although I knew that they had convoked the deputies for a night sitting."

All that evening there was danger of rioting, and the royalist troops were withdrawn within the palace grounds. At midnight Lafayette arrived at Versailles with twenty thousand National Guards. Now at last an air of security was established, and the Court feared the rebellious people no longer. There was darkness and comparative quiet in the palace, and the queen slept. But the wakeful deputies continued discussing and confabulating in the National Assembly, still surrounded by unwashed women in soaking rags, who occupied the seats usually reserved for beauty of the highest rank, richly apparelled.

And Théroigne slept too, or says she slept. On the truth of her statement a great deal depended. She was accused of being one of those who broke into the palace in the early dawn. It is difficult to believe that she slumbered through the sitting of the National Assembly, because she never missed the meetings if she could help it, and this was an important one.

She had taken lodgings at Versailles for the sole purpose of being present at them all. But if she had owned to wakefulness it would have been difficult to prove her innocence.

The queen had rested perhaps three hours when an unexpected noise aroused her. She heard cries, and a curse coupled with her name. The crowds were breaking into the palace. She heard the snapping of bars, the crash of doors breaking inwards, the feet of the rebels in the passage. It was growing light, and she fled from her apartments for her life.

Théroigne swears in her *Confessions* that she knew nothing of this attempt on the queen's safety. At the time she was hastening back to the National Assembly. At six o'clock the doors were not yet opened. The National Guard was on duty before the palace, and she saw a huge crowd assembled. She declares:

> I moved about amongst the groups of people in order to over-hear what was being said. They spoke about the aristocrats, and I joined in and spoke no good of them. Then I attempted to glide in among the ranks of the National Guard, attracted by the clamouring of the people as they were fighting with the Bodyguard. But I could not see what was going on distinctly. At last the Assembly opened its doors. I went to my usual seat in Tribune No. 6. The Hall was almost empty. Only a few of the deputies of the *noblesse* were present. Under the circumstances they demanded that the National Assembly should be transported to the Hercules Gallery in the palace. It seemed to me and to all those present in our tribune that a removal of the representatives would wound and violate the decrees of the National Assembly. We made strenuous opposition to this. All thought it would be better if a numerous deputation was sent to the king. This was agreed upon.

In the courtyard a group of armed men and women surrounded a squad of the National Guard and made them fire on the king's men. Two of the Bodyguard were seized and their heads cut off and impaled on pikes. Lafayette, ever on the alert, ordered the National Guard to fire, and averted further bloodshed.

The mob roared "Bring the king to Paris." Louis showed himself on the balcony. Marie-Antoinette came too, pale and dignified. She held the hands of Madame Royale and the child *dauphin*, but the people cried "No children, no children," and they were sent in again. It is all so well known; it was all so tragic. As she stood there a man in the crowd levelled his musket as though to fire on the queen. She did not flinch, and Lafayette stooping to kiss her hand put an end to hostile demonstration.

By one o'clock the king had promised to leave Versailles. At this news men and women danced together with a new sense of fraternity. Holding hands, they sang and splashed in the last night's mud. It was a masquerade of death and hunger and captivity. Whither were they about to drag the royal family? A start was made towards the capital. The people, having captured the baker, the baker's wife, and the baker's boy, were temporarily content. They marched on foot, they rode in carts, the women bestrode the cannon. The heads of the slain soldiers, raised on pikes, were an emblem of their triumph, and on the route a halt was made at the hairdressers' shop to have the hair powdered, curled, and daubed with cream. Women carried loaves on pikes or branches of trees. Many who marched that day were to remember it till they died.

The king was in the capital, the legislative body followed and took up its position in the riding-school. Théroigne was to be found near her source of inspiration. But the debt she incurred on those October days was still to be paid. On August 6th, 1790, a warrant was issued by the *Châtelet* for her arrest. Referring to this she wrote to Perregaux on August 26th, from Liège:

> I have been very astonished to learn this news. Was it to be expected that having taken no part in all that was said or done on the days of the 5th and 6th, I should be accused of complicity in the supposed conspiracy? .... As I am unable to judge how far the malignity of those who have denounced me has gone, if you wish to do me a service it will be well for you to learn as much as you can of the crimes of which I am accused. If they are serious, I shall have to defend myself, and to do this I should have to utter nothing but the simple truth.

There was very little definite evidence against her. The *Châtelet* began the inquiry into the events of October in the following December. By July 1790 it was completed. As many as four hundred depositions were included in the printed report, and of these only two or three contained a reference to Théroigne. One man deposed to having seen a lady he believed was Mlle Therouene de Montesurt (*sic*) on the morning of the 6th, amongst the "brigands "who came from Paris to Versailles, dressed as a man, with a tall gentleman dressed as a woman.

A *curé* of the name of François-Xavier Veytard declared that on the evening of the 5th, when the Regiment of Flanders was drawn up in two lines in the Avenue of Versailles, a lady dressed in a red riding-habit, as far as he could judge of the colour in the dim evening light, went up and down the ranks of the soldiers, holding a basket in her hand, from which the soldiers took small packets and soon afterwards withdrew to their barracks. He understood that this woman's name was Therouenne. His evidence was given on March 9th, 1790.

A priest called Tournacheau de Montveran made a deposition on

May 1st following, in which he stated that he was staying at an *hôtel* in the Rue de l'Orangerie, and, in company with several friends between 4 and 5 o'clock on October 5th, he noticed from the window several women and men disguised as women, amongst whom was one attired in a scarlet riding-habit, on horseback. She was followed by a jockey also dressed in red. He had been told that this woman, whom he had seen previously at the Assembly and had recognised since, was Mlle Therouenne de Méricourt. She had approached the sentinel who guarded the gate near the Orangery, and very soon afterwards the sentinel had closed the gate. Everyone imagined that this was done by the instructions of the said Therouenne, who thereupon, followed by the same women, went off through the Rue de la Surintendance.

There was also a Mlle Gauthier who, looking from a window in the Rue de l'Orangerie, saw a woman who was so tall that she thought it must be a man, and this person was accompanied by a woman of ordinary figure on horseback, dressed in a riding-habit, who dismounted and spoke to the sentinel at the gate of the Orangery.

When questioned about the closing of this gate, Théroigne admitted that she might have spoken to the sentinel, but that when she did so the gate was shut, and consequently she could not have been responsible for giving an order. Nor would any soldier of the Bodyguard have obeyed her instructions, for she was not known to them.

The accounts vary so much, and are so vague, that very little weight can be attached to them. Veytard, who said he saw Théroigne distributing small parcels out of a basket, made the value of such evidence dubious by declaring that it was not light enough to distinguish whether she was wearing a scarlet riding-habit. When questioned as to the colour of this garment, Théroigne acknowledged that she possessed such a costume, as well as a similar one in white and in black, but that she could not remember what she wore on that particular day. She treated with contempt the statements of the witness who declared she was on horseback. "If anyone can prove that I was riding," she answered boldly, when faced by this accusation, "I consent to any punishment they may care to inflict."

She deliberately denied having seen any woman moving about among the soldiers of the Regiment of Flanders for the purpose of inciting them to break rank and revolt. In her opinion the regiment had remained calm and ranged in battle order.

Apart from the witnesses who had named Théroigne more or less accurately, there were several who described her without mentioning

THÉROIGNE DE MÉRICOURT.

From the drawing by Raffet.

her name. A certain Cornier de la Dodinière said he saw a woman dressed in a scarlet riding-dress and round hat passing from group to group and speaking to many people. The next day an officer of the National Guard of Paris, meeting him in a *café*, had said to him that he could not forget the charming appearance of a woman dressed all in red whom he had seen haranguing and exciting his men to go to the National Assembly and to seize some captives there, whose names she mentioned, and that she had gone so far as to address the superior officer at the head of the battalion, who had given instructions that she was to be chased away.

Another soldier, of the name of Saint-Gobert, a lieutenant of Volunteer Chasseurs, described a young and pretty woman whom he had noticed in the ranks, dressed in a riding-habit, wearing a hat with black plumes, who spoke to the volunteers of his company, and that this lady said to him and to his comrades that they were to go to the National Assembly, and that she would then indicate the real enemies of the nation. He had begged the lady to withdraw, and not to cause disorder in the ranks, but not succeeding in making her take her departure, he had fetched the captain, who, when he arrived, expressed his wish that the lady would go away without delay. She had at last submitted to his repeated commands, but unwillingly, remarking scornfully as she went that she had believed she was appealing to good citizens.

Whatever proofs may be put forward to clear Théroigne's name of all imputations of evil-doing, this account is remarkably characteristic of her methods. It may or may not have been she, but it sounds exactly like her.

La Valette in his accusation said that, during the riots at Versailles, Théroigne, dressed like a man, had mingled with the crowd and distributed bread. At her orders, he declared, the gates of the Orangery had been closed to hinder the people from entering the palace grounds. When she was captive, and they were driving towards Coblenz, he tried to sound her on these points, and said to her;:

Mademoiselle, I still seem to see you leading the market-women to Versailles. It was an imposing sight. And you at their head on horseback, you looked—

But she interrupted him:

I? There you make a great mistake, *monsieur*. I was not in that famous procession at all. I was not living in Paris at that time. I stayed at Versailles the whole of the summer of 1789.

He apologised for his error. He said he must have seen her in the streets of Versailles.

"I did what others did," she answered, "neither more nor less. I wanted to watch the mob arrive from Paris."

"But in the evening, you entered the palace——"

"No, *monsieur*. I did not go into the palace, nor even into the palace grounds. The Bodyguard refused admittance to anyone. I only went as far as the park railings. The gates were all shut."

When asked why the crowd had massacred two of the guard, she said she thought that the soldiers were themselves to blame for this horrible catastrophe. The people regarded them as inveterate partisans of the court. Irritated by the sullen and equivocal conduct of the aristocracy, they wished to give weight to their demands by showing activity. It was greatly to be regretted that they should have resorted to murderous violence. But at that moment it was perhaps inevitable that it should have happened, for it was necessary to use force to obtain liberty from despotism. If royalty had voluntarily acceded to the more than legitimate claims of the people, who had been reduced to slavery for long enough, if the clergy and the nobility had freely renounced feudal rights, there would have been neither licence nor spilt blood.

"Misery begets misery," she cried, "crime begets crime." The peasant who is born into the world has no other heritage than the ill-treatment of his lord. More than this she refused to admit to her captor. It was the parrot-like cry of the people, which she had had a thousand opportunities of hearing. She continued:

In my eyes, aristocracy, however illustrious its origin, is of no more importance than the lowest of the middle classes, or the most obscure but honest peasant. All these titles and dignities are often but a cloak for worthlessness. . . . Hereditary nobility is a ridiculous anomaly. It is high time to open the eyes of the people, who are purposely kept sunk in brutishness. The peasant is obliged to work and to moisten with his sweat the land which belongs to another, whilst the other declares that he has a right to exact this toil. The lord of the land illtreats his subjects. He demands from them a blind obedience, and inflicts tortures worse than death. The revenues obtained from the soil do not belong to those who cultivate it, and the fruit of their rough toil is foolishly dissipated by the capitalists. They scatter and waste enormous sums in gambling and other vices.

These remarks aroused her hearer. In a passion he enquired how she dared to speak of the aristocracy with such disdain, "Everyone is free to dispose of his goods as he may wish, *mademoiselle*," he cried angrily.

She replied:

I do not deny it, but it is none the less true that it is the result of flagrant injustice that a small portion of society is gorged with wealth whilst thousands, nay, millions of brave people are living a life of misery—to die a death by starvation. What has the Government done to remedy this fearful state of things. Nothing! Absolutely nothing! Ought the people to consent to suffer for ever and to want necessities when so many aristocrats have superfluities, and plunge into the grossest of pleasures! Never! It is just and necessary to expel all these sluggards and idlers. They are useless; nay, worse, they are harmful. . . .

The Comte de la Valette trembled with passion. She had touched on a weak spot, his aristocratic pride. He thought that her words were meant specially to humiliate him. He cried out that she lied, that there was not a word of truth in all she had said.

She replied boldly that, on the contrary, she had spoken nothing but the truth. The abuses which she had described must end. The country would never know happiness until it was delivered from the crushing privileges enjoyed by the clergy and the nobility. It was necessary that all should enjoy freedom as well as the bread to which they were entitled. Then she began to discuss the Rights of Man.

La Valette refused to listen to her any longer. At that moment the carriage in which they were travelling gave a jolt, and almost overturned. The count, mastered by his ill-temper, jumped out, and, snatching the whip, beat the driver soundly for his clumsiness. Théroigne begged him to desist in the name of all that was human. Her prayers only augmented the fury of the blows. He ceased when the handle of the whip smashed in his hand, and throwing away the pieces, he cried, "So much for the Rights of Man,"

Théroigne was silent. She was weeping bitterly.

CHAPTER 3

Théroigne's Club

The French have always been gregarious and communicative. They have always loved to discuss their interests, and to express in words their fears and agitations, as well as their rejoicing and admiration. This national trait was remarkably noticeable throughout the eighteenth century. It was the age of opinion. The thinkers of the day emulated one another in making public their ideas. An irresistible impulse to teach, to lead, to convert, or at least to state probabilities and possibilities, began somewhere near the close of Louis XIV.'s reign—that is to say, in the youth of Voltaire and Rousseau—and increased slowly throughout the Regency, more quickly in the second half of Louis XV.'s reign, whilst in the seventies and eighties the impulse became uncontrollable. To speak one must have an audience, and to gather an audience one must have a meeting-place.

In the early part of the century people met at the *cafés* and in the *salons* to air their views and imbibe the new philosophical ideas that were spreading rapidly through the country. No sooner was there a whisper of revolt than these places became inadequate to hold the masses who wished to utter volumes of complaints and to formulate plans for the amelioration of conditions. A new outlet had to be found for them, and was found in the shape of political clubs. At first these were few and held in secret, but after the opening of the States General they multiplied in numbers, subdivided and re-formed until they became a recognised institution of revolutionary France. They were the best medium for an interchange of ideas, and they issued pamphlets and journals in a never-ceasing, ever-increasing stream.

One of the most important was first formed by a small section of the deputies of Brittany, and was called the Breton Club. Although its members were full of the new ideas which were spreading everywhere, they did not in any way hold extreme views at this time. They were frankly royalists. But as time passed a new tone entered into the debates. On June 9th, 1789, Boullé wrote of the society:

For some days our *salon* has been the rendezvous of all good citizens.

Meetings were then taking place every evening. As most of the members were in the National Assembly, the meeting-house of the club was at Versailles, but in October it naturally followed the Court and legislative body to Paris, and was presently installed in the Convent of the Dominicans or Jacobins in the Rue Saint-Honoré. Although the official name of the club was changed in February 1790 to the *Société des Amis de la Constitution*, it was soon to be known far better by the title of the Jacobins Club, and under that famous name became a political force.

The great difference between this society and other political clubs, such as had already been known in England for a century and a half, was its system of affiliation. The number of members had grown so rapidly, the ideas disseminated by the club's adherents were so popular, and its endeavour to reach Frenchmen—and even Frenchwomen—in every part of the country so insistent, that it was decided to form a nucleus in each town of people who held the same ideas, and had similar aims to those who had easy access to the mother-society in Paris. Thus, was born a mighty organism, spreading its tentacles throughout France. As was to be foreseen, with the growth of revolutionary ideas, the opinions with which the club had begun its sittings evolved on similar lines, the strength of the extreme Left becoming ever more and more a predominating factor.

There is no room in a volume which purports to be a biography to tell the history of the clubs. The ramifications of the old ones, the forming of new and ever more daring ones, the gradual change of thought from monarchism to republicanism would fill volumes of their own. But because one aspect, and an important aspect, of Théroigne's revolutionary career was closely bound up with the clubs—she frequented them, she did her utmost to be elected a member of one of the most important, and she helped to organise one of her own—some digression on the subject of clubs is necessary. Her interest in them led her to study them carefully and to endeavour to grasp and explain the changes in Paris life which had been brought about by the great upheaval, one of the most noticeable being connected with this very question of the growth of the political societies.

It is a baffling point in the character of Théroigne that, considering her irregular youth and upbringing, she should not merely have turned to the exciting and stimulating side of the people's fight for freedom, but preferred to throw her whole heart into her desire to understand the causes of their wretchedness and the serious questions involved in attempting to obtain a better state of affairs. She must have been possessed of powers of reasoning and observation superior to those usually bestowed upon women who are content with a livelihood so precariously obtained as hers had been.

But Théroigne was a law unto herself, and must not be judged by the standards applied to other women of her class. When she studied the matter of clubs, she found that they were springing up around her like mushrooms. The first one in Paris which was really worthy of the name had been opened in April 1782, by Boyer, in the Rue Sainte-Nicaise. It was called the *Club Français*. Three years later the Duc d'Orléans, who admired everything English and American, opened a *Club de Boston*. But it was not till the outbreak of the Revolution that the real utility of club life became apparent, and the idea spread so quickly that there were soon several hundreds in Paris.

The most advanced club of all was the *Club des Cordeliers*, run by Danton, Camille Desmoulins, and Marat. The *Club de 1789*, installed near the Palais Royal, revelling in dinners under the auspices of Siéyès, Lafayette, Bailly, and Mirabeau, was turned into the *Club de la Constitution Monarchique*, its members being friends to despotism under the mask of moderation, and later it became the *Feuillants*. The motto of the *Club des Impartiaux* was "Justice, Truth, and Constancy." The Cercle Social had a branch society, named the *Confédération Universelle des Amis de la Vérite*, and there were numerous others of importance, all with views more or less advanced, because clubs with moderate ideas had but little hold on the popular imagination.

So enormous was the influence wielded by these ever-spreading organisations, that the legislative body began to see a danger to the peace of the country in their continued growth, and in 1791 adopted certain propositions limiting their powers, which were chiefly exercised in two directions. They had the right to petition, and used it by presenting to the Assembly addresses which were in reality orders in the disguise of requests, and they had the right to stick bills in public places. This made it possible for them to placard Paris over at any moment with declarations which, being assimilated speedily by the man in the street, evoked a chorus of similar opinion throughout the breadth of the country.

These privileges were to be curtailed, and for that purpose the assembly drew up certain clauses, declaring that no society, club, or association of citizens could have any recognised political existence, could exercise the slightest influence over the acts of constituted powers and legal authorities, nor appear under any pretext collectively to present petitions or form deputations, or to assist at public ceremonies under various penalties. A decree to this effect was adopted on September 29th, but in practice it very soon proved inefficacious.

As well dam a flood with shifting sand. By that date the clubs had become an ungovernable, an incalculable force, and no legislative means could stop their clamour. The journals alone which poured from their presses were capable of swaying public thought. Their discussions and articles filtered through their own institutions to the more general if less highly organised groups which met in the salons, the *cafés*, the restaurants, the booksellers', and libraries, to the wine-shops, and the gatherings at street-corners and in the public gardens. All these were centres of commotion. The *cafés*, which for the past fifty years had been the resort of men of letters, wits, dramatic critics, lawyers, and artists, intent on discussing the latest achievements in their own particular profession, were now used as places where the political measures of the day were brought up for debate, and where the latest news from the Assembly could be gleaned at all hours.

The Café Hottot on the terrace of the *Feuillants* and almost at the doors of the Assembly Hall, and the Café de Foy, at first patriotic, and then monarchic, were two of the most important. The latter in its second stage was the refuge for aristocratic disputants. Knights of Saint Louis, soldiers, and financiers, with huge wigs and square-toed shoes, armed with cudgels, sword-sticks, and canes weighted with lead, who read nothing but monarchical propositions, uncovered their heads whenever royalty was mentioned, and played dominoes to while away the time when waiting for news. The Café Procope, once of theatrical fame, had to change its style, and was held in suspicion by all good partisans of the Revolution.

Unless a *café* took a political tone, the people had no use for it, as was proved by the speedy passing away of the Café Flore, whose *habitués* were bound by a vow not to mention affairs of government. The Café de la Justice was frequented chiefly by excited legal lights, the Café de la République by patriots who were keen on being informed in the speediest and most reliable manner of what was going on. The Café de Valois was another rendezvous of royalists—Rivarol, for instance, Champcenetz, who wrote a satiric letter about Théroigne, and Peltier, who was one of the fairest minded of her opponents. In May 1790 this *café*, which had originally been founded by Abbé Siéyès under the auspices of the Duc d'Orléans, became such a hot-bed of aristocracy that the patriots made a descent upon it and cleansed the Augean stables with fumes of gin.

Booksellers' shops were found convenient for the sale of royalist and counter-revolutionary journals, brochures, libels, pamphlets, and printed questions of the order of the day. They were sold openly and secretly. Sometimes there were printing-presses on the premises, issuing and manifolding publications of a seditious nature without place or date or name. One of the most notorious monarchical booksellers was Gattey, whose business was in the Palais Royal. He was said to be a police spy, and his shop was invaded more than once, his stock burned, and the place "disinfected of the breath of bad citizens" by fumigations of vinegar and sugar. A complete edition of the *Actes des Apôtres* was sacrificed at one of these holocausts, and at length Gattey found it too dangerous to sell this scurrilous royalist paper and announced that he would take no further part in its publication and distribution.

The editors and chief contributors, Peltier, Rivarol, Champcenetz, Mirabeau, Tonneau, and Suleau—Théroigne knew them well by name, and hated them well—usually held their meetings at the house of the Marquise de Champbonas. The paper was discussed and made up at the Restaurateur Beauvilliers, near to Gattey's shop, where *dîners évangeliques* were held to which only the initiated were admitted. The apostles took copious notes of the conversation and dished it up in spicy insults addressed against the patriots.

Théroigne was as frequently the subject of their coarse jests as any one. The attacks on her make astonishing reading. By what virtue—or vice—did she become the butt of fifty satirical publications? Why was she chosen especially to be pilloried in a hundred ways, as patriot, Amazon, orator, and mistress? She had splendid enemies—the aristocrats—and there must have been something remarkable about her to have kept her so persistently an object of their spite. It was said that she was driven to madness by their satires and caricatures, and the *Petit Gauthier* described a raid she made on her own account upon one of the places where these libels were on sale:

The brazen-faced Théroigne, after walking the day before yesterday in the *Camp des Tartares*, in the Palais Royal, entered a shop where caricatures were sold, and had the effrontery to say to the dealer in them, that if she continued to display those which ridiculed other people besides the executive powers, the nobility and the clergy, she would come, accompanied by some patriots, and tear them up.

The saleswoman threatened the "*ci-devant pucelle*" with a burning torch, causing her to flee and leave one of her shoes behind her in her haste.

Besides the *Petit Gauthier*, otherwise called the *Journal de la Cour et de la Ville*, and the *Actes des Apôtres*, her chief calumniators, the *Sabbats Jacobites*, which brought into fashion the word "*canaillocratie*," and the *Apocalypse* were among the worst offenders. The standing joke referred to by them was her supposed marriage with the Deputy Populus, *i.e.* the People. Of this *bon mot* they never seemed to tire. It was turned this way and that way and exploited for all and more than it was worth. A play on the subject ran through many numbers of the *Actes des Apôtres*, and was eventually published separately in 1790 under the title of "*Théroigne et Populus, ou le triomphe de la démocratie, drame national en vers civiques*." (See Appendix A.)

Attached was a "*Précis sur la vie de Mademoiselle Téroigne de Méricour*," in which her supposed lover is described in satirical terms. Beaulieu asserts that she had never met the deputy for Bourg-en-Bresse, who was at this time aged about fifty-five. The writer remarks, describing the real man:

Although Populus is only four feet seven inches and three lines tall, he possesses that agreeable sloping curve of the shoulders which denotes profundity of thought, multiplicity of studies, and the habits of meditation. Moreover, although he is between thirty and sixty-five years old, he does not wear the dissipated air which distinguishes many young Frenchmen. His hair, of the most beautiful dappled grey, arranged in curls and plastered down behind his ears, suits his face remarkably well, giving it more breadth and importance; and behind it is fastened tightly in a net and bobs about on his shoulders, giving the impression of the august and majestic character of one who represents the nation. Never has any deputy had more the air of a deputy than this honourable deputy.

Naturally enough the form in which the satires were couched was one that had especial power to wound. Théroigne was not the only one subjected to the drastic wit of the royalists. Monarchism in the press never ceased to aim poisoned darts at the people, and ironic raillery, lies, and calumny fanned the flame of hatred and gave rise to insurrectionary outbursts. In many respects the journals have small historical value, and throw little light on the course of events. It is enough to say that the obscene diatribes of the aristocrats denote a significant lack of dignity unpardonable in the governing class.

The Revolutionary journals, on the other hand, were distinguished by an earnest belief in the justice of their cause. Whilst the royalists were content to jest coarsely in and out of season, Desmoulins, Brissot, and Marat were voicing the call of freedom in their respective journals—*Les Revolutions de France et de Brabant, Le Patriote,* and *L'Ami du Peuple.*

The clubs, the *cafés,* the book-shops, with their vast stream of topical publications, were thus the means through which the new and revolutionary ideas spread like wildfire to the bulk of the people, indiscriminately, without favour or that personal and social note which relationship, acquaintance, or friendship gives. Yet this element existed and must not be undervalued. It was to be found chiefly among the feminine gatherings in the semi-privacy of the salons. Those of the capital had changed in tendency at the first signs of the struggle between the classes and the masses. Philosophy, reform, and revolution formed the new keynotes of intercourse; charm, culture, literature, and learning—all the graces of the old regime, in short—were relegated to the background.

Earnestness superseded gaiety, discussion took the place of chat and gossip, and personal ambition pushed aside social intimacy. Some of the gatherings were turned into conferences "like tragedies without women," some were political whirlpools of rage and ferment, some were training-schools for orators and pamphlet-writers, and again others were not unlike forcing-houses where guests were to be converted with the least possible delay to a belief in the "illusion of the happiness of humanity." All of them without exception were touched by the dread shadow of coming trouble and were enshrouded in the dark cloud of suspense.

In Mme Necker's *salon* friends of the ministers assembled, and she tried to win from the Abbé Siéyès and Clermont-Tonnerre the good opinion of the National Assembly for her husband. Mme de Staël's social-political activity dated from 1786. Mme de Simiane and Mme de Coigny's receptions were at their height. Mme de Tessé opened wide her doors to exponents of the new ideas. The Princess von Hohenzollern received politicians of the Left, amongst them Beauharnais, Abbé Dillon, Barnave, and the Lameths.

At Mme de Beauharnais's house Dorat, Collé, Pezay, and Bonnard held meetings, which were homely in character. The Comtesse de Genlis—Walpole referred to her later as the too-well-known woman who fled to Switzerland—entertained Brissot, Camille Desmoulins, and the friends of the Duc d'Orléans. The Duke of Bedford gave balls to the Revolutionaries. The wife of Talma, the *sprituelle* Julie, gathered in the Rue Chantereine many guests of political importance, Roucher, Roland, the painter Greuze, the orator Vergniaud, and Marie-Joseph Chénier, who was later to be associated with Théroigne in the organisation of the *fête* to the soldiers of Châteauvieux.

After the death of her husband Mme Helvetius settled in her country house at Auteuil with her two daughters, Mme de Mun and Mme d'Andlau, whom Franklin had rechristened "the stars." A large number of thinkers frequented this *salon*—Condorcet, the aristocrat-republican, Cabanis, Mirabeau's doctor, who married Mme de Condorcet's sister, Volney the traveller, Chamfort the witty moralist, whose sallies, said Mme Roland, "make you laugh and think at the same time—a very rare occurrence." Mirabeau was his friend, and Siéyès profited by his ideas.

"I have just composed a work," said Chamfort one day to de Lauraguais.

"Oh, a book?" inquired the latter.

"No, not a book; I am not so foolish. Only the title of a book; but the title is everything. I have given it to Siéyès. He can say what he will; people will remember nothing but the title"—which was *What is the Third Estate? Nothing. What ought it to be? Everything.*

Morellet, having deserted the *salon* of Mme Helvetius, commenced rival gatherings of his own on Sundays, at which the Suards were present. At the houses of Mme Lameth and Mme Dumas there were a great number of Montagnards, at Mme Roland's many of the Girondins. At Mme d'Angivillers "all the Revolution" was made welcome, and, as might be expected, the number of her guests was not exceeded in any other drawing-room. She was a very fascinating hostess. Gouverneur Morris went there as well as to the Condorcets', whose house he described as the centre of thinking Europe, where distinguished

MARC-ETIENNE POPULUS, DEPUTY FOR BOURG-EN-BRESSE.

From an engraving in the Bibliothèque Nationale.

persons from far and near were to be found, perhaps the most attractive feature being the philosopher's lively and sympathetic wife. This *salon* was presently known as the Foyer de la Republique, and all with monarchical tendencies avoided it thereafter.

After these important and representative *salons*—and there were many others—the unpretentious gatherings held by Théroigne in her apartments at the Hôtel de Grenoble, Rue de Bouloi, may at first seem insignificant. Nothing like as powerful, they nevertheless had a great deal in common with the political assemblies organised by Mme Roland. Their aims were the same. Théroigne would have scorned the word "*salon*." She preferred to use the word "club." Her receptions had little that was social in their aspect, everything that was political, and it was necessary for her to minimise their importance as much as possible when questioned on the subject by the examining magistrate at Kufstein. She succeeded in making it appear that the organisation of the club at her *hôtel* was one of the most harmless in existence. She was afraid of being implicated in plots and conspiracies, and denied having been connected with any revolutionary receptions. Yet nowhere was the purpose more definite, the labour for liberty more earnest and from the heart. She tells something of the origin of these meetings in her *Confessions*:

> When the National Assembly was installed in Paris, I followed it. I lodged at the Hôtel de Grenoble in the Rue de Bouloi. I continued to be present at the sittings morning and evening. Everyone knew me from seeing me so often. The people and the deputies liked me as much on account of my patriotism as for my private conduct.... I proposed to those who came most often to the tribune of the *Feuillants* to join in making a political society. They approved of my idea. Whilst this growing club assembled in my house it numbered some twelve or thirteen members.

The society was called the Club of the Amis de la Loi, but must not be confused with one of the same name founded in 1791 by Osselin. The chief person associated with Théroigne in founding the society was Gilbert Romme the mystic. The friendship of this high-minded idealist—it has been said that he was one of the purest characters of the Revolution—does more to reinstate Théroigne amongst the virtuous than the constant reflections of the royalist pamphlets to prove her abandonment. Michelet says:

Romme, with the face of Socrates, had his profound understanding, the austere mildness of a sage, of a hero, of a martyr.

Like his brother Charles Romme, the mathematician, Gilbert consecrated himself to the sciences. He was born at Riom in 1750 and had many followers among his countrymen in mountainous Auvergne. He sat in the National Convention, was a Montagnard, helped to produce the republican calendar and in 1793 stabbed himself to cheat the guillotine. At the time of his association with Théroigne he had under his charge a son of a Russian noble, Count Strogonoff, familiarly called Otcher. This descendant of despots was educated by him, in the latest ideas on liberty, and accompanied him to the sittings of the National Assembly and the clubs,

Romme was the president of Théroigne's society, and amongst the members were several of his countrymen, Beaulieu, Larminat, Sponville, and Romme's nephew Tailhard. Otcher was made librarian. The meetings took place three times a week—on Tuesdays, Fridays, and Sundays from seven till ten in the evening. A month later only two meetings were held, on Tuesdays and Thursdays.

Théroigne did everything she could to make the club a success and worked hard to recruit new members. She proposed that her brother should join it, but the idea was negatived on the ostensible grounds that he knew very little French; actually, it was said, because he had lived at his sister's expense on money none too honestly come by.

When the club started Théroigne was put in charge of the papers and documents, but she soon handed over this responsibility to Chapsal. She took part in all the discussions, knew as much as the other members concerning the legislation of the country, and championed more hotly than any of them the rights of her sex. She thought women should be far more independent and rely less on the protection of men than they had been accustomed to do.

From March 10th onwards M. de Larminat presided at the meetings, Sponville and Daguet were secretaries. Maret, the future Duc de Bassano and de Bosc d' Antic, son of Louis XV.'s doctor and friend of Mme Roland, joined the society about this time. The members sought to affiliate popular committees with the departments. The aims of the club were written out by Romme under the title of *Association Populaire*. (MS. by Romme in the possession of M. Marcellin Pellet. *Théroigne de Méricourt*.)

Romme said:

The project is the result of several conversations in which Mlle Théroigne pointed out that it would be of great importance at this moment to have an establishment which made it an object to learn the degree and the means of influence possessed by each member of the National Assembly.

This idea resulted in the formation and development of the society. Other plans were added and the whole grew into an important organisation, its purpose being:

To give a new impulse to manners; to educate the people to an understanding of the dignity of its rights; to enlighten it upon its real interests and upon the degree of confidence and esteem that it owes to the zeal, the knowledge, and the virtues of its representatives in the National Assembly; to display before it the advantages of the Revolution; to spread, as far as possible, a knowledge of the daily workings of the Assembly; to reawaken the patriotism which had become extinct in the souls of some who were discouraged or fearful.

To hold back some of the too excitable spirits who might be carried away by their excess of zeal; to spare impatient readers the laborious and objectionable research among the multitude of pamphlets and periodical publications with which we are inundated; to offer to good citizens a choice of literature already prepared for their use in a reading-room open to associates; to correspond with the provinces, to spread information concerning good books and fine deeds, and to gather from these sources fresh inspirations, new motives of encouragement.

To focus the scattered rays of public opinion and to dissipate the clouds, with which black, vile, and hypocritical souls intentionally obscure them in order to alarm others; and to direct a searching light upon the tribunal without censuring its decisions, in order that those marked by wisdom and maturity may acquire an impressive and redoubtable character in the eyes of those who would betray the public cause, but may inspire with confidence those who believe in the people's good.

A society with such aims should surely have been above reproach, even though its archivist was "a woman who was fatally dangerous to the young and inexperienced." (*Romme le Montagnard*, Marc de Vissac.) Romme was absolutely convinced that the members of the Amis de la Loi were as blameless in their morals as they were upright in their opinions. Théroigne appears in an altogether new, but perhaps none the less fascinating light. It is easy to picture her in a Quakerish gown of grey, her flamboyant riding-habits laid temporarily aside, her smile subdued for the time, the merry twinkle of her eye veiled by her lashes, her forehead puckered by a little frown in token of her earnestness, and her brain ever busy with fresh plans for the furtherance of the club's purposes. Her ideas were carefully sifted by Romme, and carried out practically. The work was divided into various departments.

There was a committee of annotation, whose duty it was to attend the sittings of the National Assembly; a bibliographical committee, charged with the examination and censorship of the publications and documents for the perusal of the society; an information bureau, which gathered in the news and rumours of the town, and attended the sittings of the Commune and of the *Châtelet*; and an editorial department, which issued weekly reports of the work done by the various committees. Neither Romme nor Théroigne spared themselves in perfecting the details of this somewhat complicated machinery. The arrangements for the library and reading-room were left chiefly to the young Russian Count. For the sake of the number of his own countrymen who were members, Romme desired that a translation should be made of *The Declaration of the Rights of Man* into the vernacular of Limagne d'Auvergne.

Théroigne describes a little ceremony that took place at one of her meetings:

One day, I had the idea that it would be a good thing if the people gave civic crowns or cockades to the best patriots of the National Assembly. A motion to this effect, directed by M. Romme and others, and signed by the people, was adopted. Seven cockades were given to the seven members of the Committee of the Constitution. All the world wished to contribute to the small expense which this occasioned me. But by reason of my patriotic zeal, I did not accept. I took the cockades to M. l'Abbé Siéyès, whom I considered the most worthy of public gratitude and esteem. *Monsieur l'Abbé* came to my house in person to thank me.

This account of a club, with all its dry-as-dust details of organisation, not differing much from many similar institutions, may be contrasted with an imaginary one—for the French have the power of caricature developed to a marvellous degree, and when they told the story of a revolutionary political gathering they knew how to make it humorous, even to the point of fantasy. Such a description was published in the *Actes des Apôtres* at the beginning of 1790, and is worth repeating, if only because Théroigne played an important part in it, and figured in the accompanying illustration. The skit was entitled the *Club de la Révolution*, and tells a long-winded story of the Marquis de Condorcet, who conceived the clever plan of converting the Pantheon opposite the Palais Royal into a Temple of Liberty, and calling it the Club de la Revolution, or Portico of France.

The opening of the establishment took place amidst solemn celebrations. Some five hundred members, chosen from amongst the most zealous defenders of the people, lent it brilliancy. The Abbé de Siéyès was chosen president. A like number of ladies, being the most ardent upholders of the Rights of Man, were adjudged worthy of the privilege of being incorporated in the society, and Mlle Théroigne de Méricourt was elected *présidente* by her *concitoyennes*. She was installed on the spot, and presented with the instrument proper and necessary to the rights and duties of her post. The functions required of her were more onerous than those expected of the president. The little bell usual in such cases was enlarged upon this occasion, and was provided with a handle and clapper of remarkable size. The hall was especially decorated, and there was dancing, four *quadrilles* serving to open the ball.

Everybody who was anybody among the revolutionists was present. The Duc d'Aiguillon, dressed as the Queen of Hungary, danced the minuet with the Chevalier Malo de Lameth attired as the King of Prussia. In spite of their good disguises these two were recognised. This dance was followed by a contredanse, in which M. de Clermont Tonnerre took part, wearing an iron mask. M. de Champcenetz *fils* danced with a lady disguised as Venus. M. Guillotin, the political doctor, danced not to his own instrument of torture, but a solemn minuet with Mlle Samson. Robespierre, disguised as a cherub, thought it would be better to substitute a tight-rope dance, but to this the grave doctor objected.

A *pas de quatre* followed, performed by Mirabeau attired like a royal tiger, with a mask of Paris mud, Brissot dressed like the wandering Jew, Mme Olympe de Gouges disguised as a young *Indienne*, and Mme de Condorcet masquerading as the *Infanta* of Zamora. The *fandanga*, the *caloula*, and the *bamboula* were danced, Talleyrand being among the many who took part in these fantastic steps. Next came a performance by Target, who walked the tight-rope, and to him Siéyès presented a colossal pyramid, which being reversed he was ordered to balance to the best of his ability on its point. This ingenious symbol represented the Constitution, Thouret, in the garb of a harlequin, then sang a song entitled, "*Ah! comme il y viendra*," and Target, in the endeavour to respond with "*J'ai plus que vous le poignet ferme*," took a false step and came toppling down, pyramid and all.

After some more turns of a similar character, Mirabeau, disguised in red, white, and blue, danced a figure representing the Constitution of England, which had remained unaltered for a complete century. Barnave was also present, and, masked in the head of a shark, and with his coat laced with principles, was intended to represent the Rights of Man.

Much more of the same kind of satire followed, including a detailed description of the illustration to the scene, which was called the *Opening Ceremony of the Club de la Revolution*.

Mlle Théroigne de Méricourt is here to be seen directing the orchestra and handling two bells which weighed no less than forty-four pounds each. Harmonious as were the musical instruments, the noise from the boxes on the left, rising above them, often made it impossible to hear oneself speak. The costume of Mlle Théroigne is the same she wore at Versailles when, at the head of the national army, she routed a brigade of the bodyguard. Her scarlet riding-habit, her black plumes, her chestnut locks, were the rallying-sign. She was always to be found on the road taken by the routed. *Mediae inter coedes exultat Amazon.* In a manner similar to the lictors of the Roman Consuls, the august *coupe-téte* carried national forces in front of our heroine, who commanded a detachment of five hundred warriors as dependable as herself.

The picture also shows Target doing his tight-rope act, Siéyès climbing up the folding ladder to give him the inverted pyramid. Not far from Théroigne is Barnave wearing the shark mask, and in the background, Mme de Stael is arm-in-arm with M. de Champcenetz.

But to return to Théroigne's club. Naturally enough both her friends and enemies were quick to express in complimentary or derogatory terms their opinion of her attempt at establishing one of her own on purely political lines. Champcenetz was perhaps the most satirical among her opponents. His account, or supposed account, appeared in a letter purporting to be from him, and printed in the *Actes des Apôtres*. It forms a remarkable contrast to her own simple story of the meetings at her house.

Chance gave me the acquaintance of Mlle Théroigne de Méricourt. The charm of her face, the graces of her wit, and, far more than that, her ardent love of liberty, attracted me to this adorable woman. She might be called the muse of democracy, or, still better, Venus giving lessons on public rights. Her society is a lyceum, her principles those of the portico. She might have those of the arcade if she desired. Among her pupils may be counted Abbé Siéyès, Pétion de Villeneuve, Barnave, and the happy Populus, whose prodigious arts of pleasing and inexhaustible love she will soon crown, alas! by a marriage which will be the misfortune of my life. The pieces most applauded, most eloquent, most civic of their discourse at the Assembly have been composed or inspired by her.

The Hôtel de Grenoble, Rue de Bouloi, where she lodges, has become the central point of the great interests of regenerated France. There the discovery was made of that administrative power, unknown to the ancients, so simple in its organisation, so imposing in its details, and so ingenious in its progress that it will immediately replace the three other powers, however little the mechanism of political societies is perfected. There the foundations of this royal democracy, which has all the advantages of republics, without having the inconveniences of monarchies, are laid; there is built, with the hands of philanthropy, the edifice of the liberty of the blacks, already so advanced in Martinique; . . . there the project ripens of making d'Avignon the eighty-fifth department of France; there the enterprises of aristocrats are disconcerted; there, in short, are prepared those luminous motions which are at the same time the admiration of the capital and the stupefaction of the provinces.

Le Rodeur, which endeavoured to protect the much-maligned Théroigne from her arch enemies, "The Apostles," had also a word to say on her startling enterprise. In its columns she was described as an amiable young lady of two-and-twenty, who hastened to return from Rome to the banks of the Seine in order to protect the dawning liberty of the French. She took up the people's cause, and her enthusiasm for the rights of man soon made itself felt. Revolutionary committees, it was declared, were held at her house, where a thousand nails were driven into the machinery of the Constitution, and a policy was followed which so enraged the forty-five apostles that in their utter aristocratic impotence they permitted themselves every outrage, every poignant atrocity, that jealous fury could devise.

Among this more or less excellent fooling, the general opinion appeared to be, especially in royalist circles, that she might have turned her unquestionable charms to better account. All sorts of lies were told concerning the number and identity of her associates. The deposition of the Comte de la Valette, entitled *Dires et Aveux*, represented her as being in close relation with the heads of the democracy, whom she received frequently at her house. He declares:

> Besides the Duc d'Orléans, who was her great and principal friend, one might meet at her salon the Ducs de Liancourt and de Broglie, the Comte de Mirabeau, Abbe Siéyès, and many others, all of them deputies and partisans of the people.

Baron Mengin Salabert on the same subject said that when the States General was assembled, she invited to her house the most rabid democrats, among them Barnave, Robespierre, Chapelier, and Mirabeau. He continues:

> This new Laïs turned their heads, and they soon made of her a veritable Aspasia to whose house they came to take lessons in politics, eloquence, and legislation. The continual association with courtesans usually enervates both soul and body, and often is conducive to the loss of fortune, health, repose, and honour. The four philosophers mentioned did not fear such effects, least of all from the financial point of view. They were soon reinforced by twenty other deputies, among whom were the Abbé Siéyès and the Abbé Gouttes, in spite of his white hairs.
> They took an *hôtel*, at which they lodged this marvellous young woman. There they conspired. It was at her house that they formed the project of corrupting the French guards. Dressed as a man, she went alone, from one end of Paris to the other, through all the barracks. She harangued the soldiers hour after hour, and in the end distributed money amongst them. Thirty thousand *livres* were given by her in a fortnight! The memorable manifestation of the 5th and 6th of October was prepared by her. The Duc d'Orléans frequented her *salon*. He used to go there at night, as well as several of those attached to his house. They gave themselves up to their usual orgies.

All this is the creation of a vivid imagination. Théroigne denied that she had ever spoken to the Duc d'Orléans. She said, moreover, that, though she knew Robespierre, Chapelier, and the Abbé Gouttes by sight, she had never spoken to them and never invited them to her house. If she had been intimate with them, she would have thought it a great honour. When asked whether she had given supper-parties at Versailles, she denied that too.

Beaulieu, a more reliable authority, says:

When Paris was filled with clubs, she was to be seen at one or two every evening, after having harangued crowds in every quarter of the town all day long, giving out at the clubs her motions and instructions, and hurrying back to her house to do the honours for her visitors. It would be difficult to find another example of such activity.

He accused her of having utterly ruined certain persons of considerable repute. He continues, in his *Essais Historiques*:

Rather neglected at the outbreak of the Revolution, weary of pleasures which had been too well paid, the little Méricourt thought of taking up a political career. She dressed herself in a riding-habit, crowned her pretty head with a little hat *à la Henri Quatre*, and in this attire mixed with the crowd of speakers who never ceased to discuss affairs of State in the tribunes and gangways of the National Assembly.

Her singular appearance soon attracted much attention. At first it was thought she was there to win the admiration which means much to one of her sex and age. But this was quite a mistake.

The most innocent gallantry made her frown, and the voluptuous Cypris was suddenly metamorphosed into a grave and severe Minerva. This clever pretence imposed on everybody, pricked their dignity, provoked the affections of those who thought she was pretty, and little was wanting to turn all the politicians into passionate lovers.

Several of the deputies paid court to the courtesan, among others the famous Pétion, with whom she often had conferences. They also pretended that Populus, the deputy, was one of her lovers. But the truth was that she did not know him. The authors of the *Actes des Apôtres* made a pun on the word Populus, meaning people, and her marriage to Populus meant the marriage with the people.

No one gave more praise to the philosophic sentiments uttered by the fair Théroigne, in Beaulieu's opinion, than the Abbe Siéyès. He was her particular god. She openly paid homage and adoration to his talents and virtues. Mirabeau's immorality she sternly deplored. She was told to make allowances for him on account of his weakness for the fair sex, but this she refused to do, and went so far as to show her disapproval in strong terms.

The authors of the *Histoire de la Révolution par deux amis de la Liberté* said much the same. It is suggested that Beaulieu collaborated with Kerverseau and Clavelin in this work, and he may have written or revised their account of Théroigne. They say:

> We have seen wise men fall in love with this small person, who rejected their advances with a Lacedemonian pride. When they learnt that this scrupulous beauty was nothing more nor less than a *fille entretenu*, abandoned by a lover she had ruined, they laughed heartily.

The most intimate connections of this "Luxemburg prude," as they call her, were with the brother of Abbe Siéyès and Romme, one of the most zealous followers of the *abbé*. Romme, who had since become deputy in the national convention, was at that time tutor to a young Russian noble. Count Strogonoff, who was amused by the intimacy between the two. Théroigne was pretty, Romme was a sort of Quaker, affecting the most austere modesty; he took no care of his person, and was not good to look upon. He was an obscure metaphysician, a political alchemist whose ridiculous dissertations it was quite impossible to follow. Nothing was more comic, they said, than to hear the little Théroigne trying to appreciate her master's mysticism, and to see these two, so different in appearance and manner, laughing together at their audacious discoveries.

The *Deux Amis* put her age at twenty-three or four at the time they knew her. They admitted her prettiness, but said that she pushed her reserve to extremes, that the most innocent pleasantries made her blush and the least coaxing annoyed her. Nevertheless, men were usually her companions. She joined in all the groups, was to be found in all the clubs and at all the revolutionary *fêtes*. After spending the morning in the public tribunes of the National Assembly she spoke in the evening at the Cordeliers and at the Jacobins.

Lamartine and Goncourt have taken their accounts of Théroigne's *salon* from the less accurate sources, of which there are many. Both make Mirabeau her guest as well as Camille Desmoulins. Goncourt adds the names of Brissot, Chénier, Clootz, Fabre d'Eglantine, Momoro, Saint-Just, and Robespierre. Lamartine mentions Danton and Ronsin also:

> Romme, the mystical republican, infused into her mind the German spirit of illuminatism. Youth, love, revenge, and the contact with this furnace of a revolution, had turned her head, and she lived in the intoxication of passions, ideas, and pleasures. Connected at first with the great innovations of '89, she had passed from their arms into those of rich voluptuaries, who purchased her charms dearly. Courtesan of opulence, she became the voluntary prostitute of the people; and like her celebrated prototypes of Egypt and of Rome, she lavished upon liberty the wealth she derived from vice.

Duval is quite as extreme:

> All who had vowed hatred against royalty, all who thirsted after royal blood, were admitted with enthusiasm to her lodging, and *fêted* and caressed there. She was the Duchesse de Montpensier of the gutters, as well as the wicked and vindictive sister of the Guises.

A remarkable picture of a vampire which, as far as Théroigne was concerned, was scarcely true to nature!

In spite of all that was written by those who preferred to depict her as a bloodthirsty individual marching through the dramatic scenes of the Revolution with the intention of slaying and destroying, it is evident that at this time at least she was far more the *dame politique* than the warrior. She had put her whole heart into the success of the society which had its headquarters at her house, and when it became obvious that the venture was not going to succeed, she was sincerely grieved. She found it impossible to recruit new members, and suggested every means of sustaining the dying interest in the club, which had only had a lease of three months of life. She says:

> When the association which had first held its meetings in my rooms was dissolved, I proposed to form a new one. I was guided in all my propositions only by the love of good and the glory to be acquired by rendering myself useful to the nation. But I had not enough talent for this, nor enough experience, and, alas! I was only a woman.

THÉROIGNE CONDUCTS THE ORCHESTRA AT THE CLUB DE LA RÉVOLUTION.

The idea of forming a new club having been abandoned, a proposal was started that the original members should join the *Club des Cordeliers*, but some of them objected to this scheme. Théroigne herself would have rejoiced in being permitted to work on an equal footing with the men who were giving time, money, and life itself for the good of their country. But here too she was debarred by sex. The ambitions and patriotism of a woman were not to be taken seriously at that date. She had done her best to draw Siéyès into her little circle, feeling convinced that with his authority behind her she would be able to secure a certain amount of attention wherever she wished to make herself heard. In this respect her project failed and she had to remain contented with receiving the great constitution-builder by proxy in the person of his brother.

Nevertheless, she obtained a considerable, though by no means unlimited, influence. According to Beaulieu her assistance was regarded as invaluable in cases where stragglers were to be won over, or the discouraged to be strengthened, so remarkable were her powers of persuasion. She was always present in the tribunes or neighbourhood of the Assembly, sometimes dressed in a Greek costume, at the head of the shouting rabble, and to her was relegated the duty of leading the applause or hooting. She had an extraordinary vivacity, an alert imagination, and but little wit, declared the same writer, whatever may have been said by those who in 1789 regarded her as a prodigy. Her head was full of verses by those great poets who had the most exalted Republican ideas. She repeated them with wonderful fire, in a jargon which was half French, half Flemish, which amused her hearers and sounded delightful on lips that were to all appearance sweet and innocent.

Théroigne had undoubtedly the gift of oratory. Some of her worst detractors admitted so much. The *Petit Gauthier*, royalist among the royalists, and full of coarse and satiric jesting, described "the Brabantian nymph" as carrying away her audience by sheer fervour when speaking at a bookseller's in the Palais Royal, in spite of the fact that what she said was so unreasonable that the aristocrats "shrugged their shoulders for very pity," and forced her to cut short her remarks before she had done her speech.

Baudet, who often saw her at gatherings near the Tuileries, declared that she spoke more with confidence than with the word of the orator. Her costume was neither elegant nor bizarre. It consisted of a common green riding-habit and a hat with a black feather. She was small and well-shaped, with good features and a complexion the colour of a russet pear, owing to the out-of-door life she led.

Evidence of her oratorical abilities was given by Hyde de Neuville, a royalist whose grandfather had fled from England with Charles Stuart in 1745. Hyde de Neuville had followed the royal cause staunchly from the opening of the Revolution, and wherever he could gather a crowd he harangued it upon its duty. He declared that Marie-Antoinette had become to him an object of romantic devotion and that he could see no higher aim in life than to work for her in this manner. However, much he ran the danger of being menaced and pursued, he never allowed his zeal to lessen.

He writes in his *Memoirs*:

> One day, I was so little circumspect as to apostrophise Théroigne de Méricourt, already known by her audacious immorality and revolutionary declarations. She was haranguing the people from the *Feuillants* terrace, and did not refrain from trying to persuade them by the use of pompous phrases, born of the Revolution, which were the shameful products of fanaticism, ignorance, and the perversity of our political charlatans. We began by discussion and we ended in dispute.
>
> This orator in petticoats gave vent to a thousand coarse insults and endeavoured to excite the crowd against me, but for once the populace was inclined to be generous. People listened to me without murmuring. A man entered the group and shouted in an imperious tone that I was an aristocrat and must be left in peace. He was disappointed that I did not get angry, for he liked to hear plain speaking. Then he came close to me and said in a low tone, 'Now you have done enough, little aristocrat; get out of this,' and I followed his advice, which was good.

Hyde de Neuville described Théroigne as an unfortunate courtesan, who although still young in years had aged before her time. He remarked on the facility with which she expressed herself, and described her carriage as upright, her figure as fine, and her personality as stamped with shamelessness and effrontery. Conflicting accounts lead to the belief that Théroigne, who was usually shy, retiring, and modest, lost all appearance of bashfulness when roused by the excitement of her cause and made a bold impression upon her hearers. Her first serious attempt at a speech which has been recorded was made at the Club des Cordeliers, the fiery off-shoot of the Jacobins Club. It was reported by Camille Desmoulins in the *Révolutions de France et de*

Brabant, and, it must be confessed, is coloured by the eloquent personality of its transcriber. Théroigne was imbued with the idea that it was time the National Assembly should be housed in a palace worthy of its great aims. She came to air these views before the tribunal of the club.

An usher announced to the president of the gathering that a young woman desired to enter. Everyone thought that she must be a petitioner. No one expected that a preliminary question was going to be put, so that the surprise was enormous when the celebrated Mlle Théroigne came forward and asked leave to speak and propose a resolution. It was unanimously agreed to admit her to the bar. One honourable member was overcome by his enthusiasm on seeing her. He cried, "Here is the Queen of Sheba who has come to see the Solomon of the districts."

Théroigne replied to this challenge, with much presence of mind:

Yes, it is the reputation of your wisdom which brings me into your midst. Prove that you are Solomon, and that you have been chosen to build a temple, and then hasten to erect a temple to the National Assembly. That is the object of my motion. Can good patriots much longer endure to see the executive power lodged in the finest palace in the world, whilst the legislative power has to dwell in tents; sometimes in the Salle des Menus-plaisirs, sometimes at the tennis-court, sometimes in the riding-school, like the ark's dove that has nowhere to rest its feet?
The last stone of the last cell of the Bastille has been brought to the Senate, and M. Camus regards it every day with delight where it lies deposited in the archives. The ground on which the Bastille stood is vacant; a hundred thousand workmen require occupation. Why do we delay, illustrious Cordeliers, model of the districts, patriots, republicans, Romans, who hear me? Hasten to open a subscription in order to erect a palace for the National Assembly on the site of the Bastille. All France will hasten to second you in this. She only awaits the signal! Give it. Invite all the best workmen, the most celebrated artists; send for the famous architects; cut down the cedars of Lebanon, and the firs of Mount Ida. Ah, if stones could move of their own free-will it is not for the building of the walls of Thebes they would do so, but to construct the temple of Liberty! We must give our gold and our jewels to enrich and embellish this edifice. I will give mine first as an example. You have been told that the

French are like Jews, people who have become idolaters. The crowd is moved through its senses. It is needful to give it outward and visible images upon which it may bestow its worship. Turn its glances from the Pavilion de Flore, the colonnades of the Louvre, to let them rest on a *basilica* more beautiful than Saint Peter's at Rome and Saint Paul's in London. The veritable temple of the Eternal, the only worthy one, is a temple in which the declaration of the Rights of Man has been spoken. The French in the National Assembly claim the rights of men and citizens. There without a doubt is a sight upon which the Supreme Being can turn His gaze with delight; there is the form of worship He will accept with greater pleasure than tenor and bass voices raised in the *Kyrie eleison* or a *Salvum fac regem*.

"Imagine," added Desmoulins, "the effect of a discourse so animated and sparkling with symbols borrowed indiscriminately from Pindar and the Holy Scriptures."

When the outburst of applause which greeted her speech had calmed down, her motion was discussed and adopted. The club charged its President Paré, its ex-President Danton, its Vice-President Fabre d'Eglantine, as well as Camille Desmoulins and Dufourny de Villiers, to draw up an address on the subject and distribute it in the districts and departments. Enthusiasm ran riot.

But in the end the idea came to nothing. It was not altogether new. A month before a certain Mme Desormeaux had brought forward a similar scheme. Perhaps Théroigne borrowed it from her. Her eloquence certainly drew more people's attention to it. Théroigne's grammar was not perfect by any means, but she never lacked inspiration. She had an ulterior motive in making this appeal to the people. She hoped to be admitted to the district with a consultative vote— that is to say, she desired to be accepted as a member on the same terms as a man might have been. But this was denied her.

The Assembly agreed with its president, who moved a vote of thanks to this charming *citoyenne* for her resolution. He declared that since the Council of Mâcon had acknowledged the fact that women are possessed of a soul and intellect like men, no one could prevent them from making so good a use of their faculties as Théroigne had done, and that she or others of her sex would be listened to with pleasure if they wished to propose measures they believed to be advantageous to their country. But—and then came the bitter pill—it was impossible to admit her to the club as a member with a right to speak, leaving out of the question altogether the power to vote.

Although this repulse was a great disappointment to her, she did not dwell on it, and in her own account of the affair only referred to her success. She says in her *Confessions*:

I went to the *Club des Cordeliers*, and made the following proposition: 'It is necessary to open a subscription list to build a hall which may be worthy of the representatives of the nation, and to invite the most celebrated artists in Europe to hold a consultation regarding plans and a style of decoration. Women must renounce their jewels and all such superfluities as are incompatible with the austerity of manners and simplicity of habits which ought to be the rule in a time regenerated by liberty. These vain ornaments ought to be sacrificed on the altar of our country.' My motion was adopted."

Théroigne's attitude was not received with acclamations from the press. The *Observateur* of March 4th, 1790, whilst it described her as a young heroine who played a role in the Revolution as brilliant as that of Gildippe and Clorinda at the siege of Jerusalem, nevertheless poohpoohed her idea of building a palace for the National Assembly, on the grounds of the expense at a time when the kingdom was plunged into profound and universal misery. "Had she any idea," they inquired, "as to the immense sums which would have to be consecrated to such an enterprise?" Before this was done, it would be better that the effects of the monstrous inequality of private fortune should be removed. The *Observateur* continues addressing their victim:

Imagine, if you have the courage to do so, four thousand invalids cooped up in one house, placed four by four, even six by six, in beds where air so pestilential circulates that the most robust health does not come in contact with it without peril. . . . There, if you have eloquence to spare, would be an object worthy of your talents. Moreover, it would be absurd to wish to add to the edifices of a town which is already almost deserted. Would it not be better, to keep within the bounds of a modest silence than to make oneself conspicuous by making such illtimed propositions?

The *Observateur Féminin*, which should have supported the doings of a woman, merely stated that Théroigne had astonished the Cordeliers, had made all Paris laugh, and had laid claims to great notoriety. The royalists made very sarcastic comments on the affair.

This heroine of the *boudoir* proposes resolutions in her district. She considers the king is too well lodged and the Assembly too badly. Mlle Théroigne, by her masculine courage, her patriotism, and her flashing eloquence, is in a fair way to make people forget her sex.

But that was just what Théroigne failed to do, to her own great regret. Without being unwomanly she desired to be a reformer, and that was denied her. It seemed to her hard and cruel that this should be so. She tells an incident in her *Confessions* which emphasises the annoyance to which she was subjected.

The day when the deputies went to Notre-Dame, to sing the *Te Deum*, they sent me a ticket to be present at the ceremony. But I arrived there too late, and could not get through the crowd. Several patriot deputies invited me to walk with them in the procession. The desire to see such a solemn spectacle, and also the honour of joining the deputies in a public ceremony, made me accept their offer. So, I went part of the way in their ranks. There were many who cried 'Ho! A woman deputy! That is singular!' Some priestly aristocrats who noticed this expostulated with me. I took their advice and retired. There were a great number of people who, like myself, were marching in the procession with the deputies without being deputies themselves. But they were men. At this moment, feeling extremely humiliated, I acknowledged the force and the persistence of the masculine pride and prejudice which oppressed my sex, and kept it in bondage.

Urged on by such experiences, Théroigne devoted herself to the cause of women's emancipation.

CHAPTER 4

The Citoyennes

Théroigne's enthusiasm on behalf of her sex was to lead her far; through martyrdom, through triumph, through degradation, to an appalling fate at last. Many women there were who loved as much and suffered as much and were as much in earnest as she, and probably not one of them all regretted or felt remorse for what they had done.

The Revolution gave them many opportunities. They were longing to show their mettle, their powers of endurance, their patriotism, and their unselfishness. A common cause urged them to do the thing that has always seemed a difficult task for women to achieve, namely, to unite in a common purpose, to form a combination which should give them power to solve the problems of their existence. Théroigne saw the need of this union and advocated it with all her strength.

That she was not more successful as a leader was perhaps the fault of circumstance and conditions rather than of herself, and yet she was lacking in some quality which should have brought her into closer sympathy with other women. She understood men better, and was perhaps not tolerant enough of feminine scruples nor faithful enough to the laws of social convention. But any deficiency in tact and intuition was counterbalanced by her application to practical detail and her genuine desire to understand and master the situation. Had she realised more clearly the temper of the women with whom she had to deal her task would have been easier and more prolific in results.

Serious upheavals which have for their aim the establishment of new and improved conditions have always found women ready to participate in bringing about social reforms that touch them closely. So, it was at the time of the French Revolution. The ideals, aims, and faith in the future which dwelt in the hearts of men stirred also in the bosoms of the women of the country. Yet there was this difference. Men were fighting for the liberty of the race; women desired in addition the liberty of the sex. The misery, poverty, and degradation from which the masses suffered were shared by them equally, but the political and civil rights for which men struggled were doubly debarred to them.

They not only determined therefore to stand side by side with men in the great forward movement, but they desired to make their powers so much appreciated that their companions would realise their worth, and bestow freely upon them the reward they were seeking. This was no easy task. Men were ready in that day, as in any other, to ridicule the claims of women to a political and social equality with themselves. But although the great body of men had still to be converted, women were not without advocates amongst them. Their chief champion at this time perhaps was Condorcet, marquis and republican, who wrote in his *Lettres d'un Bourgeois de Newhaven à un citoyen de Virginie*, etc. (1787), that women should be considered as both eligible and elective, and that the idea must be combated that they were illogical and incapable of being placed on a footing equal to men.

If, he said, the number of women who have received an exact and continuous education be compared with the number of men who have enjoyed the same advantages, it will be seen that the repeated opinion that the former possess no initiative cannot be regarded as proved, and he added, "I am afraid of getting into bad odour with them if they read this article, for I am speaking of their claims to equality, and not of their natural empire."

Condorcet's enthusiasm was not shared by many of his colleagues, and led to but little practical outcome. Women grew discontented and felt that justice was not being done to them. Those who were most in earnest demanded definite rights as women citizens, but they could not master the art of unity and combination, and isolated appeals received no attention.

In spite of the fact, however, that they were refused their chief demands, the efforts they made towards more freedom were not entirely in vain.

They won privileges of speech, of conscience, of appeal, as well as the right to petition, which was valuable; they could no longer be arrested or imprisoned except as directed by law, and they gained, at least temporarily, a right to divorce.

Considering that they were ready to sacrifice their all, life itself if need be, to obtain their desires, these advantages may seem but an inadequate result of strenuous labours, but it would be misleading to suppose so, for much of the emancipation of women has been based upon the exertions of that period, and the real origin of the feminist movement, although the word "feminist" was not then applied to it, dates from the revolutionary attempt to emancipate humanity.

The political weight of their opinions may be largely discounted, perhaps, but the fact of their presence and personal influence in all that went on cannot be denied. Women were in the vanguard of the mobs; they swarmed in the galleries of the Assembly and of the clubs. They marched in processions, festive or riotous, and invaded the bakers' shops. They filled the prisons, surfeited the guillotine, and joined with men in acts of bloodshed and violence which proved the state of desperation they had been goaded into, but did little credit to the restraint and modesty always regarded as among the more feminine virtues. Women were keenly interested in all the debates; they prepared speeches, they wrote discourses, they organised meetings, they embroidered flags and banners, they made shirts and knitted stockings, they sacrificed their jewels and other luxurious tastes on the altar of liberty.

Gone were the habits and frivolities of the old regime, gone the *coquetry* and dilettantism of the days of monarchy! From the highest to the lowest they demanded work—a legitimate means of earning an independent livelihood, bread that they might eat under terms of liberty, and they asked further that men should not be allowed to exercise such trades as they considered were essentially suited to women. "Leave us at least the needle and the spinning-wheel," they pleaded, and then with a sigh of revolt they added "Is our device always to be 'Work, obey, and be silent'?"

Truly their lot in the Revolution was a hard one. They had so little glory, so much suffering and sacrifice. They were prevented, except in isolated cases, from distinguishing themselves on the battlefield, or in the legislative house, side by side with men, but their punishment was as heavy as that meted out to their brothers. Olympe de Gouges cried:

> Women have the right to mount the scaffold, they ought to have an equal right to mount the tribunal.

Where was justice? Whilst in the hope of receiving their due, women searched ardently for an outlet for their pent-up energies. Not content to work and wait passively in the home, they desired to give some picturesque or dramatic exhibition of their eagerness to play an active part. This led some of them to offer their jewels publicly to the country on September 7th, 1789. The president of the National

Assembly rose to ask the house for an audience for those ladies who wished to vouchsafe this proof of patriotism. There was a sudden hush in the Assembly, and then a burst of applause as the women filed in, simply attired in white, without ornament of any kind. An usher was appointed to show them into seats, and a discourse was read which set forth their willingness to give up their jewels, "which they would blush to wear when patriotism demanded the sacrifice."

Then the president thanked these generous women in the name of the Assembly, and one by one they stepped forward, casket in hand, to place their offerings on the president's table. By these and similar means some hundreds of thousands of *francs* were collected and distributed among the poor.

But the real centre of attraction to women was the club. Even as Théroigne had quickly realised the growing power and importance of this institution, other women saw also that here might be found the very opening which they were seeking for their enthusiasm. But if they imagined that men would admit them even here on equal terms with themselves, they were utterly mistaken. In a few instances their presence at meetings was allowed within certain limits, and before long many of the societies organised a joint or branch section which was open to both sexes; but those women who believed themselves to be born orators, and were anxious to air their views upon a platform, were, with a few exceptions, doomed to disappointment. And this state of affairs led eventually to the formation of women's clubs.

One of the first of the clubs to see a woman on its platform was the *Cercle Sociale*; the incident, however, was unexpected and unrehearsed. This society had a hall in the Palais Royal, capable of seating some three thousand people. It had a large membership at a subscription of eight *livres* a month, and its motto, inscribed in prominent lettering above the speaker's head, was, "*Bring each a ray of light.*" On November 26th, 1790, one Charles Louis Rousseau was endeavouring somewhat unsuccessfully to perform the injunction of the motto with reference more particularly to woman's political position, he asked:

Have women influence in government? and, if so, by what means can this influence be used in enhancing the prosperity of the State? What civil and political rights should be possessed by women in the best-governed country? (and other questions bearing on the same subject.)

Instead of dealing with the matter in a straightforward and practical

GILBERT ROMME.

fashion, the speaker strung together a number of platitudes, interspersed his speech with ill-timed complimentary phrases meant to flatter his fair audience, and punctuated the whole with theatrical gesticulations which wearied the less impressionable of his hearers, so that at last the president, fearing that this uninspiring speech would never end, took it upon himself to suspend the sitting. This was an unexpected blow to feminism, and a woman of commanding figure rose and asked a question in ringing tones, plainly heard throughout the hall.

> Gentlemen, is it possible that the Revolution, which has for its object the attainment of the rights of man, can be the cause of Frenchmen showing injustice and dishonesty to women? Other speakers have been listened to with patience. Why should the one who pleads the cause of women be interrupted? I demand, in the name of the women citizens present, that M. Rousseau be allowed to proceed.

At these remarks there was general applause. The speaker was asked herself to continue. But her modesty prevented her saying more than a very few words. She blamed the Frenchmen for having become corrupt and enfeebled. "Since our compatriots have imitated the Romans, let us imitate the virtues and patriotism of the Roman women," she cried. There was a general desire amongst them to elect her *présidente*, but she refused.

This woman, Etta Palm by name, of Dutch extraction, and called Aelders before her marriage, worked as well or even better than Théroigne in her sisters' cause. She did several notable things in the movement, attempting to federate the women's societies and establish a correspondence among them similar to that carried on by the Jacobins. The oath taken by the members of these societies was worded as follows:

> I swear to be faithful to the nation, to the law, and to the king. I swear to help my husband, my brothers, and my children to fulfil their duties to the State as far as possible. I swear to teach my children, and all those over whom I have authority, to prefer death to slavery.

Etta placed herself at the head of those who pleaded for civic and intellectual education. Théroigne, after seeing her own club fail, and realising something of the ever-increasing dangers in which France was becoming involved, veered over to those who desired military

102

privileges and made their chief aim a share in the national defence. Etta desired to raise a statue to the wife of Phocion, in order that women might have before their eyes a model of wisdom, modesty, and simplicity—virtues which were both moral and civic. Théroigne, realising the futility of opposing force with humility and goodness, would rather have constructed a temple to Bellona, so that she might command her votaries to kneel before the altar of the goddess and utter a prayer for strength and ability in arms.

But this warlike attitude developed its full force only when constitutional measures had failed. This was not until after her return from Kufstein. Until then she remained watching the work that other women were doing in the very field, she was trying to enter herself, the field of political labour. Busy as she was with her own affairs, she found time to appreciate the efforts that other women were making to join the clubs or, this being denied them, to found societies of their own.

Etta Palm was one of the prime movers in this direction. She set forth in the following terms the part she thought women ought to play in these institutions:

Citizens, she declared, have united in the eighty-three departments to defend the Constitution. "Do you not think, gentlemen, that their wives and the mothers of families could unite in imitation of them to make it beloved? *La Société des Amis de la Vérité* is the first society which has admitted us to patriotic meetings."

Then she referred to the provincial towns, Creil, Alais, Bordeaux, and others, that had followed this example.

> Would it not be useful, if a patriotic society of *citoyennes* was formed in each section of the capital, and if a central and federative circle invited all the societies of the eighty-three departments to correspond with them?

And then followed a detailed and apparently practical plan of federal organisation. Among other duties, women were to combine to protect young country girls who arrived in the capital without friends, acquaintances, or money, and who ran great perils in an unknown city, to look after public education and bring up the rising generation to be strong and healthy citizens. Charity schools were to be under their immediate supervision, and workshops were to be founded at which girls from six to thirteen were to be taught some suitable trade in order that later they might help to support the family: in short, every form of poverty or misery, every unfortunate or starving woman, was to have a sacred claim upon the assistance of the club.

Unlike Théroigne, Etta Palm was no orator.

If, the construction of my phrases is not according to the rules of the French Academy, it is because I consulted my heart rather than the dictionary.

She declared that women were superior to men in vivacity of imagination, in delicacy of sentiment, in their resignation during trouble, strength in grief and pain, patience in suffering and both in generosity of soul and patriotic zeal. Thus, she summed up the feminine virtues. She spoke of the sacrifice of jewels and adornment, and thought that as a reward civic crowns should replace the *gew-gaws* which could only be regarded as the outward signs of frivolity and luxury. She also advocated union to be achieved by the elimination of all personal hate and enmity. This was one of the chief doctrines preached by Théroigne.

"In that case," cried Etta Palm, meaning if they were all united, "what could fifty thousand vile aristocrats do against three hundred thousand soldiers of liberty?"

All these arguments were used by the chief women leaders in the movement. On April 1st, 1792, only a few short months after Théroigne's triumphant return from her imprisonment in Austria, Etta Palm appeared at the bar of the Legislative Assembly as spokeswoman of a deputation of women who demanded:

Firstly, that public education as already established for boys should be extended also to girls.

Secondly, that women of twenty-one should be declared of age. Thirdly, that perfect equality of rights should exist between boys and girls.

Fourthly, that divorce should be legalised.

Although these suggestions were bold for her day, Etta was not among the most advanced of the women reformers. Her strength lay in her restraint. She had no militant plans like Théroigne, and took no violent measures like Rose (or Claire) Lacombe, who from 1793 onwards became the leader of the most revolutionary women's club and allied herself with the *émigrés*. Long before that date mixed societies had been formed which became a distinctive feature of the club organism. These *Sociétés Fraternelles des Deux Sexes*, as they were called, were very distinctive in their way, and gave to the women who were longing to find an outlet for their turbulent feelings the opportunity to join in political meetings and express their utter contempt for all existing conditions, especially those which limited their civic powers.

Théroigne was one amongst those who availed herself freely of these privileges, and it is therefore interesting to trace the origin and growth of these hybrid institutions. The first of them was opened at Paris in the early autumn of 1790 and held its sittings in one of the halls at the Jacobins. The original instigator was a poor and very earnest boarding-house proprietor of the name of Claude Dansard. Moved by a spirit of patriotism, he caused to assemble many artisans, street vendors of fruit and vegetables, and labourers with their wives and children. The meetings took place in the evenings and on Sundays, and their object was the reading and interpretation of the laws framed by the National Assembly and the Declaration of the Rights of Man. Dansard provided the light required at these gatherings. He always produced from his pocket a candle-end, flint and tinder-box. When the sitting was prolonged the light threatened to fail, and a subscription was raised among those present to purchase more candles, and the reading was continued amidst general satisfaction.

At first these humble reunions had something of a social importance, and probably the admission of wives and children was an astute move on the part of Dansard, but presently the social side was merged entirely in the political influence they assumed. In the spring of 1791, the club took the name of "*Société Fraternelle des Patriotes des Deux Sexes*. Defenders (later Friends) of the Constitution." Well-known individuals, both men and women, appeared there. Mme Robert, *née* Keralio, wife of the journalist, who edited and translated many works, was one of the most noteworthy. She advocated reform in the hospitals:

> Those places founded by public philanthropy for the relief of suffering humanity, where humanity is perhaps most shamefully ill-treated and persecuted.

She endeavoured to obtain the appointment of female as well as male inspectors, believing that the details of administration which would escape the notice of men would be observed by the quick eye of a woman. "They would taste the soup and see whether the meat was fit to eat," she said. But these women were not to be chosen from the luxurious and idle classes. They were to be working-women who understood their business. Mme Robert desired to institute hospitals for the diseased, workhouses for the poor, and houses of correction for the evil-doers. Mme Roland, who joined the society after the flight to Varennes, did not like Mme Robert, and described her as a small woman, intellectual, clever, and proud—but a little inconsistent.

Mme Moitte, who had led the women on to sacrifice their jewels on the altar of the country, was a member of the society, and Etta Palm, as well as Pauline Léon. Théroigne was not in Paris during the days of its early popularity, but she attended the meetings after her return in the spring of 1792. Among the men were Danton, Tallien, Roederer, and Hébert.

Mme de Genlis writes in her *Memoirs*:

> Curiosity took me a single time only to one of the public sittings of the *Société Fraternelle*. It was a spectacle at once original, terrifying, and ridiculous. The women of the people spoke there, although they did not mount the tribune, but they frequently interrupted the speakers, and uttered long dissertations without leaving their places.

Lamartine compared the fraternal society very favourably with the more violent assemblies organised by women.

> This union was composed of educated women, who discussed with more decency the social questions analogous to their sex, such as marriage, maternity, the education of children, the institutions of relief, and the assistance of humanity. They were the philosophers of their sex. Robespierre was their oracle and their idol. The Utopian and vague character of its institutions was conformable to the genius of women, more adapted to dream of the social happiness than to form the mechanism of societies.

If this were the truth, it represents but a small section of thought, for the usual temper of the women who joined these clubs was to the highest degree electrical.

Another important fraternal society was the *Société Fraternelle des Deux Sexes de la Section Saint-Genevieve*—later called, of the *Panthéon Français*. The original regulations were issued on December 16th, 1790. In November 1793 this society gave a civil *fête* in honour of Lepelletier and Marat at the unveiling of their statues in the Place de l'Estrapade. Théroigne was an active member of the *Société Fraternelle des Minimes.* Its president was Tallien, and it had rather more warlike aims than some of the fellow-societies. The *Société Fraternelle de la Section des Sans-Culottes* was one of the more advanced in its views regarding the position of women. Its regulations, which were published on July 17th, 1793, declared that:

> The right of acquiring and spreading instruction and enlightenment belonged to both sexes equally, therefore *citoyennes* were admitted without distinction to share the patriotic works of the society.

The *Société Fraternelle des Amis de la Patrie* held meetings in Trinity Church, Rue Saint-Denis, and was composed of all good citizens and *citoyennes* who were true patriots and republicans. Persons were admitted to membership on presentation by four members. They took an oath as follows:

> We swear to be faithful to the French nation, to which we have the happiness to belong, and to the law; to maintain the Republic, one and indivisible; Liberty and Equality, which yield our happiness and the destruction of tyrants; to defend individuals and property or to die defending them.

The women's names were entered in a special register.

The *Société Patriotique et Fraternelle des Citoyens de la Section du Théâtre-Français* met in the Grands-Augustins, and in June 1791 published measures of safety and vigilance with regard to the careful choice of electors upon whom depended that of the deputies to the Legislative Assembly.

Most of the sections had fraternal societies, and most of these societies made special rules for their women members. A clause in the rules of the *Union Fraternelle des Gobelins* explained that *citoyennes* admitted into the society would be separated from the citizens. Women were not expected to contribute to the working expenses of the club. But neither were they encouraged to speak, and this was a serious deprivation to those who were burning with ideas and plans for the amelioration of conditions, and desired above all things to help their brothers in the coming struggle for liberty.

The silence thus imposed upon them was little to the taste of the eager women, and no doubt gave them the idea of organising clubs of their own. In the provinces the idea was seized upon with avidity. In hundreds of small towns, the women co-operated in arranging meetings, in holding demonstrations, in giving voice to loyal aims, in subscribing patriotic gifts, and in many other ways demonstrating their love for their country. Almost every popular society admitted women.

An important, and in many ways typical, women's club was formed at Lyons towards the summer of 1791. It was called the *Association des Citoyennes de Lyon particulierement dévouées à la Nation et à la Loi*. As the name implies, one of its chief aims was to make a study of the new laws. The flag of the society was deposited at the church of Saint-Jean. Strong religious and puritanical sentiments seem to have been characteristic among the members. They eschewed the wearing of jewels as adornments unsuited to the natural beauty of the human figure, because their brilliancy competed with that of the eyes and complexion, and because by their very brightness they drew attention to themselves which ought to be bestowed upon the individual. They refused to wear garments which constricted the figure in a manner never intended by nature, or which hid under loose folds the beautiful lines of the form.

The hair was neatly dressed without artificial adornments. Simplicity in everything was the motto. Good manners were essential. It was ruled that there were never to be more than three men present at the meetings lest a greater proportion of men to women should be deemed immodest. No girl under eighteen years of age was admitted unless accompanied by her mother or an aunt. To be eligible for membership it was necessary to be introduced by three *citoyennes*, to pay a subscription of ten *sols* per month, to attend meetings, which were held on Sundays after vespers, regularly, and to take the oath of the society, which was a strong confession of patriotism.

There were also stringent rules with regard to silence. Four officials were appointed to see that order was strictly kept. They were placed in different parts of the hall and were called *surveillantes*. Should any woman break the rule that only one speaker was allowed to speak at a time, she was liable to a fine, and if the hubbub grew general the president immediately terminated the sitting.

Naturally enough this society did not escape the gibes of those who believed it impossible to maintain law, order, and quiet among a body of enthusiastic women. But at least it appears to have been carried on in a manner which allowed no room for any breach of circumspection. Not so in the case of other clubs in which men were present. At Chauny, for instance, pleasantries were indulged in during the meetings which consisted in blowing out the lights and discharging squibs beneath the skirts of the women. One day two of the members, one of them being among the best known of the orators, were dismissed for attempting to scratch each other's eyes out.

Another day the speaker was interrupted by the cracking of nuts. The president chided the culprit and begged her to refrain from this amusement during the meeting. She replied that if he would crack the nuts for her it would save a lot of trouble. Thereupon he told her that severe punishment was meted out to those who disturbed the gathering of the popular societies. At this she burst out laughing, and before he could finish what he had to say she left the hall, skipping out in an indecorous and frisky manner.

At this club a new form of the Lord's Prayer was used, addressed to the king, which ran:

> Our father who art at the Tuileries, respected be thy name; thy reign come again; thy will be done in Paris as it is in the provinces. May all rascals who seek to steal our bread be hanged on lanterns, and deliver us above all from the machinations of the National Assembly. Amen.

At Coutances in the Popular Society the *citoyennes* were seated in a special gallery, but they overflowed into the hall so often and behaved with so much frivolity—going so far on one occasion as to embrace the speaker—that the committee thought it well to make such physical demonstrations impossible, "since the nation gained nothing from such exhibitions, and morality might lose a great deal." Jealous husbands were averse at this club to their wives sitting amongst members of the other sex "unless the galleries were well lighted." The men of Cherbourg grew tired of admitting women to their gatherings, and from August 30th, 1791, members of the fair sex were excluded. Nor were they allowed to be present at private sittings of the Amis de la Constitution at Saint-Servan on account of the "proverbial incontinence of women's language."

At Villenauxe-la-Grande disturbances also took place, and it was found necessary in order to secure public tranquillity that all women should be seated on the left side of the house and all men on the right. It was here that a rumour was rife of women sticking pins and needles in the president's chair.

Women were allowed in the hall of the *Amis de la Liberté et de l'Egalité* at Colmar; but upon complaints of flippancy being made, they were relegated to a separate gallery. Once, when there happened to be no speakers, the president adjourned the house and proposed that all present should go and dance the carmagnole round the Tree of Liberty; a proposition which was very well received.

The *citoyennes* were so *coquettish* at Bayeux that by the aid of silky ribbons they transformed their cockades into a gay and unseemly adornment so unsuitable in the eyes of the Popular Society that a request was made to them not to wear their cockades *en bazin* and to cease looking like actresses.

Although such incidents make it appear that the women of the provincial clubs were not as serious-minded in their work as the men, this must not be regarded as the truth. Most of them were in deadly earnest, and if, in some of the things they did, lighter feminine moods became apparent, these were only in contrast to the business they achieved.

There were women's clubs at Cognac, Orleans, and Angouleme; and at Bordeaux, according to one account, there were no fewer than three separate feminine societies. At Valence there were two clubs which admitted women. At Bourges the Popular Society allowed women to be present at its meetings, and several members offered to make shirts for the defenders of the country. Others presented various articles of more or less value. A gift of Phrygian bonnets at Saint-Calais was received with delighted cries of "Long live women patriots!" A large number of women at Moulins made clothes for the volunteers, whilst those of Grenoble knitted socks and scarves. At Honfleur charitable women formed a Philanthropic Committee and excited the people's liberality, distributing considerable results among the poor.

Generosity was a prevalent quality among the patriotic women. When the Mayor of Beaumont-le-Roger called a meeting in the church to read the laws to the people, he took out his watch to look at the time, and patriotic women citizens demanded that he should offer it upon the altar of the country. When he refused they became riotous. The *citoyennes* of Fontainebleau, Brest, and Lorient were very active; all the children in the last place were taught patriotic songs, and the women formed a masonic lodge of their own. At Tours they swore terrible oaths to cherish the country and destroy the aristocrats. They blessed flags, sang stirring songs, and danced to patriotic music. This society boasted the youngest *citoyenne* of all. An ecclesiastic with revolutionary tendencies brought his whole family to the Popular Society and made a little speech.

My daughter Cornelia, who is eight months old, will be presented by her mother and taken on to the platform by her nurse. She will enjoy in anticipation the delights of true republicanism in the midst of you.

Children were encouraged by their mothers to show precocious enthusiasm. At Rouen, where orators of the fair sex were allowed upon the platform, a child of eight, whose name was Rose Renant, made a speech to the Popular Society.

How can I describe to you without shuddering, the terrible grief I should feel if I saw my dear papa or mamma, my relatives, friends, and neighbours suffer beneath the blows of villain aristocrats, or fall under their tyranny? Rather than that such a terrible misfortune should overcome me, I would wish that the fury of the nobility should be directed against me alone.

Rose was not the only child patriot. At Dijon there was a club called the *Jeunes Amies de la République*, of which the members were all between eight and sixteen years of age. They held meetings and harangued their mothers. One of their spokeswomen, a girl called Henriette Ecureux, deplored the fact that she was not old enough to have served her country, but she prayed for all good patriots, and had begun to weave laurel wreaths for the occasion of their triumphal return. Lamartine mentions a club of children between twelve and fourteen called "Red Children," the baptism of blood upon the heads of these precocious republicans.

Dijon, at any rate, possessed a far more serious institution in the shape of a women's club called successively *Amies de la Constitution, de l'Egalité, and de la République*. Its aim was to republicanise the Dijon ladies. The standard of the society was blessed at the church of Saint-Michel on May 30th, 1791, and was afterwards deposited in the Hall of Parlement, where the *Amis de la Constitution* met. In September of that year the president of the women's club asked the members of the men's club to send an address to all the affiliated clubs "inviting their sisters in the eighty-three departments to organise and form societies, so that they might play a serious part in the events which might follow upon war."

Meetings were organised sometimes for the strangest reasons. The Boulonnaises held a demonstration against bachelors, and gave a ball excluding these selfish individuals, "the *fête* being intended for respectable men." The women of Neuberg were so enthusiastic that young women swore not to marry any but citizens who had fought in

111

the armies. The lady members of the *Société Fraternelle des Deux Sexes de Paris* had sworn not to marry aristocrats. This example was followed at Nantes, where an oath to this effect appeared in verse:

Nous, dames du district Nantais,
Femmes, veuves et demoiselles,
Savoir faisons à tous Français.
Surtout qu'étant tres démocrates,
Nous ne pouvons voir sans horreur
Ces gens sans esprit et sans coeur
Que l'on appelle aristocrates. . . .

The Bearnaises were eligible for election as members of the Popular Society, but were discontented because they could not vote. At Blois, being forbidden to wear the distinctive tricolour ribbon, the *citoyennes* formed a society of their own.

An account of a characteristic meeting held at one of the women's clubs on December 30th, 1792, may fitly close a chapter which is intended to convey some impression of the unrest and ferment seething in the minds of the women throughout France during the earlier part of the Revolution. The gathering took place in the presence of representatives of three united administrative bodies.

After the meeting had been opened in the usual manner by the woman president, the minutes of the last meeting were read and approved, and then one of the *citoyennes* demanded that before the proceedings went any further the *Marseillaise* should be sung. A young citizen called Maitre and a woman citizen of the name of Charton sang the hymn, accompanied by music and with a chorus in which all the members joined. Music was also played during the arrival of the representatives of the three administrative bodies, who took seats near the president. They wore distinctive badges.

Citoyenne Charton made a speech from the platform, extolling the glory and felicity of the work of looking after and assisting good patriots. Then a Mme Charpin tendered a proposition that Bishop Lamourette should compose a new catechism from which children might learn not only the principles of religion, but also of true republicanism. Citoyenne Pere mounted the platform next, and spoke of the glorious Revolution, which she laid to the honour of the philosophers. She emphasised the urgency of propagating popular societies, in order that the youth of the country might be instructed in the new laws. Two other women addressed the meeting, and then a

THÉROIGNE DE MÉRICOURT.

From an engraving by Devritz of a portrait in the Bibliothèque Nationale.

young *citoyenne* recited Chapters VII. II and VIII. of Rousseau's *Contrat Social*, followed by the Declaration of the Rights of Man. Then she said a patriotic prayer. This was succeeded by recitations from other works, namely, *The Catechisme de la République* and the *Almanach de Père Gerard*, as well as further chapters of the *Contrat Social* declaimed by various men and women. After that a distribution took place of prizes given by the members of the district, of the department, and of the municipality. Citizen Chaine, who had been presented with a sabre, took an oath never to use it except for the purpose of destroying the enemies of the Republic.

The *Marseillaise* was sung a second time, and the proceedings ended.

These were sober and heartfelt doings. In other places dancing and jollity, even gambling and feasting, went on, but the women who took part in these gaieties were in the minority. Demonstrations by Catholic women who had suffered on account of the departure of refractory priests formed yet another side of the spirit shown by women in revolt.

As time went on a desperate and dangerous note entered into the club organism, and women of a different type herded together with sinister purpose. Théroigne was to come into contact with them to her cost. But that was not until a combination of circumstances had made it necessary for her to leave the scene of the Revolution, temporarily at least.

CHAPTER 5

Flight and Capture

Paris was not the safest place for Théroigne. She must have been aware of this. She pretended she knew nothing of the kind, and that the reasons which took her into the country were of the most ordinary and commonplace character. It was quite natural that, when brought face to face with her judges, she should have thought it wise to give a glib explanation of the causes which led to her leaving the capital. In order to sustain her role of perfect innocence it was necessary to appear to know nothing of any possible danger awaiting her there. In the very simplicity of Théroigne's account lies its cleverness. She says naively:

I liked Paris very much, but I had not enough money to remain there for long. Besides, I had charged myself with the care of my brothers, whom I did not wish to abandon. I was not paid my income of five thousand *livres*, and I did not know when the payment would take place. Moreover, I had anticipated my resources. I had an advance made of one thousand crowns for two years, and for a long time I had had my diamonds in pawn. I was greatly in debt, and, in short, I had no other resources except a necklace worth twenty-five *louis*.

If I had remained in Paris under the conditions in which I was then living, the whole sum would soon have been spent, and I should have been under the obligation of contracting new debts. It was therefore necessary to change my manner of living or to leave. Much in the public eye, accustomed to a somewhat luxurious existence, which I led less from taste than from *amour-propre*, it was difficult for me, unless I disappeared from the scenes familiar to me, to carry out my projects of economy.

This is not the speech of one whose heart was in the people's cause! This is not the real Théroigne, burning with ambition, reckless, impulsive, and ever ready for new adventure! She continues, as though all her life she had preferred oblivion to notoriety:

> I resolved then and there to leave society and to live apart, ignored and unknown. I took the name of Poitiers, and then I could more freely accommodate my manner of dressing and my expenses to my modest means.

Because she had done what she had done in Paris under the name of Théroigne, because the royalist journals contained that name in almost every number that was issued from their unholy presses, perhaps her object in assuming another was of more significance than the mere discarding of the gaudy amazones and other trifling extravagances she had indulged in. But still she flirts with the idea that flight had not been necessary, "I asked myself often whether I should stay in France or whether I should return to my own country," she says, and then brings out the reason why she went so far away:

> The arrival of my brother Pierre in Paris from Liège, where he had gone when he had left Genoa, decided me to take the road to my native land.

Then she becomes bolder. She refers to the annoyance caused her by the royalists; she admits that a rumour of arrests issued from the *Châtelet* had reached her, but she says nothing of her intense wish to free the people, and her heartfelt interest in the progress of the Revolution:

> I confess that I left the stage of the Revolution without too much regret, because I suffered every day from unpleasantnesses in the tribunes of the National Assembly. There were always some aristocrats there to whom my zeal and my candour were displeasing. They deluged me with sarcasms without ceasing. They annoyed me; they laid traps for me. Certain patriots even, instead of encouraging, defending, and rendering me justice, turned my efforts into ridicule. That is the truth.
>
> Besides, I was assured that they had given information against me at the *Châtelet* for the affair of October 5th and 6th. Having done nothing those famous days, I did not fear anything. Afterwards, however, they frightened me by telling me of the partiality of the tribunal. I had made many enemies, they said,

and enemies against whom all resistance would be in vain.

The underhand dealings of my enemies, my pecuniary position, which had become very precarious—all, in short, urged me to leave Paris. So, I left for Liège by the diligence.

It is a very plausible story, so plausible that it leaves a doubt as to Théroigne's sincerity as a reformer.

Had she felt deeply then, could she have concealed her feelings under so trivial a tone?

When she left Paris by the diligence, Théroigne found the vehicle full of aristocrats, who discussed the patriots in anything but gentle terms. In order to avoid the society of these "coarse people," she changed her seat, and followed the diligence in a small carriage. In the carriage she made the acquaintance of a certain M. Barrachin, and informed him in confidence that she was going into a retreat in order to study. He gave her a letter of recommendation to a bookseller in Liège, which she accepted but did not use.

At Rheims she left her carriage, which was going no farther, and drove to Paliseul in a mail-cart. There she hired a horse, and rode into Saint-Hubert. She put up at a little inn, where she met an officer and a merchant. From the latter she bought some handkerchiefs to give to her friends at Marcourt.

The officer, who recognised the moment she opened her mouth that she had come from Paris, spoke very disdainfully of the Revolution. Here apparently Théroigne forgot the part she was playing, which consisted in appearing to take but a lukewarm interest in the French position. She says she spoke hotly against despotism, and that a spirited argument ensued. It turned upon the patriots of Brabant. At this name her judges pricked up their ears, for according to more than one account the real reason of Théroigne's absence from Paris was that she had been sent in company with others by the Jacobins to spread revolutionary propaganda in this province.

She stated boldly that in reply to the officer's condemnation of the unrest among the peasants she had declared their cause was just, and that Emperor Joseph II. had wrongfully suppressed their privileges and restrained their rights. So excited was she on this question that she was unable to contain herself, she cried:

He had the intention of giving up Brabant in exchange for Bavaria, because, forsooth, he said that he liked towns that had been burnt better than those that were in revolt.

In speaking thus to the emperor's officer, she was very indiscreet, and exposed herself to insult. She merely relates that she felt this need of outspokenness, and did not try to defend it. Joseph II.'s death, in February 1790, put an end to the reforms which he had endeavoured to institute in the Low Countries, and which had aroused disturbance and discontent amongst the people. His project to annex Bavaria had already come to naught through the interference of Frederick the Great. Joseph's successor, Leopold II., did everything possible to restore order in the afflicted provinces.

Had it been true that Théroigne's mission was to Brabant, she would hardly have been likely to dwell on this episode in her *Confessions*.

From Saint-Hubert she set off on horseback to Marcourt. At an isolated farm in the midst of the forest she dismounted, and sought refreshment in the shape of new milk. It crossed her mind that she would like to remain in this quiet spot, or at least to return there when she had seen her relations at Marcourt; but the farm belonged to the monks of Saint-Hubert, and they could not give her a lodging. At last she reached her native village. She said:

> I cannot express the pleasure I felt in arriving, the joy of seeing my village again, the house where I was born, my uncle, and indeed my early comrades. I quite forgot about the French Revolution. Every evening I went to the *veillée*, when with my friends I joined in all the games of my youth. On Sundays we went to dance, to run, and to play at prisoner's base in the open meadows.

She had a dispute with the village miller because, as she thought, he charged too much for his flour, but he answered her rudely when she spoke to him about it, and she could not get him to look at the matter from the people's point of view. She also thought it wrong of the *curé* to accept an income for his work whilst his parishioners were practically starving. But, because she had known him in the days of her childhood, she wrote a letter to Perregaux begging him to send a hundred crowns that he might distribute it amongst the poor, and then she changed her mind, and ordered the amount to be spent in warm underclothing, because the *curé* would not accept a gift of money.

She had not forgotten any of her old friends, and never grew tired of telling stories about the wonderful things she had seen and done in the Revolution. De Goncourt says:

> She boasted of having prevented the queen from leaving France,

and showed proudly a fragment of one of her diamond necklaces. She gathered the young men together, questioned them closely, taught them the revolutionary ideas and songs that were in vogue in Paris, and spread the spirit of revolt around her.

If it be true that she did any of these things she was very careful not to say so. The reference to the queen's necklace may be regarded as absurd. The jewels she had in her possession were her own.

After staying in Marcourt for a month, Théroigne left there to go to Liège, where her brother Pierre was awaiting her arrival. The regret she felt at saying goodbye to the friends of her early youth was counterbalanced by the hope of continuing her musical studies at Liège.

She travelled by boat to this city, and the boatman recommended an inn he knew. Whilst she was waiting there for a room to be made ready for her, she went into the common sitting-room, which was crowded with Flemings. At first, she thought they were patriots, but she found that their opinions differed vastly from her own and that it was impossible to carry on a fair argument. She left the room to escape from their unpleasant remarks.

The very next day her brother fetched her from Liège and took her to La Boverie, a little village half a league away, where she stayed at the White Cross Inn. For a time, she lived there very quietly, seeing no friends, taking no part in the public meetings or gatherings held at Liège, and, indeed, rarely leaving her lodgings except to fetch the *Gazette* and other journals from a bookseller's shop in the neighbouring town. She soon found the country dreary. She missed the stir and excitement of the Revolution. She dared not confess that she would have liked to return to Paris, but she spoke of going to Brabant instead. She went so far as to take out her passport, and then changed her mind. She felt that she had not enough money to indulge this fancy, and discarded it for the sake of her brothers.

The only way to save expense was to remain in her retreat. If she left it, she would be wronging those who were dependent on her. By this time, she had pawned her last diamond necklace. Her income had been anticipated. Her board and lodging at La Boverie was costing her five crowns a month. Her banker, Perregaux, sent her only four *louis* every month. Many of her jewels, left at the Mont de Piété in Paris, had been sold because she could not afford to redeem them.

The Mont de Piété was at that time a recent institution in France. On December 9th, 1777, Louis XVI. issued Letters Patent stating that the good effects produced by Monts de Piété in the different countries and provinces of Europe, especially in Italy, Flanders, and Hainault, left no doubt that such establishments, both in Paris and in the principal towns in France, would result in advantage to the people. It was hoped that their existence would prevent the "disorders introduced by usury" which had ruined many families. Three days later *Parlement* registered the decree for governmental pawn-shops.

Théroigne took advantage of this method of borrowing money. Between June 1789 and May 1790, she had pledged valuables to the extent of between seven and eight thousands of *livres*, consisting of gold and diamond bracelets, sets of silver plate and spoons, cruets and stoppers, a golden casket, and diamond rings, earrings, and a necklace. The rule was that the securities for loans were kept for a year, and, if not claimed by then, were sold a month later.

Théroigne's last jewel was pledged at Liège, and afterwards her letters to M. Perregaux, whilst they make clear her devotion to her brothers, deal chiefly with her increasing financial straits.

She wrote on October 16th:

> I thank you very much for having sent me the report of the proceedings of the *Châtelet*, and I must thank you also for having accepted the little arrangement which I proposed to you. If you will kindly advance three months' money to my brother, in order that he may have my things returned, you will greatly please me. According to our arrangement of four *louis* a month, that will be twelve *louis* you will have to give him, and for three months you will send nothing to Liège. If my brother requires your help or advice in arranging my little affairs, or in having my things returned to me more cheaply, I would be obliged, *monsieur*, if you would continue your kindness to me. I should be afraid of bothering you too much if I did not rely especially on the pleasure you have taken in helping me.

She wrote to Perregaux again from Liège on December 2nd, 1790, still referring to the pledged jewels.

> Your letter was a very agreeable surprise to me when I saw from it that you had the kindness to redeem those of my effects which I had regarded as sold. I do not know how to express the gratitude with which the nobility of your act inspires me. I shall always remember your devotion. I accept your generous offer to redeem my bracelets and sell them when you can get

a fair price for them. I shall leave it in your hands. As for the silver plate and the casket, please do not allow these to be sold. I beg of you to send someone to pay the interest on a loan of eleven hundred *livres*, the term of which expires on the 9th of this month, and the acknowledgment of which I enclose in my letter with two others, one for a hundred and forty *livres* and the other for ninety *livres*. If the effects referred to in the two last have been sold they will give you the balance due, if they are not I should be grateful if you would redeem them, and hope that you will soon be able to sell the bracelet and recoup yourself for your further advances. I still have a number of diamonds to sell, and should like to get rid of them, as the interest is ruinous. I will send you my contract immediately, with the other papers, so that you will know what M. de Persan owes me. You have promised to help me with your advice, so that I and my brothers may be paid, and for this we shall be eternally grateful to you.

I am subscribing to the *Journal de 1789*, which I wish to receive at Liège. It will be necessary to add a trifle for this. You will do me a great favour if you send the enclosed receipt to the office of the paper and arrange this little matter for me. I ask you to do a great many things, don't I? If you dare to say 'yes,' you will deal me a terrible blow.

It is not often Théroigne gives such a feminine touch to her letters, but her constant demands for money grow rather wearisome.

Her dislike of inactivity soon became overwhelming, and her restlessness increased every time she walked in the meadows of La Boverie or on the banks of the Meuse and met groups of patriots from Brabant. She could hear the roar of distant cannon, and her curiosity to learn the result of the fighting was so intense that she questioned those she met. Then a strange thing took place. She was suspected of being an imperial spy, and was arrested and taken to Tilleur, where she speedily undeceived her captors and told them her real views. Nevertheless, because they were not satisfied with her statements regarding van der Noot, they wanted to take her to Namur. Her eldest brother and the people at the White Cross Inn did their best to see that she was set free at the first possible moment. She says:

It is true I was a patriot, but not with the same principles as van der Noot, for I never supported the nobility and I did not see that it was necessary for my country to declare its independence. I only desired that the people should be represented and that abuses should be removed.

To understand Théroigne's attitude towards van der Noot, it is necessary to remember that the third estate of Brabant was upholding the very principles of the social and political system which the third estate in France was seeking to destroy. Joseph II. represented in many ways the progressive spirit of the day and, finding the estates intractable, dissolved them and cancelled the form of constitution known as the Joyous Entry, together with the ancient liberties of the province. Hendrik van der Noot, advocate to the sovereign council of Brabant, a man of but mediocre talents, though courageous and animated by his love of justice, became the people's idol and organised a riot in Brussels which spread throughout the district.

Van der Noot was closely identified with the cause of malcontent hierarchy. He published a *Memoir on the Rights of the People of Brabant*, but his teachings were disputed by a growing democratic party which had imbibed French theories from the emissaries of that country, who were busy in 1790 in inciting the masses to demand a free National Assembly on the principle of their own. The Congress at Brussels employed force against the rebels. On the accession of Leopold, he offered, as already stated, to restore the liberties of the Austrian Netherlands of which they had been deprived in his brother Joseph's reign, and demanded in return that the province should swear allegiance to himself. If his terms were not accepted by November 21st, he threatened to enforce them, and sent soldiers to supplement the Austrian troops already at Luxemburg. The republican leaders made a vain effort to improve the position, and Leopold, refusing to grant an extension of time for consideration, dispatched troops on the 22nd of the month to Brussels. Resistance was impossible. Van der Noot and his colleagues fled, the Congress dissolved itself, and the Belgian Republic, after being in existence but a few months, ceased to be.

Mrs. Elliott, who was in Brussels in the spring of 1 790, saw something of the revolt in the Low Countries. When she desired to leave for England, permission was refused her, and in an interview with van der Noot she learned that this was because she was suspected of being of the party of the Duc d'Orléans. She assured him that this was not so; that she always was a royalist and ever should be such; that she was neither a van der Nootist nor a Vonckist. Mrs. Elliott writes:

I witnessed many terrible scenes in Brussels, similar to those in France. I saw poor creatures murdered in the streets because they did not pull their hats off to Capuchins, or for passing a bust of van der Noot without bowing very low. His busts were all over the town and even in the theatres. Van der Noot was a very odd-looking man. He was, I fancy, about forty, rather tall and thin. He was full of vivacity, and did not look ill-natured, though very ugly. I never shall forget his dress. It was a Quaker-coloured silk coat lined with pink and narrow silver-lace, a white dimity waistcoat, white cotton stockings, net ruffles with fringe round them, and a powdered bob-wig.

On the subject of van der Noot's flight, Théroigne wrote in her letter of December 2nd to Perregaux:

You know doubtless that the Estates, van der Noot and his satellites, formerly the idols of the people, who have today become the object of their hate and their mistrust, have been treated as they deserved. Mme Pineau's house has been pillaged, van der Noot has had to save himself from the just vengeance of the people whom he betrayed and sacrificed to his personal interests, and they have tried in vain to rekindle fanaticism by renewed processions, which have not had the slightest influence on the spirit of the people, who have had their eyes opened. They say that in the end the party of aristocrats and royalists will be crushed by one of the democrats, who, in conjunction with our old general released from the prisons of Louvain, rallies the people to resist the Austrians who are already at Namur.

Now, the general to whom Théroigne referred was van der Meersch, who had at first commanded the insurrectionary troops. He followed Vonck, the leader of the democrats, and was imprisoned by the Estates and not set free until the return of the Austrians. It was therefore impossible that he could have acted in the manner she indicated, and this mistake on her part goes to prove that she did no more than follow the course of events with interest from afar.

It is natural enough that her presence near Liège should have given rise to suspicion. Emissaries, both women and men, were sent from France to Belgium in that year. In 1791 there appeared a little book entitled *Julie, Philosophe ou le bon Patriote*, which purported to be the history of one of these women who became first the agent and afterwards the victim of the revolutions in Holland, Brabant, and France.

LEOPOLD II., EMPEROR OF AUSTRIA.

The story went that Julie was charged by Mirabeau to play some such part as was falsely attributed to Théroigne. The said Julie was born in 1760, and had several lovers—the Chevalier de Morande and de Calonne in London, Mirabeau in Paris, and van der Noot in Brussels. Mirabeau dispatched her to the latter city in charge of a sealed packet addressed to van der Noot. The revolutionist received her literally with open arms. He was charmed with her, begged her to stay for dinner, invited her to supper, and in the end refused to let her go.

Finally she broke away from him, and went over to the democratic party, and, as a Vonckist, gave vent to her revengeful feelings against van der Noot much in the same strain that Théroigne did when writing to Perregaux. Indeed, the warmth of feeling she put into her remarks to this friend contrast strangely with the colourless and guarded tone of her confessions under examination. In this same letter of December 2nd, she gives him to understand that she was charmed to hear of Duport-Dutertre's appointment to be Keeper of the Seals. The advocate had won this post through the influence of Lafayette, replacing Champion de Cicé. He was one of the presumed authors of the *Histoire de la Révolution par deux Amis de la Liberté,* and ended his life on the scaffold in November 1793.

Théroigne says:

He alone will be charged with the notification of the decrees of the National Assembly. This will enrage the party of the Blacks, who can no longer revenge themselves by trying to ridicule virtue. I hope that justice, patriotism, and good manners will accompany all the actions of the one whose elevation is an application of the principles of the rights of man and of the citizen, to which the king at first refused his acceptance; by the choice of such a minister he appears to wish to turn away the just suspicions which his past conduct inspired. If this is in good faith, it is one more triumph for the Revolution.
I shall return to France in six months. If I were there now, I would present a cockade to the generous citizen who gave such a good example by denouncing that infamous Assonville who bought votes to have himself elected *Juge de Paix.*

And she begs him, if possible, to discover the name of this excellent patriot and send it to her when he writes, addressing his letter to M. François Person, at Saint-Esprit *couronné* sur Meuse à Liège.

But in her *Confessions* she says nothing of these opinions and enthusiasms, nor does she refer to her intention to return to Paris. On the contrary, she states that she settled down so happily among her relatives that she resolved never to return to France. Some of her cousins went to see her at La Boverie, and invited her to the fair at Xhoris. She went there accompanied by her brother, and stayed with her uncle, while Pierre returned to the White Cross Inn without her. Then she sent him to Paris to fetch her remaining belongings, and ordered him to bring back her younger brother, whom she could no longer afford to keep idle in the capital. They all met again at La Boverie.

There was a distinct danger at this time that Liège and the surrounding country would become the centre of an insurrection. Numbers of soldiers were arriving every day, and it was said that they would be billeted on the inhabitants. Rumours to this effect made Théroigne decide to return to Xhoris and settle down there for a time. She went so far as to purchase a piece of land, and her uncle promised to give her a small house, for all of which she was to pay at her leisure. This plan was looked upon unfavourably by the authorities of the little village. Théroigne was still regarded with suspicion. Then it was found that the situation at Liège was not as acute as had been feared. The Imperialist soldiers bore themselves with restraint, and there was no fighting.

Again, Théroigne changed her plans. She had not yet paid for her land, and so there was no reason why she should not return to La Boverie. She was still troubled because she had not received her income for three years, and she kept up the myth that fifteen thousand *livres* were owing to her. At any rate, she made the story serve as a good excuse for a journey to Paris, which was to have the ostensible reason of looking after her business affairs. But when she had taken out a fresh passport, her brothers objected to her departure. They feared— who can say what? Perhaps that she would be arrested and imprisoned; at the best that she would become unsettled and be drawn again into the dangerous stream of a political career. After much discussion, Théroigne abandoned her plan, and to all appearances settled down to a hum-drum country life, commenced a new course of study, and busied herself in guarding her brothers' interests. She invested in a new supply of linen, and was about to make other changes in her household arrangements, when a thunderbolt fell. She was captured by aristocrats. In her picturesque language she says:

They achieved a masterpiece by drawing me pitilessly from my lair and arresting me without the slightest grounds for their action.

And she maintained her innocence to the last.

The Austrians entered Liège on January 12th, 1791. On February 15th the Comte de la Valette, with his companions, the Comte de Saint-Malon and a sub-officer Lechoux, captured Théroigne by a ruse at La Boverie. They had official authority for their daring act. Mercy-Argenteau, at that time ambassador to the emperor in the Low Countries, addressed a letter to Kaunitz on February 6th, in which he wrote:

> Zealots are arriving here. There is one of the name of Carra in the country, who is an enemy to all authority, I shall have him closely watched. They also mention the woman called Théroigne de Méricourt, who was at the head of the queen's enemies on October 5th and 6th. She is to be found in the province of Luxemburg, and carries on a correspondence with our *enragés* of Paris and of Liège. A Frenchman furnished with good letters of recommendation came to ask my permission to kidnap her secretly, herself and her papers; I gave my sanction, and ordered the escort to be strengthened by a small mounted patrol. If the capture is made, they will conduct the prisoner to Freiburg, there to await whatever fate may be decided upon as most suitable for her.

It was only natural that the man who had spent long and laborious years in safeguarding the interests of Marie-Antoinette should be strongly prejudiced against any one whose good faith towards the queen had been impugned by so much as a breath of suspicion. Théroigne, however innocent she may have been otherwise, had allowed her tongue free rein. This fact alone, and it must have reached his ears, was enough to make Mercy-Argenteau judge her unheard. Nor was it only the minister who judged. The press had a great deal to say in the matter; much of it humorous, some of it serious.

The *Journal Général* announced the news of her arrest in these terms:

> The well-beloved of Populus, the confidante of Mirabeau, the famous Théroigne, has been arrested near Luxemburg, and conducted to Vienna in Austria. They assert that the Jacobins Club intends to send an army of five hundred thousand National Guards to menace the emperor if he refuses to release this heroine, since it is of importance to their principal members that

she should not betray their secrets.

The *Moniteur* of April 10th states in its correspondence from Vienna of March 19th that:

> People speak of a prisoner of state who is being brought to Vienna; they presume arriving from the Low Countries (it is said from Brussels). Rumour reports that this individual is a woman who made herself conspicuous in France during the Revolution. They call her Mlle Théroigne de Méricourt. The oddest remarks are made on this subject. They presume that this girl, being implicated by the proceedings commenced by the Court of the *Châtelet* in Paris concerning the fatal days of October 5th and 6th, 1789, and having taken to flight, the emperor has the right to have her seized on his territory, and that His Imperial Majesty has also the right to have her judged by his tribunals, and even to condemn her to the extreme penalty of the law. This revolting absurdity is only worthy of refutation. It would be ignominious for the subjects of the emperor to suspect His Imperial Majesty of being capable of such an attempt, in which indignity would be allied with barbarism.

The royalists rejoiced greatly when they heard of the arrest of Théroigne. They celebrated the event of her consequent death in verses, beginning:

Ecoutez, grande nation,
Et pretez grande attention:
La demoiselle Théroigne
Vient d'attraper un coup de peigne
Qui défrise ses grands projets:
Hélas! c'étaient de grands forfaits!
and concluding:
Et tandis que nous devisons
Avec nos petites chansons,
Autour du cou de la donzelle,
Un bourreau tourne une ficelle.
Pleurez, malheureux Populus,
Car votre maîtresse n'est plus!

Fortunately for Théroigne things were not quite as bad as that. She had not suffered the extreme penalty of the law.

The idea that Théroigne had left Paris in 1790 to fulfil a revolutionary mission in her own country was developed in a pamphlet by M. Carra, dated April 1st, which denounced Marechal Bender to the Jacobins. The denunciation said:

> The society sent Mlle Théroigne to complete the great work of propaganda in Brabant. This heroine merited this flattering distinction in every way. She had given proofs of her powers on the ever-memorable days of October 5th and 6th. Since this epoch Mlle Théroigne has rendered the most important services to the society. Her indefatigable zeal and her unceasing activity have made more proselytes than the papers of our most celebrated journalists could ever do. You know, gentlemen, that I am more given by nature to injure than to praise people; you know, besides, that Mme Carra, my honourable spouse, merits and possesses all my affections; so that there is no reason why you should suspect my motives or my good faith when I shower praise upon the illustrious lady for whom we are all weeping. Mlle Méricourt left Paris after having received our orders, and being well furnished with assignats, to go and execute our schemes. Four or five zealous patriots set off in her company, in order to co-operate with all their might in the propagation of the great movement. She started by making an opening at Brussels, but found this stage unworthy of her talents. She made, I can assure you, some important conquests in very little time by the aid of assignats and punch, of punch and assignats. Already many of the Brabant people had adopted our principles, already general feeling was veering over to our side. I was already flattering myself that I should see my patriotic works made welcome in this country, already I had made my creditors understand that the results of our subscriptions for the Annals of the club would be sufficient to pay my debts—and all this as a result of the invaluable assistance of Mlle Théroigne de Méricourt. Oh, shame, oh, despair! Mlle Théroigne has been hanged, and our projects have come to naught.

He then went on to say that Marechal Bender, "the inhuman monster derived from the forests of Hungary," failing to be moved by the charms of the nymphlike Théroigne, had seized her person, and had had her executed in a twinkling of an eye, chasing her fellow workers out of Brabant. After a further out-pouring of his wrath against the said Marechal Bender a resolution was passed that he should be hanged for hanging the immortal Théroigne.

The royalist journal, the *Feuille du Jour*, of March 1st, 1791, after saying that Théroigne had been arrested by French officers, went on half in joke, half seriously:

> They say that having learnt that Mlle Théroigne was at Namur, these young soldiers went there, demanded dinner, paid their court to her; and since Mlle Théroigne, in exercising the apostleship, has not renounced the benefices of gallantry, the gentlemen in question had no trouble in overcoming her scruples. In the effusion of her confidence and love she divulged the motives and secrets of her mission and gave up all her papers relating to matters in Brabant. They believed that she was dangerous enough to have her pointed out to the government and to see that she was taken prisoner. Some declared that they only saw fit to give her up out of spite when they recognised that her health was no better than her politics.

This scurrilous paper added to its suggestive remarks that:

> The Comte de Mercy-Argenteau had reassured her fully, telling her that she was safe from all peril so long as nothing was laid to her charge; but if the suspicions against her were confirmed, he would use all his influence and all his credit to have her hanged.

Before the end of the month they had completed her sentence.

> They say that Mlle Théroigne has been hanged. Weep, oh friends . . .

The pessimistic views taken by these journals were never destined to be literally fulfilled, but the truth was serious enough to affect the victim of the capture and her friends to a considerable degree.

Théroigne's arrest made a great impression on her brothers. The eldest wrote to Perregaux to tell him that she had disappeared.

> They say my sister has been taken back to Paris by the police. If that is the case, can she have been kidnapped by force by any lover that she may have in the capital, or has she been accused of anything? *Monsieur*, I implore you to use every possible means to secure her release, and to inform me at the same time who could have occasioned this nocturnal removal. You would greatly oblige not only my said sister but also myself, being a great help to me in my suspense. . . .

The reference to Théroigne's possible lovers has been taken as prejudicial to the Minerva-like attitude she was supposed to have adopted since her return to Italy. But it seems natural enough that her brother, not knowing, or not wishing to appear to know, of what political crime she could be accused, should imagine her disappearance might bear a personal interpretation.

A great deal of Théroigne's charm lies in the fact that mystery constantly surrounds her actions. Apparently innocent and without reproach, invariably able to convince her accusers of her own uprightness when brought into personal contact with them, the impartial judge, when far removed from the bewilderment engendered by her presence and naive assertions, cannot fail to be assailed by many a doubt. She had had more than one lover in her youth, then why this sudden return to virtue unless, as has been suggested, her health had been destroyed by her mode of living? She had taken an active and earnest part in the revolutionary movement in Paris, then why this absolute collapse of enthusiasm when living in a district of the Low Countries where as strong an undercurrent of revolt existed?

She had never joined in any plot for the removal of the queen, then why the determined persecution by the French *émigrés?* She had, in short, been but one of a thousand with similar aims and had done nothing to justify her being singled from the crowd for vilification, then why the unceasing diatribes of the royalist press? These are problems it is not easy to answer. Innocent or not, Théroigne was to suffer penalty for even the appearance of guilt.

Meanwhile she was being borne relentlessly farther and farther from her home and from all those she loved. At Coblenz her captors were hailed by the people as saviours of the monarchy. The news of the identity of the prisoner had spread like wildfire and the *émigrés* gave a special banquet to celebrate the event. They drank to the glory of France, and were convinced that the secrets of the revolutionists were now at their mercy. From Coblenz the way led through Worms, where they stayed to greet the Prince de Condé, who had chosen this spot as his retreat. Saint-Malon communicated the story of the arrest, and so awakened Conde's curiosity that he desired to see the beautiful captive, and approached her as she was seated in the carriage that was to bear her to prison. She received him with disdain and deliberately turned her back upon him, refusing to speak a word.

After the carriage had left Worms, Saint-Malon upbraided her for her want of respect to a prince of the blood, and went so far as to accuse her of ill-breeding.

"Spare your words," she cried: "I do not need your advice. I know very well indeed to whom I owe respect."

"You are getting angry," said Saint-Malon.

She continued:

Not at all. But no true patriot can honestly greet the Prince de Condé. He is one of the worst enemies of the nation. Here, even, in this foreign country, he incites and foments intrigues against France. All the world knows the treason of which the prince is guilty. He is a traitor.

And then remembering that her words might be a menace to her own safety, she became suddenly silent.

This did not altogether suit the plan of her captors. They wanted to strike while the iron was hot, to force some admission from her which might be a condemnation from her own lips. They tried every means in their power—threats, cajoling, anger, pleading, and even love-making and flattery. Saint-Malon said:

I cannot believe, that you, so pretty, so fascinating, have renounced love for ever. Hear me, I beg of you. You must know that I love you tenderly; you are divine. I can no longer be silent. Give me leave respectfully to kiss your little white hands, fresh as the petals of the clematis.

He tried to seize her hand. She withdrew it roughly, then he endeavoured to slip one arm about her, and she, poor girl, unprotected and at the mercy of a scoundrel, struck at him savagely. Maddened by this insult, he threw aside his mask and disclosed himself in his true colours of a jailer.

"Your conduct will cost you dear, *mademoiselle*; you will not soon forget me."

"And yours has been such that I could not forget you if I would, *monsieur*. I shall always think of you as a man I despise and hate with all my soul," she replied hotly.

He gave her one more chance of reflecting, and promised to help her if she would answer all his questions frankly.

"I can only reflect that you wish to set a trap for me," she said, and added nothing but the assurance of her innocence and good faith.

The five days' journey from Coblenz to Freiburg was a period of misery, both mental and physical, to the prisoner. She arrived at the latter town in a state bordering on collapse.

Freiburg, in Breisgau, was then an important Austrian garrison town. The commander, Colonel Rudler von Greiffenstein, had his hands full at that time keeping order in the place, on account of the number of French *émigrés* who took refuge there, and the disturbances and conspiracies consequent on their presence. Her captors lodged Théroigne at the Nègre Inn, and were so fearful lest she should escape them that they asked the commander to allow them to have military help in guarding her.

Freiburg was chiefly of importance, as far as Théroigne was concerned, because it was there that her escort was changed and she was well-rid of the importunate Saint-Malon. Her new guardian, the Baron de Landresc, who had received orders to take her to Kufstein, was a very different kind of man. He treated his prisoner with kindness and respect. The baron and Théroigne, accompanied by two or three officers, left Freiburg on March 9th with the ostensible object of journeying to Innsbruck and Vienna.

When she heard that she was to be taken to the Austrian capital, Théroigne could hardly contain her excitement.

> The emperor is at Vienna. I will ask for an audience. I shall have speech with him, and he will hear me. I can tell the Court of Austria the most astonishing things.

As they proceeded towards Altdorf, Théroigne began to show more friendliness towards the baron. She felt that he was well-disposed towards her, and began to chatter freely, she began:

> As you are aware, I have joined the patriots and taken up the noble cause of the people. Our motto is Liberty and Equality. I am devoting all my efforts to promote the general welfare. Even women have their share of work to do, and can help mightily in furthering the progress of civilisation. It is only necessary that their desire to do so should be strong enough. It ought to be the aim of every well-born individual to succour the unfortunate and the oppressed. In this great work there need be no distinction made between men and women.

She denied utterly that the part she had played in the Revolution was an active one, she maintained:

> I refused to be drawn into any plot or cabal. This fact has made me wonder over and over again how I come to be in this posi-

tion. I have never committed a crime. I am innocent. It is true that I took an interest in political questions, but I did what a hundred thousand other people have done. Logically speaking, then, if I am to be put in prison, they too should share my fate.

The next stopping-place was Innsbruck, which was usually a sleepy little town. But the arrival of a fair political prisoner had been reported in the newspapers, and the inhabitants one and all turned out to see her. When the carriage and four in which she travelled rolled up, the market-place was crowded, and Landresc, concerned for the security of his prisoner, hurried her into the inn. The Archduchess Elizabeth, who was then at Innsbruck, was vastly interested in Théroigne, and commanded an interview. It is not on record whether the daughter of the people made one of her usual blunt speeches against the aristocracy and monarchy on this occasion.

At Schwaz Théroigne was taken ill, and though she struggled on as far as Woergl, she declared at this little village that she could travel no farther, and demanded a particular kind of medicine to mitigate her fever. The Baron was in a dilemma. He was not convinced that her attack of illness was genuine. He feared she might be contemplating some plan of escape. Nor did he think it wise to give her medicine of her own prescribing. How was he to be sure that it did not contain some deadly poison which would rob the aristocrats of their prey? To make security doubly sure he made the apothecary swear that the stuff was innocuous, and even went so far as to swallow a dose himself as a precaution against treachery.

As soon as Théroigne felt better and was able to continue the journey, she expressed her earnest wish to hasten on to Vienna, convinced that there she would be allowed to resume her liberty. Landresc was faced with the difficult task of telling her the truth—that he had been ordered to conduct her as far as the fortress of Kufstein, and that there he was to leave her. At this news Théroigne was overcome by despair. Her evident grief and distress softened the Baron's heart. Théroigne had the gift of knowing how to work on any man's feelings. She asked a last favour of him.

"You are the only friend I have left," she pleaded. "Think how disconsolate those must be who once cared for me and do not now know where I am or what has happened to me. My poor brother, who loves me tenderly—"

"But what can I do?" interrupted the baron.

"Help me to communicate with Pierre. Deliver a letter to him. I should feel gratitude towards you until my dying day."

The baron uttered not a word. To consent to serve as an intermediary for a State prisoner, to help her to correspond with her relatives, would be to defy all regulations, and to lay himself open to the gravest consequences.

It says something for Théroigne's persuasive powers that even here she obtained her desire. The letter was written, was sent off, and reached its destination in due course. It would be indiscreet to expect to know definitely by whose timely assistance this came to pass.

The letter contained some account of her arrest:

My dear Brother,

Among the individuals who have seized my person there were two French officers and one *impèriaux*. They did not show me any special order. I do not know by whose instructions nor why I have been arrested, which is terrible. The two Frenchmen informed me verbally, however, that it was on account of the affairs of Brabant, but I saw that it was quite the contrary, for they never ceased to question me on the events of the French Revolution. They even employed a ruse and finesse, pretending to be just and honest, with the intention of drawing out my confidences. They did not raise their masks until we reached Freiburg, where they showed the greatest enmity against the patriots and the greatest interest in finding me guilty.

She begged her brother to go to Vienna at once, and to ask permission from the emperor for her to be taken there so that he might hear her own version of the affair she declared:

I would give everything that I have for the chance of speaking to the emperor, for I feel certain that he did not give orders for my arrest.

The thought of sleeping in a prison terrified her, she said, and she complained of ill-health, fearing she knew not what evil consequences if she were not speedily released.

But Pierre-Joseph did not dream of going to Vienna. He dreaded lest he should be implicated in his sister's alleged plots. Instead, he appealed once more to Perregaux, telling him that he had received a letter from his sister since her disappearance. In order to keep him informed of what was going on, and because he wanted him to help

THÉROIGNE DE MÉRICOURT.

in freeing her, he sent him her letter.

He writes:

> But you know, that since the day of her capture I have followed up her affairs keenly with my aunt at Liège, yet all our endeavours have been fruitless.

Théroigne's enemies were not content with seizing her person; they calumniated her, he stated, in all the public journals. Her aunt had employed two lawyers, who agreed that a memoir should be printed containing her justification, that it should be published in Paris, and that a deputy of the Assembly should be found who would take the trouble to write to Mercy-Argenteau, and to send him a copy of the memoir. Pierre asked Perregaux to help him with the printing of this document, which could not be done at Liège, as it was forbidden to print anything without the permission of the authorities, and it was not possible for him to present himself for the purpose of gaining permission.

Théroigne's brother continues:

> I have learnt, that M. l'Abbé Siéyès has spoken several times very kindly of my sister to M. ——. This man was deputy for Liège at Paris during the Revolution. I am sure that if we explained things as they are to him, he would gladly take it upon himself to write to Brussels.

He then begged Perregaux to ask his brother to see about this matter, and to speak to the deputy, who had known Théroigne well, because it was unlikely that he would think harshly of the faults she had committed in France, which, moreover, were already relegated to oblivion because the National Assembly had issued a decree cancelling all the warrants of arrest.

> I am examining the papers, but you will see more clearly than I how to act for the best. I shall owe you a debt of eternal gratitude, and would gladly pay it by shedding my blood for you.

From this letter it is apparent that Théroigne's brother was not entirely convinced of her innocence. Possibly he too was mystified by the extraordinary inconsistencies in her character.

Whilst these negotiations were being undertaken on her behalf Théroigne was passing through new and unpleasant experiences.

Chapter 6

Kufstein

On the frontiers of the Tyrol and Bavaria stands an imposing fortress, with dungeons and battlements, dominating the surrounding country. Art, brought to bear upon remarkable natural qualifications, rendered this place practically impregnable.

It was March 17th, at nine o'clock in the morning, when Théroigne and her escort arrived before the forbidding walls of Kufstein. She was overwhelmed by dread at the thought of the fate in store for her, she cried:

> Unfortunate being that I am, I have been condemned—innocent, I swear it—to a convict's cell, to unheard-of tribulations and sufferings. What you have been told of me, *monsieur*, is an infamous calumny. Help me to escape from the doom that awaits me.

Landresc, deeply moved by her piteous plight, turned away his head.

She sobbed, she gave way to hysterical shrieks, she declared it would be better to die at once than to endure captivity. Nothing could calm her.

Presently the governor of the prison, Captain André Schoeniger, appeared upon the scene. He was accustomed to these outbreaks of despair. All the prisoners enacted the same tragedy in a lesser or greater degree. All declared themselves martyrs.

Schoeniger had been well prepared for the kind of prisoner he had to expect. He had been instructed to have her strictly guarded, but she was to be treated humanely. There was to be no brutality.

The captain himself conducted "Madame Theobald" to her cell. This was an unusual honour, rarely accorded to any prisoner, except those of peculiar distinction.

The approach to the upper regions of the fortress was not one to inspire hope of freedom in the captive's breast. Hewn through huge and unscalable rocks, the way to the prison wound through a narrow and dark subterranean passage, up countless flights of stairs, climbing ever higher and higher into what was a well-nigh impenetrable fastness. After mounting more than two hundred steps a little court was reached, where there was a revolving bridge and massive doors heavily barred with iron. Once beyond that, and the prisoner said goodbye to the outer world—for who knows how long? Then more mounting upward, in a tower this time, the way becoming more narrow and more gloomy, and the air more damp.

At last a second door as black and solid as the first was reached. It led into the prison proper. Fainting and breathless the prisoner stood still, unable to move another step. Schoeniger, taking her by the arm, urged her on. No prisoner was allowed to loiter there. There was a second tower to mount, more of the huge stone steps built into walls so thick that no voice could echo there; even the breath seemed stifled. Théroigne felt she knew what burial alive would mean.

The passage widened out into a vault, and that in turn into a courtyard, open to the sky at last. Round about were high walls containing many windows, strongly barred. And here every sign of the way they had come was lost. The four sides of the court appeared alike in every particular. Which of the closed apertures was the one that led out of this horrible trap? It was impossible to remember. How could any prisoner dwell for an instant on the thought of escape through those bewildering labyrinths of brick and rock, guarded as they were at regular intervals by armed sentries. Far better death than captivity in such a place!

The cell into which Théroigne was led was not terrible. It had two windows, one looking into the courtyard, the other into the surrounding mountains. The furniture was of white wood, and of the plainest description. It communicated with a room occupied by the sentry. No one could enter her apartment without being challenged by the guard.

The captain ordered an inventory to be taken of the prisoner's possessions. They were not numerous. A hat, two gowns, a silk kerchief, a brown cloak trimmed with fur, a muff, two pairs of shoes, four undergarments, five handkerchiefs, ten pairs of silk stockings, and a belt comprised the whole of her wardrobe. There was nothing like a riding-habit, and no weapons.

The governor thought she was but ill provided for. Just then his eye fell upon some books.

"What have we here?" he cried.

The soldier read out the titles. *Works of Seneca, Complete Works of de Mably,* and Plato's *Dialogues*.

"She must be a blue-stocking," said the governor, laughing; but his manner implied a new accession of respect.

There was nothing else to account for except a few silver spoons, some silver buttons, and other *gewgaws*. These were placed in a casket and locked away. The search ended, the governor retired, and the prisoner was left alone. She heard the heavy door close and the bolts shot.

She fell on her knees and called for mercy. She wrung her hands, tears streaming down her cheeks.

There was no answer to her cry.

★★★★★★

A week passed in a kind of mental stupor; she sobbed, she raged, and then, worn out, she slept. At regular intervals meals were brought to her. She was allowed to choose her own food. Whenever the governor came into the room, which was fairly often, she asked him about her trial. "When will it begin?" was her invariable question.

"I know nothing." His reply never altered.

At last her longing for an occupation became so extreme that she plucked up courage and begged Schoeniger to allow her to have a piano. "Music passes the time pleasantly," she said in her wheedling manner.

The governor was dumbfounded at such an audacious request.

"I beg of you to obtain for me this harmless amusement," she urged, wearing the air of innocence and childlike joyousness which never failed to fascinate.

"*Madame,*" he replied, endeavouring to speak sternly, "it is quite out of my power to procure you this privilege."

"Oh!" Her disappointment was evident from her voice.

"But, you might—"

"What?" She knew there was more to come. She was all eagerness.

"Well, write to Vienna to the Conseil de Guerre. It may be—"

She asked him sweetly whether he could not do her the favour of writing himself. She felt sure her request would have more weight coming from him. He had no power to refuse so simple a plea. As he was leaving the room, she laid one hand on his arm. She said:

Monsieur, just one thing more. Could you trace for me the three receipts which were taken from me at the time of my arrest. I asked them to send them to my brother Pierre. If they have gone astray the loss would be a serious one. The amount is some two thousand three hundred and eighty-four *livres*.

To this the amenable governor also agreed. He was treating the prisoner with enormous consideration. He sent for all the papers which had been seized at La Boverie.

For a fortnight Théroigne was all impatience. Then the use of a piano was accorded her. She was overjoyed, and practised her singing every day. But soon the whole of her repertory was exhausted It was impossible to obtain any new music. When her memory failed her, she attempted to improvise, but she did not care for her own compositions and soon exhausted her resources. Then she began to complain anew of the weariness of incarceration.

Had she but been able to compare her lot with that to be endured throughout the Terror by the aristocrats in the French prisons, how happy she might have thought herself! She had light and air, good food and repose, her jailers were kind in the main, and her case was by no means hopeless, whilst they had none of these consolations and many unspeakable hardships. What were her sufferings when regarded in the light of the tortures and agony they were to undergo? Penned by the score into tiny evil-smelling cells, into which the light of day hardly penetrated, fed on bad bread, putrefying meat, adulterated wine, and rotten vegetables, subjected to the vilest insults, coarse jests, and even physical violence, unable to utter a complaint lest a murmur should produce more terrible punishment still, they waited with smiling faces and brave mien to hear the creak of the tumbril and the click of the guillotine.

But Théroigne knew nothing of these horrors, and felt her own sufferings well-nigh unendurable because her imagination called up nothing worse. Confinement in itself meant death to her.

The governor, in order to dispel the stupor of misery into which she had fallen, told her that the examining magistrate, M. François Le Blanc, would arrive before long from his home in Constance, and that then the inquiry into her case would take place.

This news threw her into a state of great excitement. "When will he come? Tomorrow—the day after?" she asked eagerly.

But no exact information was vouchsafed her.

Spring was coming, and even the stern discipline of prison life seemed to relax somewhat under the benign influence of the gentler mood of the year. Théroigne was permitted to walk in an enclosed court, where the trees were in bud, and she could hear the singing of birds.

The governor now showed her every care. He realised that she was taking her imprisonment too much to heart. Her health was breaking. She was troubled by hallucinations, torturing visions which unnerved her, and at night she suffered from ghastly dreams which left her sleepless. She sighed for her freedom, for her own country, for those she loved. There was no human being near her in whom she could confide. She was falling into a rapid decline. As the days passed Captain Schoeniger dreaded that he might lose his prisoner by death.

On May 28th Le Blanc arrived. He asked for the prisoner's papers. He had already been assured that they contained nothing compromising. He had received his instructions from Prince Kaunitz. They were definite and, at the same time, lenient. Le Blanc's aim was to arrive if possible, at the simple truth rather than to attempt to force a confession of guilt. His instructions ran:

> However probable it appears that the prisoner has committed the crime of high treason, it is impossible to have proof of it unless she furnishes it herself by her own confession. It is necessary, therefore, to ask her for a statement of the principal circumstances and conditions of her life in France as well as outside this country. It is indispensable to ascertain whether at any time in her life she played a public part, and if so, where, when, and how. Especially should it be made clear what part she took in the revolt of the women on October 6th, 1789.
>
> The commissioner is authorised to say that he is not reflecting the views of the emperor in making her feel the rigour of the law. A free and sincere confession would be preferred. She must show herself worthy of the monarch's clemency. Moreover, the result of the inquiry will depend essentially on the agreement of her confession and depositions with the knowledge already obtained concerning the most salient points of her conduct.
>
> Her fanatic enthusiasm for everything connected with the idea of democracy is well known. The prisoner should therefore be warned that the Court has in its hands several infallible means of recognising the truth of the answers she will make to the

questions put to her. The least reticence, a single lie in her depositions, will suffice to class her in the category of persons suspected, dangerous, incorrigible, and who ought to be kept away from all chance of doing harm.

In any case, all hope that she will ever see her country again must be destroyed. If, on the one hand, this causes her affliction, on the other she will feel more free to speak without fear and to adhere strictly to the truth.

Since, having nothing more to fear from the resentment of people who might be compromised by her admissions, and having no further interest in propitiating those from whom she might expect ulterior advantages, she will keep back nothing of what she knows.

Evidently she has had relations with important people. Had she really the political influence with which opinion has endowed her.? In case this is answered in the affirmative, who are her accomplices, and what are their names? Why did she leave Paris to install herself near Liège? What does she know of the organisation of the Jacobins Club? In what manner does she speak concerning the royal family of France?

These are leading questions. Answered fully they would have left but little of Théroigne's hopes, aims, and intentions to the imagination.

On all other points Le Blanc was allowed latitude. It was his wish to inspire the prisoner with confidence.

At their first interview Théroigne promised to tell the truth, the whole truth, and nothing but the truth.

Her interrogator commended this laudable decision. He assured her that the Austrian Government did not mean to punish her for any political crimes of which she might have been guilty in France. She replied excitedly:

They have deceived the emperor. By means of insidious reports, some persons have clearly influenced the prince by imputing to me certain views or actions, and this has been the cause of my detention But they will have to render me justice. They will realise that I am but a simple woman, charmed with the idea of liberty and the welfare of the people. In that I cannot be held to be guilty. On this account, and because you have said yourself that the Austrian Government is quite indifferent to my past doings in France, I hope for my release. Begin to question me

143

as soon as you like. I am ready.

Le Blanc told her that a few days would be given her for calm meditation, in order that she might go through the facts she had to tell carefully, and have them clear and exact in her own mind. This did not altogether please the prisoner. She had had so much time for calm meditation already that solitude had driven her almost crazy. Nor did the commissioner's next remark please her much better. He told her he had to wait for the clerk who was to draw up the inquiry in writing.

"Is not that clerk one of the two Frenchmen who captured me and took me to Freiburg?" she inquired suddenly.

Le Blanc was astounded by her perspicacity. "I know nothing," he answered evasively. "Surely, *mademoiselle*, you must be mistaken in thinking that your captors were Frenchmen. They were Dutch."

She repeated

Dutch? Don't tell me they were Dutch. You have been ill informed, *monsieur*, or someone has been trying to deceive you, or, perhaps, you are trying to dupe me. I maintain against everything said to the contrary that my captors were officers and French aristocrats. I recognised them not only by the details of their military dress, but also by their caustic, insidious, and hateful manners—in short, by their discourteous treatment of me, and by their speech.

And then she added angrily:

Moreover, *monsieur*, if one of those two Frenchmen comes here to perform the services of a clerk, I will not answer so much as a single syllable. I would die rather than be subjected to a process marked by such partiality. Having been born in the Low Countries, my sovereign can only be of the House of Hapsburg. And therefore, I have the right to be tried by no one but the emperor's officials.

Le Blanc was surprised to learn that she had not been born in France.

She assured him that she was Austrian. She repeated more firmly than before:

I will never consent to be judged by Frenchmen, and most certainly not by one of those who seized me at La Boverie. Take care that I am never brought face to face with either of the rascals. They have reason to know already that they cannot force me to speak.

She had in mind the intolerable degradation of the journey from Coblenz to Freiburg.

Le Blanc was stupefied by her proud and obstinate bearing. He could never have believed that anyone as much worn by illness as the prisoner could have shown such strength of will. He realised that she was not an ordinary woman. There was nothing vulgar about her manners; no bold gestures, and no coarse tones. She had a large amount of personal magnetism, a powerful charm in which energy and grace made a strange contrast. Even the way she poured vituperation on the head of her captors, calling them vile, contemptible, wanting in tact, in education, even in humanity, had something of the sublime in it. She was the image of assaulted virtue pointing the finger of scorn at vice. It was Théroigne's gift to put others in the wrong and keep her own position unassailable.

The story of her early youth and upbringing, and of her doings in Paris before the close of 1789, was told with a simplicity that was wonderfully clever.

Her answers were put in writing, and she signed a document to the effect that the questions had been put to her by the investigating magistrate and were recognised by her as being those of His Majesty the emperor and king, and that the responses were in substance those she had made.

After she had been sworn the examination began in all seriousness on May 31st, and went on for some weeks, broken only by delays occasioned by the illness of the prisoner and the arrival of La Valette at Kufstein with his indictment against Théroigne, which included some 122 articles, and was entitled, "*Dires et Aveux de Demoiselle Théroigne*." Le Blanc exercised his authority in refusing to allow La Valette to be present at his interviews with the prisoner.

In the course of the inquiry it was discovered that Théroigne had communicated with her brother since she had been taken captive. She refused to disclose the means by which she had dispatched her letter.

"You are trying to shield your accomplice," said Le Blanc; "is not that so?"

Théroigne grew red and turned away her eyes. She admitted that this was true.

"Be frank and fear nothing," said the examining magistrate. "Only tell me the truth."

She remained immovable as a statue. Her face had grown pale.

"I only desire to know the name of your accomplice. He shall not be punished."

Still Théroigne uttered not a word.

"*Mademoiselle*, answer me," continued Le Blanc.

"*Monsieur*, I must not speak. Have pity on me."

"I give you my word of honour, no harm shall come to him."

"Will you give me a promise in writing?" asked the prisoner glibly.

Pained as he was by this evidence of her mistrust, Le Blanc agreed. He inquired carefully concerning the contents of the letter.

Théroigne could not remember exactly what she had written. She was accused of using the expression:

> I beg you to address yourself to the National Assembly in order that it may force the king to claim my freedom as a Frenchwoman?

Théroigne responded:

> If I used such a phrase, it was very stupid of me, because I am not a Frenchwoman. And if I wrote the words 'force the king' I employed an Improper term. The King of France cannot be forced. He can only be requested to put his laws into execution. As for addressing myself to the National Assembly, which represents the sovereign, to whom in a free country the humblest individual can present a petition, I perhaps was within my rights in suggesting this. But I did not do it in spite of the right I had, which I can prove. I was kidnapped by French aristocrats who did not show me the emperor's warrant. Therefore, it is not surprising that I should believe they were acting on behalf of their own sovereign.

She was told that her arrest had been ordered at Brussels by Mercy-Argenteau. She added, unmoved by this information:

> These same aristocrats, never ceased to insult me and to ridicule the officers of the French Army. I know nothing of the political aspect of my arrest. But, without a doubt, from whichever point of view it is considered, it was most certainly a malicious, base, and cruel trick. The intriguing underlings who conceived the sublime plan of arresting me will not remain triumphant. The Prince de Kaunitz, whose wisdom and supreme worth are

known throughout Europe, and, above all, the emperor, who has already made his reign illustrious by various deeds of justice and humanity, will recognise the fact that they have been deceived. Therefore, I remain tranquil.

This speech throws a fresh light on Théroigne's intuition and her persuasive gifts. She was not stupid, *la petite* Théroigne; and being assured once more that no harm should come to her accomplice in the delivery of a letter to her brother, she gaily made a description of an individual easily recognisable as the amiable but unfortunate Baron de Landresc.

She was permitted to send another letter to her brother at Liège. It was dated June 26th, 1791.

I cannot express to you, the regrets and grief which I have suffered from being deprived of your company for so long. You will have experienced the same feelings. I have often imagined your sorrow and anxiety, and this has contributed no little in aggravating my sadness and exaggerating the misfortune of my captivity. Nevertheless, I must render justice to the manner in which I am treated; they take every possible care of me, but, in spite of that, my brother, it is always very hard to be deprived of liberty when one does not deserve it. I confess to you that I should prefer death to being deprived much longer of the pleasure of seeing you, my family, and my friends.

However, you must reassure yourself, my brother, and reassure those who are interesting themselves on my account in this unfortunate affair; for I have reason to hope much from the enlightened justice of his Imperial Majesty, who will free me as soon as he knows the truth. I hope to see you again before two months have passed. Imagine how much pleasure it will give me, after having had so much grief! Please express my thanks to those who have interested themselves on my behalf, and have taken steps to have me released. Give my kind remembrances to all my friends; say that I hope to have permission to write to them soon, and that I shall see them again before long—at least, they tell me I may hope that this will be so, and, if they do me justice, this hope will be realised. I have not the slightest doubt of that.

I do not know in the least how our affairs stand, my brother: whether you are still boarding with François Person; whether

you have enough money to pay for your lodgings; whether you have had a coat made, for you were in need of one before I was taken prisoner; whether you have paid what I owe at La Boverie and at Xhoris; and whether you have received three acknowledgments of loans from the Mont de Piété in Paris, which I gave to those who escorted me to prison in order that they might be remitted to you.

One of these loans had already lapsed at the time of her arrest, but she hoped the others might be redeemed. She repeated herself in her anxiety to hear how her brothers were faring pecuniarily, and to be assured that they wanted for nothing. Then she went on to complain of her health, which she hoped would soon improve, and looked forward to the time when they should all live together as they had planned, "misfortune having ceased to dog their footsteps." She recommended her brother to study diligently, to take lessons from the same masters she had had before her arrest, and to send her as much news as possible.

Her correspondence was, without doubt, intended for the eye of her jailers, who supervised all her letters. They struck a very domestic note. The most interesting of them, perhaps, and the one which throws most light on her tastes and habits, was written on July 29th, 1791.

My dear brother, I will say no more of the impatience I have to see you again, for your own feelings will give you an idea of it. I am quite as anxious on your behalf as you can be on mine. What have you been doing? Where have you been all these six months that I have been in prison? Are you continuing your studies, or have you had the misfortune, as a counter-blow to mine, to lose all this time owing to want of money or credit? I am dying to hear your news. Where is my little brother? Is he still at Xhoris, and is he studying? Tell him to write to me. I keep feeling afraid that either of you should be wanting something, although you ought to have received the three hundred *livres* which I was expecting when they achieved the masterpiece of arresting me.

And then she goes on to deplore their troubles, trusts there is money enough, and asks once more about the acknowledgments for her jewels. There is a great deal of repetition in her letters.

Unfortunately, I do not yet know when I shall be able to see you again, but I still hope to have justice done me. I have been strictly forbidden to tell you anything concerning my affairs. I shall content myself with telling you that I have been outside the fortress walking with MM. the Magistrate and the *commandant*, and that I cannot go outside the prison nor receive anybody without the permission of these two gentlemen, who are very kind to me.

Perhaps you have been obliged to sell my pianoforte for very little, in spite of the fact that it cost me thirty *louis*. That would grieve me, because I love music, and I shall no longer have the means to get another one; but, after all, it is but a small misfortune. . . . Have you looked after our belongings at La Boverie? I am afraid lest my dresses should be spoilt, especially the woollen ones, if you have not had them put out to air. Above all things, I recommend my books to your care. Do not lend them to anybody. Use them for your instruction, and that of our brother.

Besides, you might ask the farmer's wife whether I forgot a parcel when I went off in the night with those who arrested me. The parcel contained some dresses, books of Seneca and de Mably. Please go yourself and see whether it was not left on the table. And be sure and let me know if you have found it, or if the farmer's wife found it, yes or no. Do not forget to go yourself and look for the five volumes of Seneca's letters which were in the parcel, and three volumes of de Mably, and my Indian morning gowns.

★★★★★★

According to the inventory of Théroigne's possessions taken by the governor at Kufstein, these books were in the parcel of her belongings there. It is possible she was kept in ignorance of this.

★★★★★★

And then she proceeds to tell her brothers to study day and night, to arm themselves with noble pride, to remember that virtue is the only good, to write to her often, and to remember her kindly to her friends.

Perhaps Théroigne's brothers were hardly worthy of the love and forethought she lavished upon them. The whole family seemed cursed with shiftlessness, which indicated that they came of a bad stock. Théroigne had done her brothers but a mistaken kindness in providing for their wants from her own purse. If her gains were really ill-gotten, as appears to have been the case, she did them a very bad service indeed. No sooner was her support withdrawn than Pierre-Joseph, thrown upon his own resources, which were of a most uncon-

vincing nature, was at his wit's end to discover any means of livelihood. He tried to obtain money from his sister's banker, Perregaux,
from the sale of his sister's jewels, and from a certain Baron de Selys,
governor of the principality of Stavelot, who had received Théroigne
at his *château* in a more or less friendly spirit during her recent stay in
the neighbourhood.

It was said that Théroigne's father had once been the baron's ten-
ant, and that he had known her when she was a little girl. He had
been inspired to renew the acquaintance partly by curiosity, partly by
a desire to find out her views and her motive for leaving Paris and
visiting her own country. In a letter dated October 1st, 1791, he wrote
that he had only invited her and her brothers so that he might be
kept informed of their acquaintances, their doings, and any plans they
might attempt to put into execution "in order to be useful to the good
cause." He took this step at the instigation of the Comte de Maillebois,
who was the principal agent of the French *émigré* princes. As he learnt
nothing which could in any way incriminate Théroigne, this would
appear to be additional evidence in favour of her entire aloofness from
an active part in the insurrection at Liège.

Although he had little to complain of in her political attitude, his
friendship for her was to be the cause of great annoyance in other directions, both domestic and financial. The Baron de Selys had married
a charming lady some twenty years his junior, and had daughters of
his own. Unaware of the risk of introducing a woman of Théroigne's
character into the bosom of his family, or perhaps in spite of it, he had
once or twice invited her to dine at his Château de Fanson.

During these visits she had fulfilled their purpose by being em-
boldened to tell him some of her private affairs. In order to strengthen
her pleasant relations with the Selys family Théroigne had asked to
be allowed to give lessons on the harpsichord to his daughters. This
privilege was refused her. Moreover, it was discovered that during
some walks they had taken in company she had given several French
books to the eldest girl, who was called Victoire, and to prevent any
such communication the parents took Victoire to Maestricht. The girl,
however, found means to receive news of her friend. The mother discovered that letters passed between them, and this underhand traffic
was put a stop to. Soon afterwards the family returned to Liège.

On the first day of the year 1791, the baron returning at midday
to the Hôtel de la Cour-de-France, where he was then staying with
his family, found to his surprise that Théroigne was with his wife, and

that she was weeping bitterly. Victoire was also in tears. Théroigne had met them as they were coming from mass, and followed them to the *hôtel*. She had begged anew to be allowed to give the girl music lessons, but the baroness refused as before. She forbade her to continue any relations whatever with Victoire, and threatened to have her shut up in a convent if she attempted to communicate with her daughter. At this Théroigne had screamed loudly, and had begged her to show respect for the rights of man. Thereupon Mme de Selys ordered her haughtily to take her departure. At this moment the baron appeared on the scene. There was renewed bewailing. Théroigne, exasperated, flung the strongest epithet she knew at him. She called him a *zealous defender of monarchs!* The baron put an end to this absurd situation by gently and politely showing her to the door. They separated without bearing each other any ill-will, but Théroigne, as is not unusual with women of her type, insisted on having the last word.

"Oh," she said scornfully, "how can a brave and gallant man like you live with a woman so insupportably proud!"

Various causes were at work to involve the baron in expense on behalf of the woman, who, attractive as she might be personally, had made it definitely clear that she was not an individual worthy of great confidence, and that all services performed on her account were likely to be but ill repaid. A very short time elapsed before Pierre Théroigne began to importune de Selys both for himself and for his sister. The baron wrote on March 6th, 1792:

> Very soon after Mlle Théroigne was so rudely captured near Liège, her brother, who often stayed with an aunt half a league from my castle, made the acquaintance of a certain R. Labeye, who for many years has supervised the workmen on my estate. Through this Labeye, M. Théroigne and his uncles and aunts asked me to try to obtain information as to what had become of his sister. I made some inquiries, and found she had taken the route to Breisgau.

Pierre-Joseph went to the castle frequently, and, complaining of not receiving help from Paris, begged de Selys to do what he could to assist him. In order to rid himself of these importunities the Baron suggested that the young fellow should make a journey to Kufstein himself in order to obtain definite news of his sister, and he even bestirred himself to obtain a passport for Pierre, which described him as a young man of good reputation, aged about twenty-four, well made, and above the average height, with chestnut-coloured hair. But this proposed journey came to nothing, which was perhaps fortunate, under the circumstances, as Théroigne was then on the point of leaving the prison for Vienna, and her brother would probably have arrived too late.

She, on her part, was moving heaven and earth to have the pawned jewels restored to her, and set about this task in the most diplomatic manner imaginable. She began by thanking M. le Blanc for all his kindness to her at Kufstein.

"You have been a benefactor to me," she remarked. "I feel convinced that you will never abandon me. And I do not doubt that you will do everything you possibly can to obtain for me the favour of an audience with the emperor."

"That will not be altogether easy," replied Le Blanc. "You have too high an opinion of my influence. Don't delude yourself in that belief."

Théroigne seized upon this occasion to express her views on humanity in general and politics in particular. She grew wonderfully animated, and her powers of fascination increased with her excitement. She was well informed upon all the questions of the day. She expressed accurate ideas of right and justice, and defended them with all the single-mindedness of which a woman led by intuition can be capable.

She declared boldly:

I have learnt to know men, and I esteem them but little, for I have been deceived over and over again. You, too, must admit that the feeling I have against the French *noblesse* is a legitimate aversion. I might be able to pardon the persecutions and personal insults which they have showered upon me, but can I ever forget that they have sought to ruin me and reduce me to beggary, as well as all those who are dear to me?

"What! what's that?" asked Le Blanc in astonishment. "Where do you get that dreadful idea from?"

If am not set free speedily I shall lose the remainder of my fortune. Do you wish to know more? Well, I will tell you. Here is the receipt for a diamond necklace which was left at the Mont de Piété of Liège. The interest is overdue; and if I remain a prisoner, and am unable to redeem the pledge, my necklace will be sold, and—

Her voice broke.

Le Blanc inquired what sum was owing. She told him that the necklace was worth more than six thousand *livres*, and that two thousand were required to get it back.

"It means a small fortune to me," she cried, "and the loss of it would be a terrible blow both to me and mine."

"That is true," said Le Blanc. "You must let me have the receipt. I will send it to Coblenz. Metternich will have the interest paid up to date before your trial comes to an end. We will save the necklace."

Théroigne hardly knew how to express her gratitude.

Le Blanc sent his report, and the minister put the matter in the hands of the Baron de Selys, who was then living at Liège. Inquiries were immediately made.

Meanwhile Pierre-Joseph had told Labeye about the necklace, and begged him to ask the baron to redeem it. Mme de Selys, hearing of the jewels, obtained the influence of some relative at the Mont de Piété and went to inspect them.

Selys, wrote in the letter of March 6th:

> At the close of 1791 my wife saw the necklace, and at the prayer of Sieur Théroigne wished to redeem it. But as Sieur Théroigne was unable to produce the receipt, *madame* was obliged to give security at the Mont de Piété in case the receipt was produced by anybody else. I learnt, on returning from a voyage, that the necklace had been redeemed, and was at my house, which did not give me any particular pleasure.

M. de Selys told this story of the necklace to Perregaux, and added that, in spite of his displeasure, and somewhat against his will, he had taken charge of the receipts sent to Pierre-Joseph, and had redeemed, from the Mont de Piété at Paris, two ear-rings and a ring. He was not rewarded for his trouble. It came to his ears that Pierre's real reason for not going to the Tyrol was that he feared to be arrested himself because he had been told that the Baron de Selys was partly responsible for the capture of his sister, and was waiting to seize the brother too before appropriating Mlle Théroigne's redeemed jewels for his own uses.

The baron was naturally disgusted when he heard of these absurd aspersions on his character. He wished to rid himself as quickly as possible of all Théroigne's relatives, and, hoping to obtain her consent to sell the jewels for the benefit of her brother, he wrote a letter to her personally, and took steps to assure himself that it would reach her. In it he told her that her relatives were all well, and greatly desired to see her again. Leonard Clamend, her uncle, who lived at Xhoris, had lost his mother. Her youngest brother, Pierrot, had left Xhoris for Marcourt. Pierre-Joseph was still at Liège, and told him he was making good use of his time.

Having thus dismissed the trivial family gossip, he explained that he had helped both her brothers several times with sums of money, the last being an amount of five *louis* the very day before the one on which he wrote. He had also redeemed her jewels as she had directed, and informed her that her brother Pierre wished to sell them and buy himself an interest in some business, which, he was told by Pierre, was a plan of her own. He asked her to agree definitely to this arrangement, as her brother was without resources, and could get no answer from Perregaux although he had written more than once.

Before this letter reached Kufstein Théroigne was on her way to Vienna, and Le Blanc himself replied to it on November 21st, 1791, informing the Baron that she would soon be free, and able to answer his questions in person.

This, to her, highly desirable state of affairs was brought about by Le Blanc's conviction that the prisoner had been arrested under a misapprehension.

Finding that her account differed in almost every particular from that of her chief accuser, La Valette, he decided to confront the two of them, in spite of her objection ever to be brought face to face with her persecutor. La Valette was introduced into the prison under the name of Legros on July 6th, and this dramatic interview was to be the final act of the inquiry into the charges brought against the prisoner.

When Théroigne recognised the *Chevalier,* who had been brought into her cell without warning, she rose from her bed like an infuriated tigress. She was trembling and gasping with the strength of her emotion. Her stifled breathing and the glare of anger in her eyes showed plainly the hatred she bore this adversary. Le Blanc, who was present, began to fear the result of so much excitement upon her already enfeebled health.

After repeating the substance of his accusations, La Valette said proudly: "I persist in my declarations, and maintain all my depositions to the letter."

"And I refuse to alter a single word of what I have said," added Théroigne. Her voice rang out; she drew herself up, and at that moment she held herself like a great lady, and faced her accuser with a dignified pose that was both graceful and full of energy. Her conscience was at rest, and she was inspired by a knowledge of her own innocence.

Le Blanc saw that nothing was to be gained by prolonging the interview. Influenced, no doubt, by her obvious honesty, by the straightforwardness of her replies, and no less, it must be confessed, by the personal magnetism which affected even better men than the inquiring magistrate, he became convinced, little by little, that she had never made an attempt to assassinate the Queen of France, and, as no proof existed of her having incited the people of Brabant to rebellion, he could not bring home to her any worse accusation than that of being a misguided young woman.

At the end of June his sympathies had been deeply enlisted by her evident sufferings and ill health. He sent for the local doctor, who seemed unable to cure her. Then he called in an illustrious physician, Dr. de Méderer, who came all the way from Constance, where he was enjoying a holiday, at the request of his old friend and colleague.

Méderer had a world-wide reputation. He arrived at Kufstein at the end of July. He recognised at once that Théroigne's physical condition was anything but satisfactory, and that her mind was deeply troubled. Continuous excitement, unrelieved suspense, and grief had worked havoc on her constitution, and had reduced her to a state bordering on mental aberration. Something had to be done at once to relieve the strain upon her mind, lest her brain should become unbalanced. At all costs her thoughts must be distracted, unless it was possible to offer her the only remedy which could be thoroughly efficacious—namely, the release which would naturally terminate her anguish.

The doctor's report is interesting, both as it stands and as evidence of the strange effects of "Revolution fever" with which many people in France became afflicted about this period. The report ran:

In accordance with an order given me on the 14th of the month, I went on the 23rd to see the French prisoner detained here. I stated that her physical ills were easily curable, and I gave instructions to that effect. But I found her moral condition utterly degenerate, and, as a result of continued physical and mental strain, I feared she might at any time give way to a serious disorder, and that the abuse of her constitution might lead to the contraction of a dangerous disease.

I therefore considered it to be my duty to report this state of things, and the condition of the prisoner's mind to the authorities, and to beg that she might have every possible care, because if she did not, the treatment I had ordered would be likely to fail, and immediate aggravations of her state were likely to set in. How many people gifted with these extraordinary powers, if they employ them continually on one idea, as occurred and still occurs in the case of this highly-strung prisoner, are liable to weaken and destroy both body and mind so completely as to have great difficulty in restoring them! This is an acknowledged fact, and is so generally known that it is unnecessary to furnish proofs of it.

Kufstein, 25/7/1791.

Le Blanc, having received this report, communicated it at once to Kaunitz, and demanded his authority for transferring the prisoner. Kaunitz put the matter before the emperor, who ordered Théroigne to be brought to Vienna.

In the early days of August 1791, a coach and four left Kufstein on its way to the Austrian capital, and its occupants were Théroigne, Le Blanc, Méderer, and a clerk.

The greatest precautions were taken to ensure the prisoner's safety. So far, she had been known as Mme Theobald, now she was called Mme Lahaye. The journey was made by very slow stages. Théroigne's health did not permit of quick travelling. At this time a number of *émigrés* were making their way to Vienna, amongst them the famous Mme de Polignac, who was accompanied by her family. Her *cortège*, consisting of several carriages and many servants, traversed the same road on the same day that Théroigne passed that way.

At that date Vienna was still a fortified town. The travellers arrived late at night, and certain formalities had to be gone through before they were admitted. The heavy carriage was at last allowed to proceed, and rolled on through deserted streets until it pulled up before a small house where one called Antoine Schlosser lived with his wife. This domicile had been designated by the secret police as a suitable house of detention for Madame Lahaye. She was very well looked after there, and had a servant of her own to wait on her. She was permitted to take walks, and was treated, in short, as though she were no longer in prison.

By August 31st Le Blanc had drawn up a long report of her case for the court in which she was to be tried. Delays ensued, as invariably happens in such cases. Théroigne had, perforce, to remain idle and in suspense. She was pursued by fresh anxieties. Supposing her persecutors should succeed in prejudicing the Court against her! Nothing could satisfy her but the one thing she desired above all others—her liberty.

Le Blanc provided her with money, and though she accepted considerable sums from him they were not sufficient for her requirements. Théroigne, like most women of her class who have the capacity for getting their friends to supply them with means, had neither a knowledge of economy nor arithmetic to help her to make good use of funds. *Ducats* burnt her fingers. She spent them here and there prodigally or out of sheer generosity. She had soon disposed of many hundreds of florins. The only friend besides Le Blanc she had in Vienna was her uncle, the banker Campinado. She went to him and asked him to obtain more money for her. Then she persuaded him to dispatch a letter to Perregaux expressing her needs. In doing this she broke her parole. She had promised Le Blanc to write no letters and send no word to her friends concerning her whereabouts. The letter was dated September 15th, and was very guarded in its statements:

Monsieur,

I can say very little except that my affairs are not yet settled, and that I am not yet free. Whilst waiting to examine the depositions of the generous French *chevaliers*, they are treating me very well. I am no longer in prison. I am in a special house where they look after me as well as they possibly can. I can walk about everywhere, and go into the public streets with a companion. I think they would even let me go alone on parole. But although I appreciate all that has been done to ameliorate my unjust position, I confess frankly that I am none the less unhappy. Nothing gives me pleasure if I have not liberty, and besides, although I can go everywhere and speak to everybody, I am nevertheless isolated and cannot speak to anyone of my affairs, nor say who I am, nor describe the position in which I find myself.

Therefore, I can make no real friends, nor receive advice from a living soul. I am forced to remain inactive whilst I have reason to fear that my cowardly persecutors will do everything possible to prejudice those against me in whose hands my fate lies. Nevertheless, the conclusion of this intrigue approaches. I hope that they will no longer take the emperor's religion in vain, that truth and justice will triumph, and that I shall be free to go where I will, because I defy them to discover that I have

MARIE-JOSEPH CHÉNIER.

done wrong, unless they attribute it to me on account of my opinions from which they greatly differ. Besides, it would be a bad way to correct patriotism by impeding liberty. I beg you to send as soon as possible twenty *louis* to my brother. I do not know how our money matters stand. If you have received the half-yearly payment of my income of 3,200 *livres*, please send the money to my brother, who is at Liège, *chez* François Person, at the Saint Esprit couronne sur Meuse.

Théroigne.

P.S.—I cannot tell you where I am, but perhaps I shall soon have permission to write freely to my friends. Give my kindest regards to all those who know me, and who speak of me. I require forty *louis* for myself. I shall try and let you know where you can send them. Sell my diamonds, which are ruining me in interest. I pray you to take heed of all my requests.

On October 4th she signed a declaration in which she agreed to live in whatsoever place might be fixed upon by the authorities. This limitation did not trouble her greatly. Her chief desire was to be set free.

The delay had made her terribly impatient.

"Will your report never be done?" she asked Le Blanc nearly every day.

He counselled her to keep calm.

Then she varied her question. "Will they let me go?" she pleaded.

"I cannot tell you," replied the magistrate.

When she heard that a formal verdict was to be issued, she was delighted. She was determined to have a copy of the criminal proceedings. She knew that every Dutch citizen was entitled to a copy.

Le Blanc reminded her that the report would embody all her letters and private papers, and that the mystery of her life would be bared for everyone to read it. But this did not seem to trouble her. All she desired was that her motives should be understood, and her innocence vindicated. As for her private life, that concerned no one. Le Blanc made a quiet reference to the Marquis de Persan. Even the thought of this episode becoming public property did not distress her.

"What did the old man matter to me?" she replied ungratefully. "I hate the very thought of him."

Le Blanc took it upon himself to scold her for her rashness in wishing to be regarded as a political prisoner of importance, and for posing as a martyr. He dissuaded her from her plan of having the report of her trial published and distributed. He gave her a hint that there was a chance of her obtaining compensation for her imprisonment, and casually inquired the age of her brothers. She told him that one was eighteen, one twenty-two, and the third was married in Paris. Le Blanc praised her for the anxiety and solicitude she showed on their behalf, and suggested that possibly the emperor might allow them to enter the army—as lieutenants.

"That would be magnificent," she cried.

Le Blanc's trust in the prisoner was somewhat shaken when she told him that without his knowledge, she had been allowed two interviews with Prince Kaunitz and one with the emperor. She declared triumphantly that the latter had given her permission to return to her own country.

The examining magistrate was furious because she had managed to arrange all this behind his back. He threatened to have her clapped into prison again.

A fortnight later, on November 24th, Mme Lahaye was summoned to the court.

She was received sternly by the judge, who reproved her in a long speech.

So, *madame,* it is not enough that we should have to read columns of lamentable details concerning the incidents of the French Revolution in your *procès-verbal* and other documents relating to your affairs, but you consider it necessary to add your personal opinions with regard to the causes of this catastrophe. Not content with describing terrible and bloodthirsty scenes in poetical language, you do not hesitate—madly anxious to proselytise as you are—to try to persuade us that the reasons you give for your revolutionary frenzy are excellent ones. . . . It is your democratic fanaticism, and that of others like you, which is at the root of the evil. It is culpable and is the cause of the present impossible state of France. Is his Majesty Louis XVI. the author of the troubles and scandals of Paris and of Versailles? Not at all! It is the mad folly of such as yourself. Without the demoniacal passion which possesses you and blinds you, you and your coreligionists in Paris, there would be no cries, no tumults, no struggles, no tears, and no blood in the streets of the capital. And you call this the fulfilment of your duties as a good citizen. . . .

And he proceeded to heap vituperation upon her head. She replied proudly:

"My ideas are what they are, and it is useless to use such grand words and gestures to contradict them. The truth is that I am a fervent patriot and a good *citoyenne*. You condemn the republic: that is your duty. I, on the other hand, condemn the monarchy: I think I am right in doing so. Besides I have only one hope. It is that the principles of '89 and the acknowledgment of the Rights of Man should spread throughout Europe and to every country in the world. In this work I have tried to help. I have not committed any crimes, and nobody can produce a proof to the contrary!"

"You think so! But the *Châtelet* of Paris has nevertheless stigmatised you as a dangerous person . . . it would be a good idea to shut you up in a convent. There, submitting to a severe but human rule, you would lead a tranquil life and be set free on the day you gave an understanding never again to rail at society."

"That day would never come! . . . I swear—"

She uttered the words in a strident voice.

After pointing out to her that, in accordance with the doctors' depositions, it was within his power to have her shut up for the safety of the public health, he explained at some length that she ought to know that her fate—nay, life itself—hung entirely in the power of the government and the emperor.

At his first words Théroigne seemed to feel every vestige of the hope of freedom in which she had indulged oozing away, and she was overcome with despair, but at his mention of the emperor she raised her head, and gravely looked at the man who was torturing her. She had faith in the clemency of Leopold II.

There was a short pause, and then she heard the deep tones of the judge once more addressing her.

"Hear the emperor's will."

"Yes, *monsieur*," she replied. "I am ready to face the worst. Speak."

"He has ordered a change of residence for you."

A smile spread over her face.

"Tomorrow you will leave Vienna. Councillor le Blanc is instructed to hand over to you the sum of six hundred florins."

"What is that amount for?" she asked, her lips quivering.

"For the expenses of your journey."

"What journey, *monsieur*? Put me out of suspense, I beg, as you love me."

"Tomorrow you leave for Brussels."

"Ah!" she cried, "A thousand thanks, *monsieur*. What am I to do at—Brussels?"

"You will go thence to Liège."

"And there?" Her voice trembled with excitement, her eyes were shining, her face full of an unearthly light.

"At Liège you will be allowed your—"

"Great heavens! My liberty?"

"You have guessed right, Mlle Théroigne. Your liberty. Perfect liberty."

★★★★★★

With reference to these proceedings the *Moniteur* contains two interesting notes. The first appears in the issue of November 16th, 1791, under news from Vienna of October 29th. It reads as follows:

M. de Plank (le Blanc), charged to inquire into the case of the famous Mlle Théroigne de Méricourt, still imprisoned at Kufstein, under the pretext of an attempt on the life of the Queen of France, has just arrived here. He has submitted to the emperor the protocol of the inquiry and proceedings. The result is that it appears they arrested this young lady on insufficient evidence, and that the accusations against her have no foundation in fact.

The second note appears in the issue of December 22nd, 1791, under news from Vienna of December 3rd:

The emperor has set at liberty Mlle Théroigne, and has given orders that the expenses of her journey should be paid. This individual, having been detained for a long time in the fortress of Kufstein in the Tyrol, was conducted to Vienna to be questioned on the supposed plot against the life of the Queen of France.

The *Petit Gauthier* announced the fact of Théroigne's release in its issue of December 15th in the following terms:

The vicious (only they used a stronger word) creature who is called Théroigne de Méricourt, the same who on October 6th, 1789, planned the most horrible of crimes, is now at Brussels. She presented herself before the worthy Minister Metternich. Her savage audacity has not been diminished by her sojourn in Austrian dungeons. She had the atrocious impudence to say before the minister: Is it not just to sacrifice a handful of nobles to millions of citizens? The apparition of this wandering corpse (another stronger term) exasperates all the honest people in this country. She is staying at the sign of *l'Homme Sauvage,* who was never as barbaric as she.

But Théroigne was free. For the moment, at any rate, she could afford to ignore these coarse jests.

On January 5th, 1792, she wrote to Perregaux from Brussels:

Now that I am free, that I am sure of being able to go wherever I wish, that I am content with the justice done me by the emperor, I feel that I ought to say that during the time of my unjust detention they treated me kindly enough.

As for your aristocrats, they employed the basest means, the most infamous intrigues, in their endeavour to make me lose my liberty for ever. I assure you that if it had depended only on them, I should still be in the fortress of Kufstein. Such is the character of French noblemen!

I should be much obliged, *monsieur,* if you would send me thirty *louis,* which kindly change in Paris. If you have only *assignats* I should lose less that way. I beg you to send me what I ask by the first courier, as I have not a *centime* to pay either lodging or board. Please address your reply to the *poste restante,* Brussels.

From Brussels Théroigne also wrote to the Baron de Selys to tell him of her interview with Leopold II., but unfortunately this letter has been lost. A reference occurs to it, however, on the back of the copy of the baron's reply. De Selys jotted down notes as to the contents of the letter, consisting of an account of a talk with the emperor, and questions as to what had been done with her jewels and the amount of the money which had been lent to her brothers.

For some time afterwards the Baron heard no further news of Théroigne except vague rumours that she had returned to Paris.

The difficulty about the jewels was not settled, however. On February 23rd, 1792, Théroigne wrote to Perregaux from Paris asking him to reclaim the diamond necklace from the Baron de Fançon, as she now called him.

Altogether she had pawned thirteen articles of jewellery, and had received a sum of nearly eight thousand *livres* in loans on them.

Her pecuniary difficulties were as insistent as before, and notes of this period to Perregaux all contain requests for money.

Poverty seemed but a trifling drawback in view of her glorious liberty. Was she not free to plunge afresh into the intense excitement of the Revolution?

CHAPTER 7

To Arms! To Arms!

Théroigne had left Paris at the beginning of May 1790. She returned early in 1792, after an absence from the capital of nearly two years. The amnesty which abolished proceedings against all active revolutionists had been proclaimed on September 15th, 1791. The tide of the Revolution was sweeping on to its flood, and event after event had taken place in which Théroigne had been debarred from playing any part.

Almost the day she left there had been a massacre of the National Guard at Montauban, and this outrage was reflected in the mournful streets of Paris. About this time, too, there had been an outburst in the provincial towns of Federations, or Feasts of Union, at which all men declared themselves brothers. Inspiriting scenes of this character had been held at Lyons in May, at Lille early in June, and in other towns, causing a very fever of Federation to enter the blood of all the French people. The result of this infectious spirit was the arranging of a general *fête* for the whole of France, timed to take place on the anniversary of the Fall of the Bastille.

The story of the famous Feast of Pikes will never be forgotten. The work on the *Champ de Mars* getting behindhand, the people, both men and women, turned out in thousands to dig and delve, to wheel earth about, and fashion it into mounds for seats. Students, cavaliers, monks, nuns, shop-keepers, children, greybeards, beggars, nobles, and Court ladies took their turn at digging, day and night, in rain or shine. Who can forget that Abbé Siéyès and de Beauharnais tugged at the same cart? Even the king was not spared. He wielded his spade to the joyous accompaniment of the people's applause.

Théroigne would have been in her element here. It was a thousand pities that she could neither handle shovel nor trundle barrow; that her cheery voice was not heard encouraging others in their toil (they were few, after all, who needed encouragement); that she could not be heard chanting in flute-like notes the inspiring "*Ça ira*," which was not yet the horrible "*Ça ira*" it later became. She missed the sight of thousands of delegates from the provinces, representing tens of thousands of armed men, taking sacred oath on the altar of the country to maintain the new Constitution. The king was present, the members of the National Assembly, the Army of Paris, and an imposing array of citizens. The impressive ceremony began with a mass. It was at that mass the story was told of Talleyrand, still known as the Bishop of Autun, that when he approached the altar he whispered in the ear of Lafayette: "Whatever you do, don't make me laugh!" Absurd probably, but it is the kind of story that remains in the memory.

Through these and all the happenings of 1790 Théroigne was far away from Paris, regretting the reasons that made it wise for her to remain in hiding. She probably heard as much as most people of the disaffection in the army and mutinies among the soldiers in various districts of the country. The riots at Nancy in August 1790, involving the Swiss of Châteauvieux, led directly to the *fête* in April 1792, given to those who were taken prisoner. Théroigne helped to organise it.

At the opening of the year 1791 a great inclination to emigrate was noticed on the part of the nobility, a desire shared also by royalty. The story of that emigration is long enough and exciting enough to fill volumes. Throughout France people were stealing more or less openly to the frontiers, longing to be safely across the borders; gathering in little coteries in out-of-the-way spots; homeless wanderers setting forth in their great travelling coaches with fear in their hearts, often only too well justified, that they might never see their beautiful *châteaux* again.

In the minds of the masses the word that reverberated was Federation, in the minds of the classes it was Emigration. Both possessed but one idea—the former to be knit more closely together in the centre of things, the latter, on the contrary, to spread out and scatter. The lowest in the land were affected by the prevailing tendency as well as the highest. Even those closely related to the king—his brothers, for instance—were not immune from the epidemic of flight, and among those who carried it into effect with success were the forlorn maiden ladies, *Mesdames*, Louis XVI.'s elderly aunts. On February 19th they left Bellevue, their home, arousing a clatter of discussion over this pathetic escape. The people, unable to detain their persons, absolutely refused to allow the luggage to follow, and invaded their household with a view to seizing all their possessions.

Among the many unwarrantable calumnies uttered and written against Théroigne is one by a chronicler who goes so far as to make her play a part in the doings of that day, although, in reality, she was many miles from the scene of action. This trifler—*vaude-villiste* he has been called—is Georges Duval, who, in his *Souvenirs de la Terreur*, says of Théroigne:

> She commanded the mob of male and female bandits who came to besiege Bellevue on February 19th, 1791. They arrived, brandishing pikes and sabres, in the Court of Honour, and perceiving the door which led into the apartments of the *château* open, they entered and crowded into all the corners, inspected the coffers, visited the armouries, looked under the beds, and forced their pikes into the mattresses of *Mesdames* in the same manner as was done at Versailles into those of the queen. It was, in short, another 5th of October.

Nothing was found; their prey had escaped them; and the people gave way to transports of rage. Théroigne, in her position of leader, incited them to set fire to the castle. They were about to carry out this order when something happened to change the trend of their thoughts. Their wanderings by torchlight had brought them to the dining-room, where supper was served. The sight of food made them forget their purpose. They flocked round the table like harpies and seized upon the various dishes, nor did they spare the wine.

Meanwhile the National Guard had been summoned from Versailles, but did not arrive in time to prevent these depredations. It is here that the author of the narrative allows his imagination to get so much the better of his discretion that he accuses Théroigne of being drunk and in a fit of frenzy snatching up a lighted torch:

> "Those who love me will follow me and fire the *château*," she cried. With Jeanne le Duc and others close upon her heels, she tore through the apartments, intent on her wicked deed, when a second discovery caused a diversion. A huge chest had been found in a little-used apartment, in which at first it was thought the princesses themselves might be concealed. This was not the case, but the capture was hardly less valuable, since it yielded booty in the shape of plate, jewels, and other rich treasure. At this moment the National Guard arrived, and put a stop to the

nefarious schemes of the intending pillagers, and the phantom Théroigne disappears from the scene.

Théroigne saw none of the doings of the Day of Poignards on February 28th, nor of the immediate results of the suppression of the barriers in the spring. She was not in Paris when Mirabeau died on April 2nd, nor for his magnificent funeral on the 4th. She was spared the excitement of the flight to Varennes in June and the return of the royal family under the guardianship of her friends Pétion and Barnave. Her enthusiasm would have reached fever-heat and her tears of pride have been shed freely on July 11th when the remains of Voltaire were borne in triumph to the Pantheon, had she been there to see.

Only a few days later the people's great petition demanding the deposition of the king was laid on the altar of the country, which still stood on the *Champ de Mars*. This petition was the result of the people's displeasure with the National Assembly, which, still profoundly monarchical, hesitated to declare that the king, who had turned his back on the throne, had forfeited his right to sit there. The *Club des Jacobins*, growing more powerful day by day, and with whose ideals those of Théroigne coincided, had said, "We no longer recognise Louis XVI." The *Club des Cordeliers*, going a step farther, added, "Nor any other king." Thus, was Republicanism born.

The mighty petition was soon covered by thousands of signatures. The National Assembly, taking fright at this demonstration of feeling, ordered Lafayette and Bailly to march troops to the scene of action, and there proclaim martial law. After in vain commanding the people three times to retire, the soldiers fired on the crowd, and covered the altar of the country with dead and dying. The conflict dealt a serious blow to the popularity of Bailly and Lafayette.

From July 1789 to September 1791 the National Assembly had worked faithfully at the Constitution, according to the oath sworn in the Tennis-court. When finished, the new laws comprised thousands of decrees. When the Constitution was completed, the king, released from his suspension by the Assembly, was invited to take his oath of acceptance, and he did so on the 14th.

Afterwards the National Assembly, in whose sittings Théroigne had shown indefatigable interest, declared its work completed. Before separating, and at the instigation of Robespierre, who proposed the resolution, the Assembly decided that none of its members should take a part in the new legislative body, which, under the name of the

Legislative Assembly, met first on October 1st, 1791, the day after the dissolution of its predecessor. Like the Constituent Assembly, the new body was composed of seven hundred and forty-seven members. It sat until September 21st, 1792, and then transmitted its power to the National Convention, which proclaimed a republic.

Long before that date Théroigne had thrown herself with a new vigour into the tide of popular affairs. As she passed through the streets of Paris on her return in January she was greeted as a martyr and a saint. Little knots of people gathered round her as she told her adventures, and she was urged to mount a platform, where all could see the woman who had suffered imprisonment in an Austrian jail for the sake of liberty. She was wearing a short skirt, a soldier's jacket, and a hat with a long feather. The warm greeting of the people thrilled and excited her. All her past misery was forgotten. She shook hands heartily with those who pressed round to welcome her, and promised to put renewed energy into her labour for the cause. Thus, by slow degrees, she made her way to the *Club des Jacobins*, where she expected, and rightly expected, to be received in triumph.

Her visit was in the nature of a surprise. The usual business was proceeding.

The hall in which this influential club met was fitted up in nearly the same style as the one in which the legislative body sat. The tribune, or pulpit, from which the members spoke was opposite to that in which the president was seated. There was a table for the secretaries and galleries for a large audience of strangers of both sexes, in one as in the other. Men were appointed to walk through the hall and command, or at least solicit, silence when the debate became turbulent, after the fashion of the ushers at the Assembly. Nor had their efforts much more success here than there. The bell of the president, the cries of those whose business it was to keep order, were equally disregarded in stormy debates in both places.

That day there was no uproar in the house, only the low drone of the members' voices discussing the possibilities of the opening year.

It was January 26th, 1792. Gaudet was in the president's chair, and Lostalot described to the assembled company an Englishman's scheme for putting the people through certain new tactical exercises which in six weeks were guaranteed to render them equal to trained troops—a Utopian idea which can hardly have worked out in practice. Hion proposed that the National Assembly be asked to replace the battalions of Paris by French guards and soldiers of the people. Danton

BRISSOT.

supported this proposition. Lasource and Robespierre disagreed over the question of public contributions to funds, the latter asserting that this motion was put forward to distract public attention from more important questions. This remark caused such a tumult of objections that the president was obliged to interfere. The babel of excited voices, the splutters and ejaculations, died away. A diversion was caused by the arrival of a deputation from one of the fraternal societies.

A proposition was made by the leader of the deputation that a petition should be addressed to the Assembly requesting that certain galleries recently opened to those who possessed influence should be as free to the public as the others. Again, there were cries and gesticulations and the murmur of the crowd. Lostalot, who had taken the president's place, remarked that denunciations of this nature touched upon constitutional matters, and could not be dealt with by the society. At this moment the tinkle of the president's bell announced a new speaker. It was Dufourny. Looking round the full house, he said he had something of importance to communicate. A woman, celebrated for her devotion to the State and for the persecutions she had suffered at the hands of tyranny during her stay in Austria, was present in the hall that day. He believed the assembled members would like to show in the usual manner their appreciation of a martyrdom endured for the people's cause. He would call upon Mlle Théroigne de Méricourt—for it was she—to come forward and receive the greetings of the Assembly.

His words were drowned in loud applause, and many members rose from their seats and hastened to the back of the hall, where Théroigne was standing among a crowd of women. They insisted on escorting her to a prominent place in the centre. As she came forward, smiling, a slim, small figure, her chestnut locks loose beneath the feathered cap, her coat, her short skirt, and even her shoes adorned with tricolour ribbons, there was a moment's tense silence, then a tumultuous uproar; then silence again.

"Friends," she said, stretching out her arms as though to embrace everyone.

"*Vive Mlle Théroigne!*" came the stirring cry from hundreds of throats. She was reaping the reward of months of suffering. She was keenly alive to the interest her sex and her misfortunes had aroused.

At the first pause she spoke, thanking the assembled company for their gracious reception. Her words were simple, but her tones thrilled her hearers. Never had her gift of oratory appeared to better advantage.

When she ceased speaking Dufourny addressed a few graceful phrases to her, expressing the pleasure experienced by the members of the Jacobins Club in seeing her back in their midst.

These remarks were received by a second ovation, and many patriots, among the most enthusiastic of whom was the Abbé Siéyès, hastened to pay court to her in person.

Théroigne was then requested to continue her narrative, but this she refused to do, saying she would write down an account of her imprisonment and read it at some future date.

On January 29th Lostalot announced that Mlle Théroigne had intended on that day to give them a description of her misfortunes during her stay in Austria, but was unable to fulfil her promise. She proposed to acquit herself of the obligation she had contracted towards the society on the following Wednesday.

On February 1st, at the request of a deputy, Théroigne read the discourse she had prepared before the assembly of Jacobins. It was proposed that her account should be amplified in a memoir, but no traces occur of this having been printed.

She told her adventures with candour and picturesqueness. She praised the emperor highly, said little in favour of Prince Kaunitz, and declared that the patriots had friends and partisans everywhere—in the Low Countries, in Germany, even in Leopold II.'s palace. She urged them on to action, and succeeded that day in thoroughly rousing the Jacobins.

Brissot's Journal, the *Patriote Français,* said in its number of February 4th, 1792:

> The society bore witness to the keenest indignation against her infamous persecutors, as well as the highest admiration for the constancy she has shown. This lover of the people has pointed out the best, nay, the only, means of establishing our liberty on a firm basis; it is to bring war against the rebels and despots who menace us with hostilities, and yet fear them more than we do.

Her account finished, Théroigne stood silent, the cynosure of all eyes. The president rang his bell, and Lanthenas rose to address thanks to her in person.

> Love of liberty, placed by nature in every heart, made you cherish our glorious Revolution, *mademoiselle.* Your sentiments have drawn persecutions upon you. That is a certain claim upon our esteem. Your example demonstrates to all the friends of liberty

the power of this silent resistance, which is based on the elevated ideals of the soul, and by means of which the most feeble individuals have often made tyrants pale before them. The innate energy at the back of this resistance has often been possessed by women in such a large degree as to seem almost a supernatural gift in the eyes of ignorant people. In this enlightened age men will be moved by sheer natural inclination whenever your sex reveals grace accompanied by civic virtue, a combination which must eternally excite our enthusiasm. Brave *citoyenne*, repeat what you have done and suffered for the sake of liberty in all assemblies which public interest gathers together, even as you did here in our presence. And believe that wherever true French hearts beat, you will have accomplished something useful in the advancement of universal freedom.

Then the staunch Jacobin Manuel stood up to speak:

Once there was a time, when a certain society of men desired to know whether women possessed a soul. As a matter of fact, this society was composed chiefly of priests, double-faced gentlemen who always wear an air of contempt towards women, in order that it may not seem as though they cared too much for them. . . . If our forefathers indulged in so low a conception of womanhood, it was because they were not free, for liberty would have taught them, as it has taught us, that it is quite as easy for nature to create Portias as Scaevolas. You have just been listening to one of the first Amazons of liberty. She has been a martyr to the Constitution. I demand that she should partake of the honours of this meeting as woman president, seated by the president's side.

Delighted as she was with her enthusiastic reception, with the halo of martyrdom which public opinion had placed upon her brow, Théroigne had no intention of resting upon her laurels. She knew it was time for action, she realised in a flash the change that had come about in the attitude of the people since her departure, two years earlier. To them the alteration had been gradual, to her it seemed sudden, and therefore the more significant, the more appalling.

Whilst Marie-Antoinette sat in her *boudoir* earnestly planning an invasion that might save her husband, his country, and their child, never doubting that grapeshot would teach the rebellious French a lesson it was high time they learnt, while she wrote letters to her brother, the emperor, and to Mercy-Argenteau, in the hope of producing the result that was nearest to her heart, Théroigne in her humble and untutored way was doing her utmost to help in bringing these same schemes to naught. The queen incited men to war upon the kingdom over which she ruled; the woman of the people called to her sisters to arm themselves and try to defend the country that was thus betrayed.

Although she did not flourish a sabre as fiercely as the notorious Alexandrine Barreau, or hop as gaily in the bayonet dance as the sisters Fernig, Théroigne was all aflame in the great cause.

First and foremost an orator of the cross-roads, a clubist of the streets, she was so inspired by the military ardour of women throughout the provinces that she attempted to organise in Paris a battalion of warriors on the lines of those already in existence in the country. In Angers as early as 1789 women had desired to enrol in the auxiliary services. They said in a petition to the authorities:

> We, mothers, sisters, wives, and lovers of the young citizens of Angers, declare that if there should be an outbreak of war occasioning the departure of troops from the town, we desire to join with the country in protecting our interests; and since we are not qualified to use force, we wish to make it our duty to look after the baggage, food, and various preparations for the marching of the soldiers, which services might well depend on us, for we prefer the glory of sharing their danger to the security of shameful inaction.

Two years later these women subscribed a thousand *livres* to purchase a flag for the volunteers of the National Guard. This example was followed by the women of Brest and Nantes. At Aunay a *"corps d'Amazones nationales"* was formed by women who swore to be faithful to the Nation, to the Law, and to the King—ill-natured people added, to their husbands or lovers!

From the summer of 1790 onwards several legions of women warriors were formed.

At Creil the uniform worn was a white tunic, short skirt, plain cap, a cockade worn on the breast, and a federal badge of gilded leather which bore the Gallic cock on one side, with an inscription "*Citoyenne de Creil*," and on the other side a laurel wreath round three hearts, with the device "*l'Union fait notre vertu*." The officers wore white tunics faced with red cuffs and collars, with white braiding and district buttons, blue hats with white plumes, and a wide tricolour sash. They were armed with javelins.

The uniform of the Fernig corps was a white tunic with breeches, waistcoat, collar and cuffs of various colours, according to the division. The breeches were slashed *à la Portugaise*, and a brass helmet and flowing plume completed the equipment. These women cut their hair short in order to obviate the necessity of dressing it in a manner which might cause them to look conspicuous.

A manifesto was issued by the women of Maubeuge to the effect that they were ready to fight it ran:

> At the moment when the country appears to be menaced by a cruel war, instigated by traitors who push their rascality to the extent of themselves bearing arms against a kingdom of which by rights they should be the supporters, we hasten to make known to you our patriotism and our devotion to the country. We are determined to spill the last drop of our blood rather than to cringe under the yoke of tyrants and despots.

Their offer was not received with unmixed approval. Grateful France thanked the intrepid *citoyennes* for their sublime devotion, and, since she relied with confidence on the worth and valour of her brave soldiers, she advised the women to use their talents in deeds of a less warlike nature. At Lalinde the women swore to shed their blood drop by drop rather than live under the yoke of tyranny. Patriots of the fair sex at Limoges wished to form a battalion which might share the work of the National Guard.

The women of Vic-en-Bigorre sent an appeal to the National Assembly, saying that they desired to be regarded as an example of all the Christian, civil, and patriotic virtues, especially with reference to carrying out the laws. They had armed themselves in order to serve, in case of need, as auxiliary troops to the National Guard, thereby demonstrating to the country that their courage would not be found wanting as a last resource. Their flag was elaborately embroidered with a device on one side, "*J'élève un défenseur a la Patrie*," representing a mother sacrificing her son on the altar of the country, and on the other "*L'hymen et l'amour couronnent le guerrier citoyen*," a young citoyenne crowning a hero before the altar of Hymen.

The women of Harcourt offered a flag to the National Guard bearing the motto "*Libres ou mourir*."

On January 31st, 1792, the women citizens of the town of Belvès placed in the hands of the president of the Legislative Assembly a declaration in which they swore to consecrate their lives in upholding the Constitution, and to take up arms, either for the defence of their homes or to fight side by side with their sons and brothers.

As early as January 1789, owing to riots at Grenoble, the women of that town wrote to the king to say that they objected to bring children into the world if they were destined to live in a country overridden by despotism. Battalions of these women were formed, and they shouldered their pikes with a bold air that was truly edifying.

The women of Versailles were enthusiastic warriors. In white uniforms with tricoloured sashes, they formed a deputation which marched into the Assembly Hall in August 1792, and announced that they were prepared to guard the town while the men went to the front. At Rambervillers the women swore to do battle beside their sons and brothers on the ramparts. Two hundred women enlisted in the *Legion Juste* at Frie, and on August 9th, 1790, elected a certain Mme Feurier to be their colonel. A few days later, on the occasion of the consecration of their flag, mass was said, then there was a review, a banquet, and a ball. So great was the enthusiasm that "the troop of both sexes embraced to the sound of repeated *vivats*."

When the National Guard was reorganised at Pérouges in the spring of 1793, it was found that over one hundred women were serving in the ranks. Others were enrolled in various sections of the republican armies, and some women certainly saw active service, but no body of *citoyennes* had the glory of facing the enemy's fire. One at least took the command of soldiers. At Mormant a Mme de Moulins wrote to the volunteers:

My nephew, who is an aristocrat, has refused the honour of acting as colonel of your National Guard, so I propose to command you myself.

Her bold plan was hailed with enthusiasm. A fine military reception was given to the lady in question, and she was so deeply touched by this exhibition of feeling that she displayed the national cockade and armed herself with a sabre.

Théroigne knew how to appreciate the spirit which animated these women. All over the country they were ready to defend themselves. Their warlike attitude was expressed very clearly indeed in a letter printed on February 27th, and distributed at the instigation of Tallien in his capacity of president of *La Société Fraternelle séante aux Minimes*. Théroigne was a member of this society, and made one of her most telling speeches on presenting the members with a flag. She thoroughly approved of the sentiments contained in the letter which appeared immediately after her triumph at the Jacobins, and to which over three hundred signatures were appended.

The appeal was made to the Legislative Assembly:

Legislators, women patriots present themselves before you to claim their individual right to defend life and liberty.

Everything warns us of a speedy and violent upheaval. Our fathers, our husbands, and our brothers may perhaps fall victims to the fury of our enemies. Is there anyone who can hinder us from the privilege of avenging them or of dying beside them?

We are women citizens, and can never be indifferent to the fate of our country. Your predecessors entrusted the Constitution to our hands as well as yours. How can we guard this trust unless we have arms to defend it against the onslaught of enemies? Legislators, we require arms, and we come to obtain permission to carry them. Our want of physical strength is no obstacle; courage and intrepidity will stand us in good stead; the love of our country and hatred of tyrants will make it easy for us to brave every danger.

Do not suppose that it is our intention to abandon the care of our family and household, always dear to our affections, for the sake of rushing out to meet the enemy. No, gentlemen, we only ask to be in a position to defend ourselves. You dare not, and society cannot, refuse us this right which nature has given us; unless it be claimed that the Declaration of the Rights of Man has no application to women, and that the latter ought to allow themselves to be slaughtered like sheep without any attempt at a struggle.

Does anyone believe that the tyrants would spare us? No, they will remember the 5th and 6th of October, 1789.

But people tell us that men are armed for the purpose of defending us. That may be so; nevertheless, we reply, why deprive us of the power to co-operate in this defence, and of the pleasure of prolonging their days at the cost of ours? Do they know for certain the number and strength of our hidden enemy? Will there be only one fight? Are our lives worth more than theirs? And are not our children as much orphans when they lose their father as when they lose their mother? Then why not make use of all the sources of civicism and purest zeal in order to dismay aristocracy and overthrow despotism—zeal which level-headed men may call fanaticism and exaggeration, but which is the only natural outcome of hearts burning with love for the public welfare?

Doubtless, gentlemen, most perfect success will crown the justice of our cause. In that case we should enjoy the delight of having contributed to the victory. But if by the cunning of our enemies, or through the treason of any on our side, the victory should remain in the hands of the unjust, would it not be cruel to condemn us to await a shameful death in our houses, and all the horrors which would precede it, or, worse still, the doom of surviving all we hold most dear—our family and our liberty?

Gentlemen, you cannot contemplate such possibilities unmoved; and if, for reasons we cannot grasp, you refuse our just demands, the women whom you have raised to the rank of *citoyennes* by giving this title to their husbands, the women who have enjoyed the first-fruits of liberty, who have conceived the hope of bringing into the world free men, and who have sworn to live free or to die, these women will never consent to give birth to slaves; they will die sooner, and to keep their oath a poignard thrust in their bosom shall deliver them from the degradation of slavery. They will die thus, regretting not life, but the uselessness of their death; regretting that they were prevented from dipping their fingers in the impure blood of an enemy to the country and avenging some of their fellow citizens.

And then followed their demands:

We hope to obtain from your justice and equity, firstly, permission to procure pikes, pistols, and sabres, even guns, for those who have strength to use them, in accordance with and submission to the police regulations; secondly, to assemble on *fête* days and Sundays in the *Champ de la Federation*, or other convenient place, to exercise and manoeuvre with the said arms; and thirdly, to name as our commanders certain former French Guards, always in conformity to the regulations prescribed by the wisdom of the mayor for good behaviour and public tranquillity.

Such, then, was the temper of the women, and all the early months of 1792 this warlike spirit seethed in Paris. Everything possible was done to obtain arms. They collected money for the fabrication of pikes, and numbers of these weapons were made specially for women. One may be seen at the Carnavalet today, (1911), beautifully finished, light, yet strong, and the handle adorned with a design of laurel branches and a Phrygian bonnet. Naturally enough the royalist journals expressed their views on the matter, and pointed out Théroigne's aims with a satirical finger.

The *Sabbats Jacobites*, describing the day Théroigne arrived to read her statement before the club declared:

> A superb deputation of women arrived armed with pikes. They opened the discussion by warning the honourable members of the house that their visit was only a rehearsal of a farce which they intended to perform the following day in the National Assembly. The colonel of this feminine squadron was the incomparable Mlle Théroigne de Méricourt. This new Penthesilea, having made the most charming remarks to all the members of the sublime Aeropagus, closed her discourse with lines sung to the air *'Ne v'là-t'il pas que j'aime'*:
>
> *Il faut pour être utile enfin*
> *A notre République*
> *Que chaque femme ait à la main*
> *Une superbe pique.*

The *Petit Gauthier* of March 14th said:

> The martial fire which the *Bourrique des Jacobins*, Mlle Théroigne, put into her command last Sunday of the patriotic manoeuvres of those ladies who are ready to shed their blood in order to keep the Assembly in its place, was so active that the moustaches of the said lady came unfastened and were lost.

But such poor jesting as this was not likely to damp the ardour of Théroigne herself nor of the numbers who sympathised with her.

The *Patriote Français* praised her warlike language, and pointed out that her leaning was towards the Brissotins, as opposed to the Robespierrists. On the question of war, she was prepared to side with those who were presently known as the Girondins. But her great wish was, as already stated, to do for Paris what others had done for the provinces, namely, to organise a battalion of women soldiers.

A reference to her scheme appeared in an article on pikes in *Les Révolutions de Paris*, dated February 18th:

> On July 14th next, twenty-five millions of pikes will exist in

France. In imitation of our early ancestors, who never assembled in the *Champ de Mars* without being armed with lance and shield, twelve million citizens able to bear arms and to carry a pike will gather on the *Champ de la Federation*. Pikes, however, are forbidden to women; let it not displease the famous Théroigne and the *phalanx* of Amazons that she proposes to establish and to command!

Apart from drilling and manoeuvring, there was enough occupation for the eager women. Petitions, discourses, presentation of flags, and the acquirement of pikes were the chief signs of activity at this time. A tricoloured flag of Liberty and two pikes were presented by the affiliated *citoyennes* to the *Société des Cordeliers* at their sitting of Sunday, March 11th. The presentation was made with the usual speech. The spokeswoman said:

> The women who bring you the flag of Liberty, know well how to speak the language of freedom. Though our arms may be too feeble to defend it, at least our hearts' desire is to inspire you with sentiments no less worthy of a Pompey or a Brutus. For long enough you have rotted in the degradation of servitude. The hour has struck. Arise!—(with much more to the same theatrical effect.)

A reply was made by Lebois, president of the *Société des Amis des Droits de l'Homme*.

Generous *Citoyennes*,
The Society of the Friends of the Rights of Man receives with the deepest gratitude the tricolour flag which you have presented, accompanied by two pikes. Beneath this august emblem of liberty, it swears to march towards victory, for victory is certain when one fights for the safety of the country, and under the eyes of wives and sisters. You have doubled our courage, you will share our triumphs.
The gift you have made to us will never perish. Your standard will float in the enclosure of our assemblies like a living gauge of your civic virtues and of the fraternity which unites us.

Only a few days later Théroigne was the chief figure in a similar ceremony.

She made a stirring appeal to women to emancipate themselves. At that day most women's ideas, especially on religion and politics, were coloured by those of husband or father. In her struggle for liberty Théroigne applied particularly to women for help. She desired them to realise for themselves the duties of citizenship and their civil rights. She desired above all that her sex, without neglecting their duties in the home, should have a share in the direction of the affairs of the country. Her remarks were delivered in the declamatory style of the day, and show signs of an incomplete education, besides being reminiscent of certain authors—for instance, de Mably, who based his ideals on the political civilisation of Greece and the Republic of Sparta,—but they display her views and aspirations in a manner both brilliant and intelligent, and throw a great deal of light on the feminist movement of that day.

The discourse was delivered to the *Société Fraternelle des Minimes* on March 25th, 1792, the fourth year of liberty, by Mlle Théroigne, in presenting a flag to the *citoyennes* of the Faubourg Saint-Antoine.

The hall was crowded, hundreds of women were there, excited and gesticulating; the tense expectancy which is always startling among French audiences was tuned up to breaking pitch. Of a sudden there was silence, and a thousand eyes were turned upon the slim figure of the speaker as she rose from her seat on the platform.

Citoyennes, although we have gained victories, although a tyrant is dead, a treacherous minister has been accused of high treason, and the Assembly exhibits an energy which revives the hope of the Friends of the Country, we are, nevertheless, still, and always, in danger. Without entering into the details that are already known to you, I will only repeat those things which I believe cannot be recalled to your memory too often, in order to beg that you may reflect seriously upon the present situation. Do not lose sight of the fact that the torches of civil war are ready to be lighted, that the standard of the counter-revolution is displayed in various parts of the empire; that it is visible everywhere, but more especially in Paris; that paid scoundrels have formed a plan with regard to the internal disunion of the country, which they are following up with the utmost determination, with a view to organising parties who will prove fatal to liberty if your vigilance does not defeat the criminal plots concocted by our enemies.

Citoyennes, do not let us forget that we owe ourselves wholly to our country; that it is our most sacred duty to tighten our bonds of union and confraternity, and to spread the principles of steadfast energy, in order to prepare ourselves with as much wisdom as courage to repulse the attacks of our enemies.

Citoyennes, we can destroy the thread of these intrigues by generous devotion. To arms! To arms! Nature, as well as the law, gives us the right to arm. Let us show men that we are not inferior to them either in virtue or in courage. Let us show Europe that Frenchwomen know their rights, and are amongst the most enlightened of eighteenth-century people, in despising those who are prejudiced, who, because they are prejudiced, are absurd, and often immoral, in that they make a crime of virtue. The attempts which the executive power can make in the future to regain public confidence will be nothing more than dangerous traps which we must distrust: whilst our manners are not in accordance with our laws, authority will not lose the hope of profiting by our vices to put us in chains. It is quite obvious, and you may expect it, that they will put the loud talkers and scoundrelly pamphleteers forward in order to try and shake our purpose, in order to employ the weapons of ridicule, of calumny, and all the lowest methods which are usually employed by vile people to smother the transports of patriotism in feeble souls,

But, Frenchwomen, since the progress of enlightenment calls upon you to reflect, compare what we are now with that which we ought to be in the social order. To understand our rights and our duties it is necessary to take reason as our arbiter, and to be guided by her; thus, we shall distinguish the just from the unjust. What then can be the consideration which could stay us, which could hinder us from doing the right thing when it is evident that we can do it and that we ought to do it? We will arm because it is reasonable that we should prepare to defend our rights, our hearths and homes, and that we should not do justice to ourselves and our responsibilities to the country if the pusillanimity which we have acquired in bondage should still have sufficient sway over us to prevent us from doubling our powers.

According to all accounts, it is impossible to doubt that the example of our devotion will awaken in the souls of men public virtues and an overwhelming passionate love of glory and of the country. We shall thus maintain liberty by emulation, and the social perfection resulting from this fortunate concurrence. Frenchwomen, I say to you once more, let us rise to the utmost height of our destiny, let us break our chains; it is time at last that women should throw aside their shameful inactivity in which ignorance, pride, and the injustice of men have kept them bound for so long. Let us return to the time when our mothers, the Gauls and the proud Germans, spoke in the public Assemblies, and fought beside their husbands to repulse the enemies of Liberty. Frenchwomen, the same blood runs in our veins today. What we did at Beauvais, at Versailles on October 5th and 6th, and in several other important and decisive circumstances, proves that we are not strangers to magnanimous sentiments.

Let us recover our energy, then; for if we desire to preserve our liberty it is needful that we should prepare to do things the most sublime. At the present moment such things appear extraordinary, perhaps even impossible, owing to the corruption of manners, but shortly, when enlightenment and the progress of public spirit have had an effect, they will become simple and easy.

Citoyennes, why do we not enter into rivalry with men? They pretend that they alone have rights to glory. No, indeed no. . . . We also wish to merit a civic crown, to sue for the honour of dying for a liberty which is perhaps dearer to us than to them, because the effects of despotism weigh still more heavily on our heads than on theirs.

Yes, generous *Citoyennes*, all of you who hear me, let us arm, let us go and exercise two or three times a week in the Champs Elysées, or on the Champ de la Fédération, let us start a list of French Amazons upon which all those who really love their country will come and enrol their names. We will meet again immediately to discuss means for organising a battalion on the lines of that of the pupils of the Patrie, of the Veillards, or of the sacred Battalion of Thebes. In conclusion, may I be allowed to offer a tricolour flag to the *Citoyennes* of the Faubourg Saint-Antoine.

Amidst a thunder of applause she sat down.

It was arranged that the first Assembly of the *Citoyennes* would be held on Monday, April 2nd, at five o'clock in the afternoon, in the hall of the *Société Fraternelle des Minimes, Place Royale*.

Théroigne's military plans, although not entirely her own idea, were not derived directly from any special individual. Paris was in a state of intense anxiety and ferment. The people were arming against internal enemies, and war from without appeared to be inevitable. From the beginning of February, the nation had accepted the situation. From the beginning of March, which opened with the decision of Prussia to join Austria in invading France, and also by the death of Emperor Leopold, which retarded the actual movement, the suspense had grown more and more acute. It was felt that no stone should be left unturned, and Théroigne thought she recognised available material for use in defending the country among the earnest and eager women.

But the ways of a capital are different from those of provincial cities; and in exploiting her scheme for mobilising legions of women Théroigne found herself face to face with various difficulties which in the end proved insurmountable. She had failed on the purely political side when endeavouring to organise her *Club des Amis de Loi*; her attempt to raise a club of armed women was no more successful. In the early part of April, she worked hard to enrol members in the Faubourg Saint-Antoine, but on the 12th of the month her enthusiasm received a severe check. She made herself unpopular among the very individuals she was trying to help.

People at this time were growing fickle, and suspicious of their best friends. The hero of today was the outcast of tomorrow. Almost every hour brought a new personality into the limelight, and relegated one who had been a favourite to the shadows in the background. New parties were springing up, new and ever more daring opinions were being expressed, and he who did not venture to the extreme of rabid republicanism was in danger of being left behind in the race, or, worse still, of being trampled to death by those who were rushing pell-mell to the limit.

Théroigne's adventure might have proved very serious. As it was, she received a shock from which it took her some time to recover. She was busy with her recruiting work in the Faubourg Saint-Antoine when the crowd set upon her and handled her roughly. She owed her safety to the intervention of the Commissioners of the Section of the *Enfants-Trouvés*, who, after making her promise not to return and cause further disturbances in that quarter, sent her away under an escort of the National Guard.

The *Folies d'un Mois* said with reference to this affair:

All the world has heard that the infamous Théroigne escaped with no little difficulty last Thursday from the chastisement which the people of the Faubourg Saint-Antoine wished to inflict upon her. The evening before she had been proposing that the women should arm themselves with the pikes that men refused to carry. She returned accompanied by prostitutes. No sooner was she recognised than the cry was raised: 'Here she comes; let's beat her!' She took refuge from her persecutors in the Church of the *Enfants-Trouvés*, where she found the Commissioners of the Section, who deliberated whether they should send her before the magistrate, as they ought to have done. In the end, however, they dismissed her without any punishment, and, to save her from the indignation of those who were pursuing her, they had her escorted to a carriage by a dozen National Guards.

She was fortunate in her escape. The time was coming when she would not be let off so easily.

But the matter did not rest there. On the 13th the *Société des Défenseurs des Droits de l'Homme et Ennemis du Despotisme*, which held its meetings in the Faubourg Saint-Antoine, sent a deputation to denounce Mlle Théroigne to the Jacobins Society.

The deputation accused her of having caused troublesome excitement in the Faubourg Saint-Antoine, because she wished to assemble the women of that quarter three times a week and form a club; and had invited them to a feast or civic banquet, and had made use of the names of MM. Robespierre, Collot d'Herbois, and Santerre, probably without authorisation. The deputation, moreover, accused Théroigne of having imposed upon the women of this quarter by showing them a list of supposed signatures for this civic feast, the signature of Mme Santerre being recognised by the commissioners as in the handwriting of Mlle Théroigne.

In reply to a question put to Robespierre as to the use of his name in this connection, he declared that he had never had any special dealings with Mlle Théroigne. A year earlier she had denied a personal acquaintance with him. She knew him by sight, she says in her *Confessions*; but then, who did not? But she had never spoken to him. She would have regarded his acquaintance as an honour.

M. Santerre, when approached on the same subject, was more inclined to defend her. He announced that he had heard rumours of disturbances in the Faubourg Saint-Antoine of which Mlle Théroigne might have been the cause without actual intention. With regard to the supposed false signature of Mme Santerre, the list was not supposed to be of signatures, but of the names of those people who desired to take part in the *fête*.

Probably the trouble caused by the desire on Théroigne's part to form a women's club was the fault of the women themselves. The *filles de la Pitié* had been induced to join the meetings, and the nuns, who were responsible for their education, made objection. Then violence had been resorted to. The men of the quarter, continued Santerre, preferred to find their homes in order when they came in from work, rather than to come back to an empty house and wait for their wives to return later from meetings at which they acquired a spirit the opposite of gentle. No doubt they had looked askance at meetings which were to be held three times a week. He concluded:

All these considerations, produced the disturbances of which I have advised Mlle Théroigne to avoid a repetition, and I have suggested that she would do well to renounce her plans. I have no doubt that, after reflecting on these disturbances, which she certainly never meant to cause, as evil-intentioned people might accuse her of wishing to do, she will renounce her plans of her own free will.

What could unhappy Théroigne do? Her ardour was considerably damped by the blow she had received to a popularity which had increased by leaps and bounds throughout February and March. She was forced to abandon the idea of training women to take an active part in warfare, and instead she turned for solace to a more picturesque line of demonstration, and joined lustily in the civic banquets and *fêtes* that were dear to the hearts of the people.

That same evening, March 25th, a large number of the conquerors of the Bastille, of the inhabitants of the Faubourg Saint-Antoine, and the strong men of the Halles, met at the Halle Neuve. Thence the guests hastened to the Champs Elysées, where the banquet was to take place. Bonnets of liberty, carried on pikes adorned with the national colours, preceded the procession, which marched to the sound of drums and music. Gaiety and good-fellowship were the keynotes of this feast. Patriotic toasts were drunk, and patriotic songs and dances formed a feature of the evening. Pétion was there and Saint-Huruge.

This feast was the subject of many jests in the royalist press, and

Théroigne's presence did not escape comment. The *Folies d'un Mois* says:

> La Théroigne played a part in the *fête*. She stood upon the table and drank to the health of the patriots of Brabant, Liège, and all the universe. A Hercules of the Halle called Nicolas was there dressed in a bonnet-rouge, a white vest and breeches. The people asked him to kiss her, and she permitted it once, but she put on high-and-mighty airs and refused when all who were present shouted out *bis* to encourage Nicolas to begin again.

The *Sabbats Jacobites* described the civic banquet in a curious sketch, a "civic interlude," entitled *Mlle Théroigne's Boudoir*. The *boudoir* itself was a wonderful place.

> On a kind of toilet-table stood a pot of vegetable rouge, a poignard, some ringlets of false hair, a brace of pistols, the *Almanach du Père Gérard*, a cap, the Declaration of the Rights of Man, a red woollen bonnet, a comb, a bottle of toilet vinegar, a torn lace fichu, the *Chronique de Paris*, and the *Courrier de Gorsas*.
>
> In one corner was a cross bedstead and mattress; beside it lay an enormous pike, and a riding-habit of Utrecht velvet. On the walls hung pictures of the taking of the Bastille, the death of Foulon and Berthier, the day of the 6th October, the assassination of Favras, the murders at Nimes, Montauban, and so on. Théroigne appeared in *négligé* of the most fascinating kind— shoes of red morocco, black woollen stockings, blue damask skirt, a pierrot of white *bazin*, a tri coloured fichu, and a gauze cap of flame colour surmounted by a green pompon. Her make-up was also tricolour; white, brick red, and very deep blue. Basire comes upon the scene, and sitting down beside her takes her hand. First, he sings a song. Then growing emboldened, makes advances which she repulses, saying she is not in a playful mood. Thereupon he accuses her of loving another.
>
> "No, my friend," she replies, "but the country is in danger, and although I love you sincerely I love the country still more. In moments of crisis surely I may be permitted to forget you for her sake."
>
> Basire begins to suspect that she prefers Chabot to him, but she answers him that she never sees the "old monk." Both these men were her friends, neither were her lovers. According to a

little verse they were inseparable companions:

Connaissez-vous Monsieur Basire?
Connaissez-vous Monsieur Chabot?
Chabot vaut bien Monsieur Basire
Et Basire Monsieur Chabot.
Les talents de Monsieur Basire
Valent ceux de Monsieur Chabot,
Et lorsqu'on apperçoit Basire
L'instant après on voit Chabot,
Car Chabot n'est rien sans Basire
Et Basire rien sans Chabot.

At last Basire is forced to believe that Chabot is not his rival in Mlle Théroigne's affections, and he suggests that he is deeply jealous of Pétion.

To this Théroigne gravely replies:

"I esteem M. Pétion greatly. The friendship I have for him might easily have deepened into love on Sunday, March 25th of this year. It was on that day that *Messieurs* the Port-piques of the Faubourg Saint-Antoine gave a splendid repast to Messieurs the Hercules of the Halles. Jérôme Pétion, as mayor of Paris, was at the banquet. If you had seen with what grace, what ease, he replied to all the toasts they drank to him! He went from table to table crying 'Long live the Nation!' and humming the air '*Ça ira*'—in a word, the festivities were charming."

Théroigne had evidently not mastered the excitement aroused in her by her discourse at the *Société des Minimes* that evening. She describes the baptism of the child of a drummer's wife, when Mme Tremblay, wife of a patriot printer, and Mlle Calon, the daughter of the deputy, officiated at the font in the role of godmothers, and vin de Suresnes was used instead of holy water. Pétion was the godfather, and the baby was named Pétion-Nationale-Pique. "How sorry I was not to be chosen as godmother!" she cries. "I would have added three more names to the pretty ones already chosen which would have been quite equal to them—Lanterne, Assignat, and Bonnet-rouge."

Basire's jealousy is by no means assuaged by this story. "Then I see," he says, "that M. Pétion has really taken my place in your heart."

The adroit Théroigne.replies:

"By no means, I love M. Pétion for his civic virtues, his patriotism, his devotion to public affairs, his talent for denunciation, his earnestness at the Jacobins. In a word, it is the nation that I love in him, for he is the most worthy representative of it; but you shall be none the less my lover, I swear it by my deeds of October 6th."

And together they go off amicably to denounce the aristocrats at the Jacobins.

The same paper, the *Sabbats Jacobites*, satirised the arrangements made for the *fête* of the Châteauvieux, describing how a group of three thousand women were to be chosen from the *habituées* of the Palais Royal, the *Dames des Halles*, and the *Société Fraternelle*. They were to be dressed in red ribbons and red Pierrot costumes, bearing a pike in one hand and a pamphlet containing extracts from *The Rights of Man* in the other. Mlles Théroigne and Calon were to be at the head of the procession. As a matter of fact, Théroigne took a very active part in preparing for this *fête* to the Swiss, which was intended to revive public spirit. She had been busy with the organisation from the beginning of the month.

On March 1st Gorsas wrote to Palloy saying:

Mlle Théroigne wishes to see you and talk with you, comrade. Please fix a day and hour when I can accompany her to your house. She particularly wishes to speak to you of a proposed *fête* for Châteauvieux.

Three days later the question came up at the Jacobins, Théroigne being spokeswoman for a deputation sent by the *Société Fraternelle* to propose a plan for a patriotic feast, "in order to tune up public spirit to its highest pitch," as she aptly expressed it. She gave such a long description of the proposed *fête* that Bronsonnet interrupted her, saying that Louis XIV. had been in the habit of giving *fêtes* when he had forced other nations into submission, and that it was unthinkable that any one should propose similar measures in France now she was free, and at a moment when she might be forced to declare war against several nations.

Théroigne replied that what she proposed was not so much a *fête* as a ceremony, and she went on reading. Thuriot, the President, did not discourage her, and in the end Bronsonnet and Restaut were commissioned to examine into the plans submitted.

Throughout the month controversy raged hotly round the forty unfortunate Swiss of Châteauvieux who had been condemned to the galleys and sent to Brest for revolt, murder, and pillage at Nancy in August 1790. Opinion was divided as to whether they were heroes or outcasts, as to whether they were to be *fêted* or reviled. Collot d'Herbois pleaded for them, crying himself hoarse. Roucher opposed him, and insults were hurled from one to the other, the latter accusing the former of "rushing at him as though to strike him with the oar the Swiss had brought him from the galleys." Marie-Joseph Chénier associated himself with Théroigne in championing the cause of the soldiers; André Chénier, on the other hand, wrote immortal verses denouncing the affair.

This *fête* that is preparing for these soldiers is attributed to enthusiasm. For my part I confess I do not perceive this enthusiasm. . . . How, then, is the honour of Paris interested in feting the murderers of our brothers? . . . In a city that respected itself such a *fête* would be met by silence and solitude, the streets or public places would be abandoned, the houses shut up, the windows deserted, and the flight and scorn of the passer-by would tell history what share honest and well-disposed men took in this scandalous and bacchanalian procession.

Dupont de Nemours assailed Pétion on the same subject. The walls of Paris were covered with placards for and against. The discussion was hottest in the Jacobins Club. The press devoted columns to it; the masses, adoring everything theatrical and emphatic, were on the side of the celebrations. But Théroigne worked on steadily against all opposition, and on that same fateful March 25th presented a petition, jointly with Marie-Joseph Chénier and David the painter, to the Council General of the Commune.

M. the Mayor and Gentlemen,
In a few days from now we shall have amongst us the soldiers of the Châteauvieux. Their irons have fallen off at the vote of the Assembly; their persecutors have escaped the penalty of the law, but not the stain of ignominy. Soon these generous soldiers will see again the Champ de Mars, where their resistance to despotism prepared the way for a reign of law; soon they will embrace their brothers-at-arms, these brave French guards with whom they shared a heroic disobedience.
Fraternal liberality and well-deserved honours will acquit the country of the debt it has contracted towards the soldiers of

Châteauvieux. Thus, the efforts of good-citizenship should be encouraged. This moving *fête* will everywhere be the terror of tyrants, the hope and consolation of patriots. Thus, we will prove to Europe that the people, unlike despots, are not un-grateful, and that a nation which has become free knows how to reward the supporters of its liberty, as it knows how to strike down conspirators, even on the steps of the throne.

Numerous citizens have charged us with a mission to you, which we fill with confidence and joy. They invite you, by our voice, to be witness of this *fête* which civism and the arts will render imposing and memorable. It is to be hoped that the magistrates of the people will consecrate with their pres-ence the triumph of the martyrs of the people's cause. They have preserved, even in chains, that inward and moral liberty of which all the kings in the world are unable to deprive them. The country has engraved on their irons the oath to live free or to die, as it has engraved it on their swords, and on their na-tional pikes, as it has engraved it in your hearts, in ours, and in those of all true Frenchmen.

Marie-Joseph Chénier
Théroigne
David
Hion, etc.

The municipal body approved of the petition and invitation; the former was printed and distributed to the Forty-Eight Sections, the latter was courteously accepted.

In this enterprise Théroigne is found in excellent company. Marie-Joseph Chénier was the poet of the Revolution. He won fame with his play *Charles IX.*, of which Camille Desmoulins said: "This piece has advanced our cause better than the days of October." Like Théroigne he was pursued with venomous attacks by the *Actes des Apôtres*. His in-spired features speak of his deep love of humanity and of his lofty aspi-rations towards freedom and justice. He composed numerous patriotic and republican hymns, among which the "*Chant du depart*" shared with the *Marseillaise* the glory of guiding the soldiers to victory. David did for art what Chénier did for poetry. Not content with using his brush to depict some of the events of the Revolution, he took an active part in public affairs, especially in organising picturesque *fêtes* like the one to celebrate the release of the Swiss of Châteauvieux.

The soldiers were set free in February, 1792, and marched on foot to Paris, where they arrived on April 9th. They were accompanied by crowds of citizens and two deputies-extraordinary of Brest. From Versailles the crowd increased enormously, and the shouts of "*Vive la Nation!*" became deafening. The procession made for the Hôtel de Ville, where, after much dispute, and the matter being put thrice to the vote, they were admitted to the Assembly.

Tallien drew up on April 2nd the programme of the *fête*, which was fixed for April 15th, a Sunday.

A detachment of mounted *gendarmes* was to ride at the head of the procession, preceded by trumpeters, and followed by a battalion of the National Guard of Paris, a band, and *gendarmes* on foot. Then a number of men and women citizens, eight abreast, were to carry in their midst the Declaration of the Rights of Man; then another band. A second group of citizens and *citoyennes* carried arms and tools employed in the Conquest of Liberty on July 14th, 1789. These were to surround a model of the Bastille and the flag of the fortress, which were borne turn and turn about by citizens of the Faubourg Saint-Antoine, conquerors of the Bastille, and former French Guards dressed in their uniforms.

A battalion of veterans followed.

A third group included the flags of England, America, and France, united by tricoloured ribbons to indicate an alliance, and carried by citizens representing the free peoples. These were to be preceded by busts of Franklin, Sidney, J. J. Rousseau, and Voltaire, carried by citizens of the countries where these great men were born, and surrounded by pupils from the schools.

The book of the French Constitution, carried by fathers of families, their wives, mothers, and young citizens, to whom it was confided by the Representatives of the Nation, formed the fourth group.

National Guards marched between the groups.

The fifth group was composed of deputies, municipal officers, members of the various administrations, judges of the Civil and Criminal Tribunals, and deputies of the Forty-eight Sections.

These were to be followed by citizens who had been victims of despotism and oppression, others carrying a model of the galleys, and still more carrying oars decorated with flowers and ribbons.

Then followed forty *citoyennes* carrying as many trophies, made out of the chains the soldiers had worn, and banners bearing emblems and inscriptions in the honour of liberty. In the centre of the group was an

SAINT-JUST.

ancient sarcophagus, on which were traced the names of twenty-three soldiers immolated by an arbitrary judgment to the vengeance of their officers and to the resentment of Bouillé.

Another *sarcophagus* of the same kind was consecrated to the names of the National Guards who died victims of their zeal in executing the law. These two funereal monuments were inscribed with the legend: "Bouillé and his accomplices alone are guilty."

Then came the Car of Liberty, drawn by twenty horses, harnessed four abreast.

It was a solemn and imposing festival.

In an earlier plan for the *fête* it had been suggested that the town of Brest should be represented by a woman partly veiled and showing signs of profound grief, whilst another woman, dressed to represent Paris, was to approach, embrace, and console her with promises of blessings to come. It was supposed that Théroigne would have taken one of these parts had not the idea been given up in favour of the statue of Liberty.

A few days after the *fête* her popularity received another check, this time at the hands of her former friend, Collot d'Herbois. The occurrence happened at the Jacobins on April 23rd. Collot d'Herbois, who was speaking, congratulated himself on the fact that Théroigne whilst at the Café Hottot on the terrace of the *Feuillants* had declared that she withdrew her confidence from him and from Robespierre. This statement was received with much laughter.

Théroigne was in the women's gallery. Irritated by the speaker and the tittering among the audience, she leapt over the barrier which separated her from the main body of the hall, avoiding all attempts to restrain her, rushed to the platform, and insisted on speaking. Her excitement was intense, her gestures highly animated. A tumult ensued, which the president found it impossible to quell. At length he put on his hat and suspended the sitting. Théroigne was led crestfallen from the hall. The trouble had arisen because a rupture had occurred between the Brissotins and the Robespierrists, and Théroigne, in spite of her friendship for Basire and her recent alliance with Collot d'Herbois, had declared herself Brissotine.

A writer in the *Correspondance Littéraire Secrète* summed up the matter thus on April 28th:

MM. Collot d'Herbois, Robespierre, Chabot the ex-monk, and Tallien are opposed to MM. Brissot, Condorcet, Fauchet,

Gaudet, and Vergniaud. A reconciliation is rendered more difficult than it would otherwise be because several women are taking part in the quarrel. These are Mme de Condorcet, Mme de Staël, and Mlle Théroigne.

After this date Théroigne's name is frequently coupled in the royalist press with those of Mme de Staël and Mme de Condorcet.

CHAPTER 8

Suleau

Did Théroigne take part in the demonstrations of June 20th? The authoritative chroniclers give no definite evidence that she did. The deeds of that day were of the stirring character in which she delighted, and if she was not at least an interested spectator there must have been a good reason for her absence.

France was afflicted by additional calamity. Besides internal strife, discontent, revolt, and scarcity of food, the allied powers, Austria and Prussia, were threatening utter devastation, particularly from the north. Patriotism was ready to burst forth in the south in the hope of saving France—for the blame of the disaster rested, according to the people's opinion, on the king's shoulders. The day on which the power of the masses could no longer be kept in check was at hand. After much demur permission had been granted for a petition to be presented to the Assembly by armed men. The citizens of the Faubourg Saint-Antoine were gathered ready to march to the palace. The streets were filled with agitated crowds. National Guards, demonstrators armed with pikes, the porters of the markets, women waving branches of trees, little children joining in the general clamour.

Pétion, the mayor, had doubled the guard at the Tuileries, but took no steps to prevent the formation or progress of a procession. It was impossible. A repetition of the massacre of the Champ de Mars would have been an irretrievable mistake. The crowd swelled and swelled, until by eleven o'clock in the morning it was an irresistible human force ready to overflow in any direction suggested by its leaders. There was no talk of violence. This was to be a peaceable *fête*; one of the *fêtes* ever beloved of the masses during the Revolution. It was proposed, said Roederer, to plant a tree of liberty almost at the door of the palace. At the earliest hour of the morning this leafy symbol of budding summer and renewed hope was already hoisted on a cart in anticipation of its triumphal journey.

Surely this was a project after Théroigne's own heart. Planting trees of liberty, even though they came no nearer to the Tuileries than the garden of the Capuchins, was not an amusement to be indulged in every day. Her friend Saint-Huruge was one of the leaders of the mob; Santerre was another. Maton de la Varenne declared that Théroigne was a third. But his opinion is of little value, for his remarks concerning her are full of inaccuracies. He called her "a miserable creature, small, wrinkled, and sickly, who blushed at the least coaxing ways of men, and who by an appearance of wit, although no real powers of attraction, had captivated and ruined several," and he accused her of trying to foment an insurrection at Vienna!

With her or without her, the people, intent on their *fête*, swarmed from east, west, north, and south, but chiefly east, to make their way into the grave presence of the country's legislators. A peaceable and good-humoured crowd, but nevertheless a crowd excitable and unrestrainable. The petitioners, without asking by your leave or with your leave, rushed into the hall. The Assembly, roused by this irregularity, rose to close the sitting. The intruders withdrew. Thereupon permission was given them to make an orderly advance. The petition was read at the bar. It contained the usual plea for freedom from oppression, and in addition a demand that the king should have no will but that of the law. There was no manifestation of republicanism as yet. Dancing, singing, and full of joviality, the encouraged petitioners made their way out through the hall, and thence towards the Tuileries, accompanied at a safe distance by battalions of the National Guard. In their turn they were followed by a rabble of women, armed men carrying waving flags, a bullock's heart raised high upon a pike, with the gruesome inscription, "Heart of an aristocrat," and a pair of ragged breeches hoisted in the air, bearing the legend, "*Vivent les sans-culottes*—Tremble, oh Tyrants."

At the palace admittance was at first refused, but presently, by the king's order, the gates were unbarred. The mob shouted hoarsely for the king, and cries of "Down with the *veto!*" rang through the air. Santerre was among the last to come from the Assembly, and his followers had a cannon with them which was drawn up to the royal gate, and presently, some say, up the staircase of the palace itself. The daring of such a deed whetted the already tense excitement of the people.

Pouring into the palace, they rushed into the apartments, seeking for the king. When at length he appeared, calm and imperturbable, as was his usual attitude in the face of danger, he was urged to enter one of the large apartments in order that a petition might be read to him. There he was asked to step upon a bench, and one of the rabble held up his red cap on a pike. Amidst general applause the king placed it on his head. Demarteau, who is usually a reliable chronicler, says that Théroigne marched at the head of the people of the faubourgs, who invaded the Tuileries, and forced the king to place the *bonnet-rouge* on his head.

The extravagant Duval declares that on June 20th Théroigne appeared at the head of a crowd of brigands who invaded the king's apartments, and helped to push one of the wheels of the cannon which was hoisted into the hall where the people had forced the king to appear before them. When Pétion arrived, she went to shake hands with him; and when he commanded the people to withdraw, she said to him in a tone of reproach, "I believe we might have ended the whole matter today!"

Meanwhile the queen was with difficulty dissuaded from joining the king. She stood with her children beside her, surrounded by grenadiers, watching the rabble invading the sanctity of the private apartments with a sense of unutterable disgust in her heart and an expression of staunch indifference on her features. With her own hand she placed the obnoxious *bonnet-rouge* on the head of her little son, and when Santerre, speaking to her in friendly terms, relieved the child of this disfiguring headgear, she appeared conciliatory enough, although a shudder swept over her frame. At length, after an invasion of the palace lasting three hours, the people took their departure, induced to do so by Pétion and Santerre. The queen hastened to join the king, who, finding himself still adorned with the red cap, tossed it from him in a fit of impetuous anger.

Thus passed, harmlessly enough, one invasion of the palace by the people. Their next visit was to have more serious consequences. In July the fever of unrest became more and more pronounced; every peasant in the country dropped the handles of his plough, betook himself to the mayoralty, saw the proclamation that the country was in danger, and returned, a soldier at heart, the cockade in his cap. If in June the royal family had been exposed to a sense of unbearable humiliation, in July they were dominated by fear—fear of death by the sword, by poison, or perhaps worse, by judicial condemnation. The last hope of flight was dwindling away, the last hope of rescue by foreign forces was dead; nothing remained but the dumb pain of impotence, the inability to escape from an unrelenting fate.

And so in a slow agony the days passed, bringing nearer and still more near the crisis which was to determine the bitter end of the royal household. Republicanism had come suddenly to life. During the first days of August one word sounded ominously in the ears of those who loved their rulers—"dethronement." It was a thought which spurred the people to action; it was the keynote of the deeds of the terrible 10th.

There is no room for doubt as to Théroigne's movements on that day. She played a conspicuous role in one of the dramatic incidents which made up the tragic scenes of the attack upon the palace. In this incident she and Suleau were the two chief actors.

The de Goncourts say bluntly, "On August 10th Théroigne murdered Suleau." It was natural that so bold an assertion should lead to questions as to the motive of the crime. Various motives were imputed to her. The most romantic stories were woven about the event. At first it was supposed that Théroigne had vowed vengeance upon some young *seigneur* who had betrayed her in early life, and, coming face to face with him, had wreaked her vengeance and wiped out her wrongs by his death. Lamartine is responsible for perpetrating this dramatic but improbable version of what took place. He does not mention August 10th, but dates the tragedy as from the massacres of September, he says:

> Her ascendancy during the *émeutes* was so great, that with a single sign she condemned or acquitted a victim; and the royalists trembled to meet her. During this period, by one of those chances that appear like the premeditated vengeances of destiny, she recognised in Paris the young Belgian gentleman who had seduced and abandoned her. Her look told him how great was his danger, and he sought to avert it by imploring her pardon. 'My pardon,' said she, 'at what price can you purchase it? My innocence gone, my family lost to me, my brothers and sisters pursued in their own country by the jeers and sarcasms of their kindred; the malediction of my father, my exile from my native land, my enrolment amongst the infamous caste of courtesans; the blood with which my days have been and will be stained; that imperishable curse attached to my name, instead of that immortality of virtue which you have taught me to doubt. It is for this that you would purchase my forgiveness. Do you know

any price on earth capable of purchasing it?' The young man made no reply. Théroigne had not the generosity to forgive him, and he perished in the massacres of September. In proportion as the Revolution became more bloody, she plunged deeper into it. She could no longer exist without the feverish excitement of public emotion.

That may be fine writing, but it is not the truth. If Théroigne felt personal animus against Suleau, a plausible explanation might be that she knew of him as one of the authors who had poured forth incessant abuse of her in the pages of the *Actes des Apôtres*. But it is difficult, almost impossible, to apportion her exact share in the murder of the royalist. The crowd was thirsty for victims. Suleau was one of the most prominent and most hated of those prisoners who offered a chance of assuaging the rioters' lust for blood. Did Théroigne make any special movement, even the slightest push, to precipitate his fate? If she did, was not her action quite possibly the outcome of the mad passions which dominated the crowd rather than any deliberate desire to destroy a personal enemy?

With grave questions such as these unanswered it is not possible to be sure that an accusation of wilful intent to murder against her would be just. On the other hand, to hold her innocent is impossible. Only a few moments earlier she had been speaking to the crowd of people, swaying them to her lightest will; and though it is true that they had escaped her control, it seems probable that had she urged them to stay their hands Suleau might have been saved—at least, for the time being.

There is one important point in her favour. The first victim of all was the Abbé Bouyon, editor of *Les Folies d'un Mois*—also guilty of maligning Théroigne, and no doubt equally an object of her hate; but it has never been suggested that she was in any degree implicated in his death. Carried away by the tragic turn the Revolution was taking, she may have come to the point when she was tainted by the general belief that no measures short of violence and massacre were possible. If that be the case, she had gone a long way since the day when she had desired to take only an academic interest in the political upheaval—when she had been a reformer, and not a fighter. In this attitude she was not alone; hundreds, nay, thousands, had been infected by the same thirst for blood—the spirit which led, within the succeeding twelve months, to the excesses committed in the name of liberty under the shadow of the guillotine.

If Théroigne must be blamed for the responsibility of one man's death, she had, at least, far less upon her conscience than hundreds of the men with whom she was working and struggling side by side. In her normal state she was not by nature cruel—quite the reverse; and if she were guilty of an act of cruelty to Suleau, the abnormal conditions of the hour in which the deed was done must not be ignored when estimating her culpability.

Suleau's position was enough to bring the manner of his death into particular prominence. He was very well known by the patriots as well as by the royalists. Born in Picardy in 1758, he had studied and travelled much, returning to Paris in August 1789. He was many-sided. In his composition was a little of the soldier, a little of the lawyer, a good deal of the writer, and, first and foremost, the adventurer. He threw himself with the peculiar vivacity and gaiety natural to him into the thick of the activities. Before long he was arrested for *lèse-nation*, then newly a punishable crime, and was arraigned before the *Châtelet*. His trial was a judicial comedy. He railed and mocked at the accusation, at the judges, at the people, at the whole world. In April 1790 he was released, but he had not learned wisdom. Hot-headed as ever, he made himself well hated as a pamphleteer, being largely responsible for the notoriety attained by the *Actes des Apôtres*. Still his love of danger and intrigue were unsatiated. His characteristics won for him the nickname of "*Chevalier de la Difficulté.*"

At the close of 1791 he went to Coblenz and worked amongst the *émigrés* with more energy than discretion, conspiring with foreign princes, and acting against the national interests of France. As was not surprising for a man of his class and temperament, he gained the hatred of the patriots without ingratiating himself with the *noblesse*. Neither the French aristocracy nor the foreign powers trusted him or I took his efforts seriously, and this blow to his pride kept him temporarily inactive. But in August he had been working on the side of the royalist party. He was amongst those who, dressed in the uniform of the National Guard, were sent out to report on the condition and temper of the people.

It was said that on the morning of the 9th Suleau told his friend Le Sourd that he had been warned by Camille Desmoulins that a price had been placed upon his (Suleau's) head, and Camille had offered him a refuge at his own house, which he refused. Le Sourd met him twice during the succeeding twenty-four hours—the first time he was following in the track of Potion, who had been ordered to the bar of the Legislative Assembly to give an account of the chances of public tranquillity, the second time was shortly before his arrest, when he invited Le Sourd to his house in the *Place Vendôme* to take refreshments. His friend says:

> It was then, that, leaving the terrace of the *Feuillants* and crossing the court, he was arrested. The too famous Théroigne de Méricourt was established there on a makeshift platform. She did not know Suleau, but he had been pointed out to her by the chiefs of the conspiracy as a necessary victim. One of the furies round her having named him to her, she designated him to one of the hired assassins near to her, who thereupon massacred him. His body was dragged to the right-hand corner of the Place Vendôme, under our very windows, and was placed there with those of eight other victims.

A dramatic account of the affair, which, however, in many details is wanting in accuracy, is from the pen of Baron Thiebault, Lieutenant-General in the French Army.

On the night of August 9th preparations had been made at the Tuileries to repel the threatened attack of the people. False patrols had been ordered to sally forth dressed as National Guards, their apparent object to keep the peace; in reality to slaughter the people if the chance came. Drums rolled, there was the clash of arms, the tocsin boomed. A skirmish between the false and the real Guards was in progress, and many of the former were carried prisoner to the guard-room in the *Cour de Feuillants.*

Hearing this news, the people crowded into the court early in the morning of the 10th.

Thiebault writes:

> The courtyard was getting fuller and fuller, and the cries became appalling, I determined then to send La Fargue to the officer commanding the Butte des Moulins battalion, which waff assembled fourteen hundred strong in the *Place Vendôme*, asking for reinforcements. He would only have to cross the Rue Saint-Honoré, while two hundred men would suffice to clear the courtyard of the *Feuillants,* and enable us to close the gates and disperse the rabble. But the commander, whose name I have forgotten, replied that without orders he could not detach a man outside his section. La Fargue replied, 'Well, sir, if they cut our throats and murder our prisoners you will have one advan-

tage, namely, that of being in a front-row box.'

Thiebault tried a last resource, since he could not get reinforcements. He rushed into the midst of the crowd, mounted on one of the two guns which stood in the courtyard, and harangued the people from this improvised platform:

Are you Frenchmen? So are we no less. Are you patriots? So are we no less. But you will cease to be worthy of one or the other title if you cannot get beyond the detestable idea of replacing justice by assassination. You will indeed be rebels, for the Assembly has put the prisoners under our guardianship. What have you then to demand? It can be only one thing, namely, that the prisoners—against nearly all of whom, by the way, there is no charge—should not escape. Well, I answer for them on my honour. I will be responsible with my own head, and, if that is not guarantee enough, I will add to their guard any three of you whom you like to choose.

Some of the crowd made answer, to which Thiebault replied, endeavouring by every means in his power to gain time. Just as he was congratulating himself on the success of his efforts Théroigne de Méricourt entered the courtyard. She was dressed in a black felt hat with a black plume, a blue amazone, and carried pistols and a dagger in her belt. Thiebault writes:

She was a dark girl of about twenty, and, with a sort of shudder I say it, very pretty, made still more beautiful by her excitement. Preceded and followed by a number of maniacs, she cleft her way through the crowd, crying 'Make room! make room!' went straight to the other gun and leapt upon it. . . . Having heard what was going on, she had hurried up from Robespierre's house, and, confident in her influence with the populace, she had come to restore all its ferocity to the mob. As long as I live that creature will be present before my eyes; the sound of her voice will ring in my ears as she uttered the first sentence of her discourse. 'How long,' she shrieked, 'will you let yourselves be misled by empty phrases?' I tried to answer, but I could no longer make myself heard. A thousand voices greeted with applause every word that she uttered.

Compelled to silence and at the end of his wits, Thiebault got off the gun and forced his way through the angry crowd back to the guardroom. He shut and locked the door behind him. Furious, the mob hurled themselves against it. The upper part was of glass; it splintered, the broken panes flying into the defenders' faces. At the end of a narrow passage were a score of men armed with bayonets and loaded muskets. To force their way through the passage or through the iron-barred window meant loss of life to all who attempted it. The mob halted.

Thiebault continued:

> They found it more dignified, to put me on my trial, their beautiful fury, Mlle de Méricourt, presiding, and to condemn me, unanimously and by acclamation, to death. I never saw her again after that day, but, though I am as susceptible as most men to the influence of women, I certainly never met another woman who, in half an hour, could have left on my mind a recollection of her which a thousand years would not weaken.

Suleau's handsome face and upright bearing made him appear a conspicuous figure. Seeing the danger of his fellow prisoners, he cried: "Comrades, I believe that the people mean to shed blood today, but perhaps one victim will satisfy them. Let me go to them. I will pay for all." He accompanied these words with an attempt to leap from the window, but he was kept back by the National Guard. It was at this moment that the mob burst into the building. The first victim was a harmless dramatic author of the name of Bouyon, who was carried forth into the courtyard and rent limb from limb. Suleau was seized and despoiled of his uniform and arms. As he struggled, Théroigne, who had rushed into the guardroom at the head of the crowd, caught sight of him.

The accounts accuse her of a fury which knew no bounds. "Where is the Abbé Suleau?" she cried, and then, coming face to face with him, she hurled more personal questions at him. "Am I the mistress of Populus? Am I old? Am I hideous?" And, throwing herself upon him, she seized him by the throat and dragged him into the thick of the murderous rabble. Hundreds of arms were stretched out to avenge her. Suleau fought like a lion attacked by twenty madmen, but before a moment had passed, he was pierced by a dozen swords, and his body was flung out into the Place Vendôme with those of eight or nine more victims.

The royalist Peltier, who was an eye-witness of these scenes, writes:

> Thus, perished the amiable Suleau, whose gaiety, candour, and

friendship endeared him to me.

At the time of his death Suleau was thirty-five, and had recently married Adela Hall, the daughter of the artist. The fact that he left a young widow to mourn his death made the horror of it more poignant. His friend Peltier wrote:

> Ah, amiable Suleau, since the hand of thy young wife could not perform the last fond duty of closing thy eyes in death, let friendship at least be allowed to scatter a few flowers over thy ashes. Thou art no more! It was thy fate to expire with French monarchy. Thy loyalty has already received its reward; in dying first thou hast not been witness to the long series of disasters which have made us every day since experience a thousand deaths.

The murder of the royalists whetted the excitement of the people. Rushing from the guardroom through the courtyard, they joined the crowd who were marching on to attack the palace.

★★★★★★

The king and queen, being informed that they were no longer safe in the Tuileries, had decided to seek refuge with the legislative body in the *Salle de Manège*. "The king is going to the Assembly; make room!" cried Roederer. At first no obstacle was placed in the way of a free passage, and crestfallen royalty defiled by the staircase leading to the terrace of the *Feuillants*, where the crowd hemmed it in. After a delay of a quarter of an hour, after urging and pleading, and the employment of slight physical compulsion, a way was cleared for the king, and His Majesty was permitted to resume the path which led for ever from the Tuileries. The queen had lost her usual fortitude, and her face showed signs of tears; Madame Royale wore the bewildered look of fear which was becoming habitual; the *dauphin*, wearied and sickly, was borne on the shoulders of a grenadier.

In the Assembly chamber the king took his seat beside the president. But the legislative body were hindered by convention from debating openly in the king's presence, and decided that the royal family must retire into a small box used by the reporters of a certain journal, which was partitioned off at the back of the hall. There for fourteen hours they remained without repose or refreshment, cramped in this prison that was but a few feet square. Inside the hall the drone of the speakers' voices continued, outside the ominous murmur of a gathering throng was heard. The hot sun poured down upon the queen as she sat there, causing her to fall into a drowsy nightmare that was but half sensation. Then a new sound stirred her into consciousness; it was the boom of guns, the crash of falling glass and masonry, the shrieks of the wounded and dying.

The story of that attack upon the Tuileries has been told over and over again, and while the details grow wearisome, the horror of it must ever seem acute. The abode of royalty had become a battle-ground. The rabble, possibly still unaware of the king's departure, beat down the courtyard gates and turned their guns upon the palace. The royalists, reluctant to fire on the people, hoped that conciliatory measures might stem the rush of the aggressive crowd. But a short parley showed their hope was vain. Shots were discharged on both sides.

The Swiss entrenched on the main stairway were subjected to a shower of balls. Rushing out from the barrier, they opened a fusillade on the *Marseillais*, and for a moment it appeared that the people might be successfully driven back. It was then that the ill-advised written order to cease firing was handed to the Swiss. The Marseillais and Bretons rallied and stormed the palace. They massacred those of the Swiss who were still within, they sacked the royal abode, destroying the last vestige of the king's authority. The republicans were the men of the hour, and with them terror reigned in Paris.

The immediate result of that day as far as Théroigne was concerned was a reward. In the *Moniteur* of September 3rd an entry occurs announcing that the *féderes* had bestowed upon Mlles Théroigne, Lacombe, and Reine Audu civic crowns for distinguishing themselves by their courage on August 10th.

CHAPTER 9

Brissotine

During many days republican fever ran riot in the blood of the people. The king and queen were in the temple. There was much to be said, much to be done, not a moment to waste. At the Jacobins Club this stress made itself felt as much as anywhere. There was something in the tone there which portended great issues. One intimate glimpse of Théroigne, showing her at this moment of tense calm before the storm, we owe to Dr. John Moore, who had been studying the events of that week to some purpose. He had obtained a full view of the queen, and had deplored the change in her appearance. "Her beauty is gone. No wonder!" he writes.

A few days later, on the 17th, he visited the Jacobins, where "there was not, properly speaking, a debate, but rather a series of violent speeches," and saw the daughter of the people.

He continues:

There were abundance of women in the galleries, but as there were none in the body of the hall where the members were seated, I was surprised to see one enter and take her seat amongst them. She was dressed in a kind of English riding-habit, but her jacket was the uniform of the National Guards. On inquiry I was informed that the name of this Amazon is Mademoiselle Théroigne; she distinguished herself in the action of the 10th by rallying those who fled, and attacking a second time at the head of the Marseillais.

She seems about one or two and thirty, (he overestimated her age), is somewhat above the middle size of women, and has a smart martial air, which in a man would not be disagreeable.

That day the partisans of Robespierre were so loud in their demonstrations that any speaker whose sentiments happened not to be quite in accord with theirs was howled down and the tribune given up to someone who had a more palatable doctrine to propound.

The great issues were about to begin at the point of the knife. The people, having steeped their hands in crime and bloodshed, were not brought back easily within bounds of moderation.

At the beginning of September massacres were carried out systematically. Butchers stalked through the jails slaughtering the prisoners like sheep. There was carnage everywhere—at the *Abbaye*, at the *Châtelet*, at *La Force*, at the *Conciergerie*, the *Bicêtre*, and *La Salpêtrière*, the place of durance vile of which Théroigne was before long to gain an extended knowledge.

It is impossible to depict the disorder that existed, or to explain the paralytic inaction of those in authority and of the masses of more peaceable inhabitants, who did not even denounce the doings of the murderers, or attempt to interfere with this wholesale slaughter. The blood that was being spilt incited all who had shared in the spilling to continue their gruesome labours. The women of the Revolution joined in these diabolical doings. Following in the footsteps of Billaud-Varennes, who, wading through blood, cried "Bring wine for the brave toilers who are about to deliver the nation from its foes," they remarked facetiously that they were carrying dinner to the husbands who were *at work* in the prisons.

In contrast to their ferocious attitude, such brave royalist women as Elizabeth Cazotte and Mlle de Sombreuil, amongst others, stand out as wonderful examples of courage, sacrifice, and filial piety. The former, throwing herself between her father and his would-be assassins, cried, "Strike, if you must, you scoundrels, but you will not get at him except over my dead body"; and the latter was credited with having gulped down without a murmur of disgust a glass containing the blood of an aristocrat—a nauseous draught forced upon her by the murderous demagogues as the price of her father's release.

It is impossible to say with certainty whether Théroigne, excited as she was by her activities on August 10th, restrained herself from staining her hands with additional crime during these days of unbridled licence. The best evidence that can be put forward in favour of her innocence is the fact that she withdrew her support from the extreme party to bestow it upon the cause of the moderates.

August 10th had put the Girondins temporarily in power. On September 21st the Convention superseded the Legislative Assembly. The Girondins formed the Conservative party, with Brissot, Vergniaud, and Gaudet at their head. On the Left were the extremists, the Montagnards, led by Robespierre, Marat, Danton, the Duc d'Orléans, now called Philippe Egalité, and Théroigne's former friend, Collot d'Herbois. The hostility was acute, and, taking into consideration the trend of affairs, could have but one end. It was the desire of the Moderates to destroy the ascendancy of those whom they believed to be responsible for the massacres, and to disperse the hired bands of assassins who were giving expression to the feeling of revenge dominating the masses. This task was no easy one.

Against them were the *triumvirate* of front-rank republicans, Robespierre, Danton, and Marat. More organising power and diplomacy, less brilliancy and oratory, would have been needed by the Girondins to bring to book such strong and obstinate antagonists. Between the extreme parties there vacillated and temporised the Centre of the Convention. Hating Marat and all his works, yet dreading the power of the Commune, they extended no definite help to the Right. The struggle, often renewed, yet never decisive, gradually strengthened the position of the Montagnards, to whom the entire sympathies of the Jacobins were now given—no mean support, taking into consideration that the galleries of the house were usually filled with their adherents, who noisily shouted down the Girondins, whilst encouraging their opponents with applause.

The internal situation, being thus unstable, was much complicated by the position of foreign affairs. For a while the French had been successful in the battlefield. War had been declared against the King of Sardinia, and French troops occupied Savoy. Custine, with 18,000 men, had succeeded in driving the Prussians before him in Lorraine, capturing Mainz and Frankfort. The allied army retreating, Dumouriez set out to invade Belgium.

At this point a vague rumour is heard of Théroigne. In the *Correspondance Littéraire Secrète* of October 20th a note states that she had returned to her native country just when the army of Dumouriez was facing the Prussians there and about to make war on the Low Country. A strange report to have come into print if it contained no truth, yet it is not substantiated by any biographer. Dumouriez, having left Paris on October 17th, reached Liège on November 27th. On the 9th of that month Théroigne wrote a letter from Paris to Perregaux, from which it is clear that she was in worse financial straits than ever before, for she sent a messenger with an appeal to No. 9, Rue Mirabeau, addressed to "Citizen Perregaux, or to his clerk, should he be absent," in the following urgent terms:

Citizen, I beg you will give the hundred *livres* you promised me yesterday to the woman who brings this letter.

On January 28th following she made another application to M. de Limbourg, friend of the Baron de Selys, who was then at Theux, near Liège, about her jewels. This note was signed "*La Citoyenne Théroigne*," and addressed from the Rue Saint-Honoré, No. 273, near the Jacobins. By that time Dumouriez was back in Paris. If, therefore, she had really been with his army, the visit to her own country was a short one and can have had but little significance. At any rate, the conqueror of Jemappes had no great opinion of her ability, for, in his *Memoirs*, after especially praising Mme Roland and Mme Necker, he classes Mlle la Brousse, Mme de Staël, Mme Condorcet, Pastoret, Coigny, and Théroigne as "either artful females, like those who haunted the courts of former times, or differing in nothing from the vulgar and furious women of the faubourgs of Paris."

Between August 10th, then, and the beginning of May 1793, Théroigne has baffled her biographers. More important personages were commanding attention. The execution of the king in January, the anguish of the queen, the slow crushing of the Girondins, the rise of the Montagnards, kept every chronicler busy. Théroigne was doubtless living in the rooms near the Jacobins, frequenting the clubs, perhaps holding gatherings of her own and mingling more or less conspicuously with the street crowds in these, some of the most anxious months in all the history of the Revolution. On the whole, she had probably a good reason for remaining comparatively quiet. In the spring the position of the Girondins was becoming critical. Failing in their foreign policy, in their attempt to save the king, as well as in maintaining any pretence of internal equilibrium, they were tottering before the downfall.

At this hour of internal dissension, of wavering in the sections, of military disaster (caused in part by Dumouriez's treachery in allying himself with Coburg), of rebellion in La Vendée, of the interference of England under Pitt's policy, of utter lawlessness and anarchy, Théroigne chose to declaim a stirring appeal to the sections, exhorting them to rally and make a final stand. There was much of her usual fire, of her wonderful power to carry her audience with her, in the speech, which was afterwards printed and placarded on the walls throughout the city.

Although diffuse and containing many grammatical errors, its fervour outweighs such deficiencies. It is a typical publication of that day, and throws a glaring light upon the desperate condition of affairs and the internal disunion of the country. It has rarely, if ever, been quoted in full, and not at all in English. Addressed to the Forty-eight Sections, it was printed by Dufart, Rue Saint-Honoré, on blue-grey paper, and runs as follows:

Citizens! Hear me! I am not going to utter fine phrases; I am going to tell you the pure and simple truth. Where do we stand? All the conflicting passions which have been aroused are liable to carry us away. We are almost on the edge of the precipice. Citizens, let us stop and reflect. It is time. On my return from Germany, almost eighteen months ago, I told you that the emperor had a prodigious number of agents here to sow discord amongst us, in order to prepare civil war at a distance, and that his plan was to cause it to break out at the moment when his satellites should be ready to make a general effort to invade our territory. That is where we stand! They have reached the point of a *dénouement*, and we are ready to fall into the trap. The preliminary altercations of civil war have taken place already in some sections. Pay attention, then, and let us examine calmly who are the instigators, in order that we may recognise our enemies.

Misfortune be on your head, citizens, if you allow such scenes to be renewed. If people come to fisticuffs, and use abusive language, unworthy of citizens, they will soon go farther, and I can foresee that their passions will be heated to such a point that it will no longer be in your power to hinder the explosion. These manoeuvres have three aims—civil war, there is no doubt, that of justifying the calumnies of kings, and of their slaves, who pretend that it is not possible that the people can assemble to exercise its sovereignty without abusing it. This is a branch of the great conspiracy against democracy.

Citizens, let us grasp democracy so firmly that it can never escape us. Baffle these intrigues by your rectitude, your justice, and your wisdom. By these means you will give the lie to your calumniators.

What about their wish to detain, for as long as possible, the remainder of the contingent which Paris ought to furnish to march against the rebels in the Vendée? They desire, it would appear, that instead of carrying help to our brothers they should have to come amongst us to restore harmony. It is actually the aim of the king's agents to create a diversion, to weaken us by setting one against the other, for, whilst we flew at one another's throats, the rebels—backed up by the English, who would not be long in descending upon our shores, if the intrigues of Pitt continue to shackle us, and to hinder us from seriously considering our position, during that time—the rebels, I say, who, to our shame be it known, are more united and firm in defending despotism and religious prejudices than we are to defend liberty, will make better progress than we are able to calculate, because we have not their passionate force, since men who have placed themselves midway between victory and death fight in desperation.

In agreement with the Imperialists, the Prussians, and the coalition of powers, they will advance from every side. Our armies and our generals, not knowing if they are fighting for the Republic, or for the parties, or for a tyrant whom they justly fear to see raise himself as in Rome to put an end to the discords, will grow discouraged.

Besides, the feeble citizens, those who up till now have remained undecided, but who would declare themselves if our unity and strength received a strong impetus, discouraged by these same motives and seduced by perfidious promises such as are contained in the Proclamation of Coburg, would remain in their wavering state. And so, if we fall into the trap prepared for us, and the kings succeed in producing an outburst of civil war amongst the most fiery citizens, and seducing or discouraging the others, how shall we save ourselves from their satellites? How shall we stem this torrent of hostility on the part of enemies who will combine their efforts at the very moment when we shall be most divided against ourselves? Oh, terrible thought! It is impossible to pursue it.

Citizens, let us stop and reflect or we are lost. The moment has arrived when it is to the interest of all to reunite, to sacrifice our hates and our passions for the public welfare. If the voice of the country, the sweet hope of fraternity, does not inspire us, let us consider our closest interests. All united, we are none too strong to repulse our numerous enemies from without, and those who have already raised the standard of rebellion. Nevertheless, I warn you that our enemies will make no distinction between the parties; we shall all be confounded on the day of vengeance. I can say that there is not a single patriot who has made himself conspicuous during the Revolution concerning whom I have not been questioned. All the inhabitants of Paris are indiscriminately proscribed, and I have heard those who wished to make me depose against the patriots say a thousand times that it would be necessary to exterminate half the French to subdue the other half. To exterminate us, vile slaves! It is you we should exterminate.

Danger is going to reunite us, and we are going to show you what men who desire liberty, and who work for the cause of the human race, can do. We shall all march forth, rich and poor alike, and those who, having the necessary means, send substitutes will be covered with infamy. Surely, then, it is in vain, tyrants of the earth, that you send your agents here, that you scatter your gold! The French are too clever to be caught in the trap you have set for them, and to go astray. We desire liberty, and will defend ourselves with our last drops of blood. Eternal justice is on our side, and only lies and crime on yours. Judge your cause and ours, and say to whom shall be the victory.

The smallest things sometimes lead to the greatest. The Roman women disarmed Coriolanus and saved their country.

Recollect, citizens, that previous to August 10th not one of you broke the silken thread which separated the terrace of the *Feuillants* from the Tuileries gardens. Sometimes the least thing will stay the most forcible outpouring of passions with greater success than all the force that might be opposed to it.

Consequently, I propose that in each section there shall be chosen six of the most virtuous *citoyennes*, the gravest for their age, to conciliate and reunite the citizens, to remind them of the dangers by which the country is threatened. They shall wear a wide sash, on which will be inscribed the words 'Friendship and Fraternity.' Every time there is a general assembly of the section, they shall gather for the purpose of calling to order every citizen who stands aside and who does not respect the liberty of opinions, which is so necessary in forming a good public spirit. Those who have gone astray, but nevertheless have good intentions, and love their country, will be silent.

But if those of bad faith who have been bribed by the aristocrats, by the enemies of the democracy, and the agents of the king to interrupt, to speak abusively, and to come to blows, show no more respect for the voices of the *citoyennes* than for that of the president, we shall at least have the means of knowing them. And a note can be taken of their names in order that inquiries may be prosecuted on their account. These *citoyennes* can be changed every month. Those who show the highest virtue, firmness, and patriotism in the glorious ministry of reuniting the citizens, and of obtaining respect for the liberty of opinions, might be re-elected for the space of a year. Their reward would be to have a special place at our national *fêtes*, and to superintend the educational institutions consecrated to our sex. There, citizens, is an idea which I submit to your notice.

★★★★★★

The nature of Théroigne's plans for those of her own sex who could share in the active work of the Revolution had undergone a distinct modification since 1792. She no longer desired that women should arm and fight side by side with men; it was better that they should occupy themselves with the spreading of propaganda and bringing encouragement to those who vacillated.

This was the work she wished her sisters to do, and to this she urged them with all the strength she possessed. But as far as can be judged her propositions were not received with enthusiasm. They were too openly Girondist, although the Gironde is not mentioned in her speech. The broadside is dated only by internal evidence. The Proclamation of Coburg was issued on April 5th, 1793, but there are still later references: firstly to the scenes of violence at the beginning of May in various sections which had been provoked by the Decree of the Commune on the 1st of the month proclaiming the necessity of raising a Parisian army to march against the Vendéans; as well as to a supplementary decree by the Convention on the 8th, relative to the numbers which each section was to furnish.

The exact date is of importance, because Théroigne had thrown her last effective die in the cause of liberty. Within a week of her proud protest she was to be utterly humbled, and her dignity was to have fled from her for ever. Like many another who suffered for an excess of zeal, she was destroyed by the very passions she had been instrumental in arousing. An event occurred in the second week of May which was a downward step in her deplorable fate.

There were women in Paris who were growing ever more lawless,

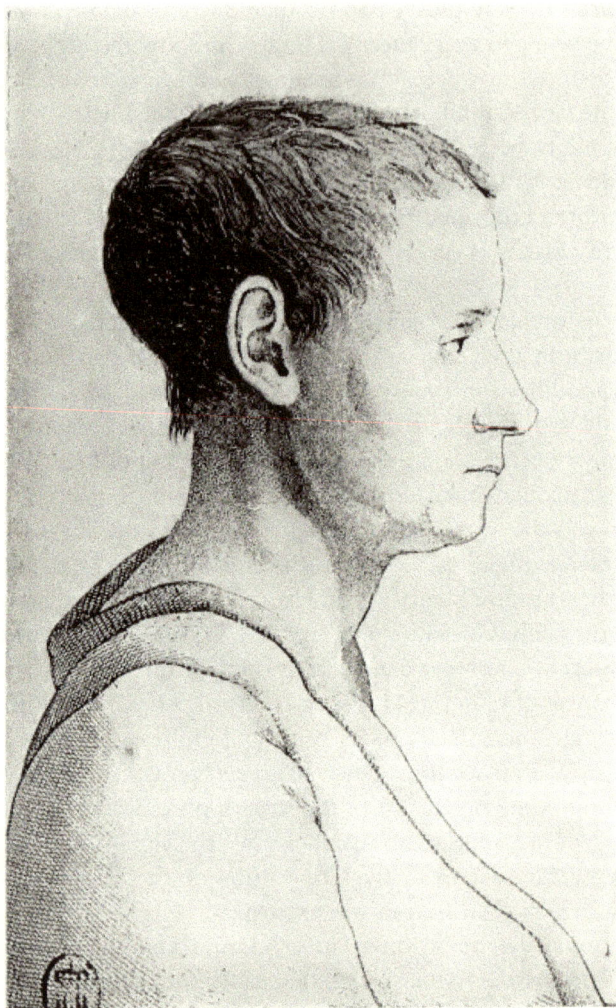

THÉROIGNE AT THE SALPÊTRIÈRE,

From an engraving at the Bibliothèque Nationale after a drawing by Gabriel.

and who were banding together in various societies for more or less nefarious purposes.

From the beginning of the year the more violent of them had formed a political organisation called the *Club de Citoyennes Révolutionnaires.* They demanded a hall for their meetings, they sent deputations to the authorities, they conspired riotously to bring about the downfall of the Girondins. They did duty as sentries, they crowded the tribunes of the Conventions, and influenced the debates by their shrieks and vociferations. They were only one step less abandoned than the so-called furies or *Tricoteuses*, Robespierre's knitting-women, who were drawn from the scum of Paris—women from the gutters, from the thieves' dens, viragoes and unfortunates.

No deeds that could be devised were too criminal, too extravagant, or too outrageous for the perpetration of these outcasts. They acted as spies, they escorted prisoners to jail and to the guillotine, hurling blasphemies in their tortured ears; they danced to the noisy, wild revolutionary songs, and gave way openly to drunkenness and debauchery. They were paid for hooting and applauding, for demanding revenge, punishment, death, or destruction according to the signal given by those who employed them, and distributed amongst them the wages of their shame.

The group of women who made it their business to do the dirty work of the Jacobins, hounding down the Girondins, gathering both within and without the Convention, mounting guard at the doors to intercept those who were not of their party, opposing all byword or action who held other views from theirs, had become a menacing feature of the days of trouble and tumult during May. On the 15th, Théroigne, passing along the terrace of the *Feuillants*, came boldly down the street and close to the door of the Convention encountered these dangerous women. Exactly what took place it is difficult to state, but a conflict between the women appears to have arisen on the subject of Brissot. The restless, scheming journalist, whom Carlyle described as "a man of the windmill species that grinds always, turning towards all winds, not in the steadiest manner," had been hunted out of the Jacobins Club in the previous October, and since that had been particularly hated by the extremists.

Théroigne's friendship for him, or at least her sympathy with his aims, was no secret. "Down with Brissot and the Brissotins," cried the Megaeras, perhaps seeing the object of their contempt and hatred. Théroigne intervened, calling to them to be silent. They hooted and derided her. Furious and outraged by their threats, she tried to gain ascendancy over the aggressive rabble by means of her old gift, oratory. But the tongue in this case was not a sufficiently effective weapon against their determination to inflict physical chastisement. She had no other resources. The excited *citoyennes* refused to listen. Seizing her roughly, they stripped her clothes from her back, and beat her unmercifully. There was no opportunity for self-defence against such numbers. Only by chance was she rescued in the nick of time, and thus escaped death. It might have been better for her if the mad and wicked creatures who set upon her had then and there been allowed to finish their gruesome purpose.

Among the accounts of the affair one occurs in the Police Report of May 16th, describing it as follows:

> The women who gather at the doors of the Convention yesterday placed a detachment of their body at the doors of the first tribunes at nine o'clock in the morning, to hinder the women favoured by the deputies from passing in with admission cards. They performed this self-imposed task with insolence of the worst kind. . . . Citoyenne Théroigne, beaten by these furies, told them she would sooner or later make them bite the dust.

Another is to be found in the *Courrier des Départements* of May 17th:

> A heroine of the Revolution experienced a slight check the day before yesterday on the terrace of the *Feuillants*. Mlle Théroigne, who, it was said, was recruiting women for the Rolandin faction, unfortunately addressed herself to the followers of Robespierre and of Marat, who, not wishing to augment the army of Brissotins, seized the female recruiter and fustigated her with great activity. The Guard arrived and saved the victim from the fury of these indecent maniacs. Marat, who was passing, took the beaten one under his protection.

The *Révolutions de Paris* of the 18th says:

> For the last few days a number of women have been policing the Tuileries gardens and the corridors of the National Convention. They have taken it upon themselves to examine all the cockades and stop the people whom they suspect of wavering. It was they who on the 15th of the month gave the whip to Théroigne, calling her Brissotine.

The story told by Barras in his *Memoirs* is somewhat different, but is interesting because it amplifies the suggestion in the *Courrier des Départements* that Marat came to Théroigne's rescue.

One of the early feminine notabilities of 1789, who had not ceased to bestir herself, Mlle Théroigne—very well known in Paris, owing especially to her democratic sentiments having become suspected of backsliding—was arrested by the populace and brought before the committee with headquarters at the *Feuillants* to the repeated cries of 'To a lamp-post with her!' The crowd became so great, so considerable and threatening, that the members of the committee despaired of saving the unfortunate Amazon; when Marat arrived on the scene the danger was imminent for the members of the committee, who were delaying handing her over to the mercies of the mob.

Marat said to them, 'I will save her.' Leading Mlle Théroigne by the hand, he showed himself to the enraged people, saying: 'Citizens, are you bent on attempting the life of a woman? Are you going to sully yourselves with such a crime? The law alone has the right to strike. Show your contempt for this courtesan and reserve your dignity, citizens.' The word of the friend of the people quieted the gathering. Marat, taking advantage of this moment of calm, dragged Mlle Théroigne away and led her into the hall of the Convention, his bold action saving her life.

Among the many accounts of the assault by her historians were those by Michelet, who accused the Montagnards; by Gabriel her contemporary, who spoke of the furies of the guillotine, Lamartine following his example; the Goncourts say by Sans-Jupons; Lalanne by women of the *Société Fraternelle; Restif de la Breton* by the royalist women of the Halles; Duval, who is usually amongst the most vivid, contented himself by saying that she was attacked "by the crowd that gathered round her." As to the result of her punishment there is little doubt. For weeks Théroigne was ill and wretched. She had suffered both in mind and body. Méderer, when he had examined her state of health at Kufstein, had foreseen that excitement and overstrain were dangerous for her and that there was a tendency to mental affliction. He might have warned her that in throwing herself heart and soul into the people's cause, she would be stricken by a fever that would attack the seat of reason itself.

One of the most reliable pen-pictures of Théroigne was written at this period by George Forster, President of the University of Mainz, who was nominated by the people of that city to be their representative at Paris in the beginning of the Revolution. He dwelt on her intellectual gifts, threw light upon her position, and foreshadowed the brain trouble that was to overtake her before long. He says:

> Imagine, a five- or eight-and-twenty year-old brown-haired maiden, with the most candid face, and features which were once beautiful, and are still partly so, and a simple steadfast character full of spirit and enthusiasm; particularly something gentle in eye and mouth. Her whole being is wrapped up in her love of liberty. She talked much about the Revolution; her opinions were without exception strikingly accurate and to the point. The ministry at Vienna she judged with a knowledge of facts which nothing but peculiar readiness of observation could have given.
>
> She is from Luxemburg, and is naturally most eager for the freedom of her own country and for Germany. She speaks nothing but French, fluently and energetically, though not altogether correctly. But who speaks it correctly now? She has a strong thirst for instruction; says she wishes to go into the country and there study to supply the deficiencies of her education. She wishes for the company of a well-informed man, who can read and write well; and is ready to give him his board and two thousand *livres* a year. She is no more than a peasant-girl, she said, but has a taste for learning. She must still have enough to live upon, although she said she had used up her income, for she lives in quite good condition here and keeps a carriage.
>
> Six or seven weeks ago the furies who sit in the tribunes of the Convention dragged her out into the garden of the Tuileries, beat her about the head with stones, and would have drowned her in the basin if help had not fortunately arrived. But since that time, she has frightful headaches and looks wretchedly ill.

The worst was to come.

CHAPTER 10

La Salpêtrière

Few of the revolutionaries escaped a violent end. Nearly all Théroigne's associates suffered the final penalty of the law. Brissot, Barnave, Saint-Just, and Basire were guillotined. Pétion's body was found partially devoured by wild dogs in a field whither he had fled from the scaffold. Romme stabbed himself to escape the executioners, Condorcet took poison for the same purpose. Collot d'Herbois was deported. The deaths of Robespierre, Marat, Danton are familiar to everyone. But the fate that was meted out to Théroigne was as tragic as all these, and many may agree more tragic still.

For over twenty years she was shut up in a madhouse, babbling of liberty, of equality, and of the rights of man.

Many of her biographers stated that she went mad as a result of the ill treatment at the hands of the Jacobins women; Lamartine, de Goncourt, and Michelet are amongst the number. Beaulieu says that soon after the assault she was in an asylum; but Forster, as we know, saw her about two months later, and there appeared to be nothing worse the matter with her than that she complained of bad headaches.

On July 5th she was still attending to financial matters and wrote a business letter to MM. Le Couteulx et Cie, bankers to the Baron de Selys, about the settlement of a sum of one thousand five hundred and fifty-six *livres* claimed by the baron. The letter contains reference to the much-disputed jewellery. A receipt was sent to her on the 9th of the month. That autumn—it was the autumn that witnessed the execution of Marie-Antoinette—perhaps not till early in the following year, she suffered from mental aberration, which caused her to commit some absurdity or other which led to her arrest.

Her brother Joseph, whom she had helped to train as an artist in Rome, published a notice in the spring of 1794, warning the authorities that his sister's mental condition did not warrant her administering her own estate, and begging that she might be put under restraint for the sake of her own safety and of those about her. It is quite probable that he knew the risk she ran of imprisonment, and feared lest harsher treatment would be her lot when confined in a dungeon than if she were placed in a madhouse. An order to this effect was made out on June 30th, 1794, but by that time Théroigne had been in a house of detention for three days. Her room on the fourth floor of the Rue Honoré, No. 273, had been entered, her papers seized and sealed, and amongst her possessions was a sabre which the police confiscated.

Then Joseph Terwagne, perhaps fearing the guillotine for her, again addressed the authorities. He informed them that the mental state of his sister being incurable madness, he was prepared to take entire charge of her, and desired to claim her liberty. He offered to make himself entirely responsible, and to provide her with every form of assistance which humanity and fraternity could suggest. Moreover, he promised to take every precaution rendered necessary and prudent by her condition. He was convinced that her arrest was the result of actions performed under aberration of intellect.

On September 20th, 1794, her madness was certified to as of some standing, and she was removed from the house of detention in the Section Le Peletier and placed in an asylum in the Faubourg Marceau, no great distance from her brother's abode in the Rue Croulebarbe. In her lucid moments she appealed to friends or strangers to assist her in getting free. Once she leaned out of the window and called to a neighbour, who interested himself unavailingly in her position. Another time she had addressed a letter to Saint-Just, the olive-complexioned deputy for Aisne, which was afterwards found among his papers, and which bears evidences of a wandering mind. This letter was written two days before Saint-Just shared the fate of Couthon and Robespierre on July 28th, 1794.

> Citizen Saint-Just, I am still under arrest. I have lost precious time. I have written to you to beg you to send me two hundred *livres*, and to come and see me. I received no reply. I do not feel much gratitude towards the patriots for leaving me here, bereft of everything. It seems to me that they ought not to be indifferent that I am here, and that I am doing nothing. I sent you a letter in which I say that it is I who said I had friends in the palace of the emperor, that I was unjust as far as Citizen Bosque

was concerned, and that I am sorry about it. They told me that I had forgotten to sign the letter. That was want of attention on my part. I should be charmed to see you for a moment. If you cannot come to me, if your time does not permit it, could I not be accompanied on the way to see you?

I have a thousand things to say to you. It is necessary to establish the union; it is necessary for me to develop all my plans, to continue to write as I have written. I have great things to say. I can assure you that I have made progress. I have neither paper, nor light, nor anything; but even then, it would be necessary that I should be free to be able to write. It is impossible to do anything here. My stay has taught me something, but if I remain longer, if I remain longer without doing anything, without publishing anything, I should learn to despise the patriots and the civic crown. You know that there has been discussion, both about you and me, and that the proof of union is in the results. There must be fine writings to give strong impulses. You know my principles. I am grieved never to have spoken to you before my arrest.

I presented myself at your house. They told me that you were *déménagé*. It is to be hoped that the patriots will not leave me a victim to intrigue. I can still repair everything if you will aid me. But it is necessary that I should be where I shall be respected, for they neglect no means of showing contempt for me. I have already spoken to you of my plan. Whilst waiting until this can be arranged, until I have found a house where I can be safe from intrigue, where I can be worthily surrounded by virtue, I beg that they will send me back home.

I shall be under a thousand obligations if you will lend me two hundred *livres*.

Farewell.

★★★★★★

By this time Théroigne had been reduced to a sad state of helplessness. Carlyle describes it well:

The poor *demoiselle's* head and nervous system, none of the soundest, is so tattered and fluttered that it will never recover; but flutter worse and worse till it crack: and within year and day we hear of her in madhouse and strait-waistcoat, which proves permanent! Such brown-locked figure did flutter, and

223

inarticulately jabber and gesticulate, little able to *speak* the obscure meaning it had, through some segment of the eighteenth century of time.

Villiers saw her at the Hôtel Dieu in 1797, and described the vacant stare, the meaningless utterances which fell from her lips. On December 9th of that year she was transferred to the Salpêtrière; from there she went, on January 11th, 1800, to the Petites Maisons, where she remained until her return to the Salpêtrière on December 7th, 1807.

Her romantic chroniclers follow her even into the retreat of the insane.

The letters "published by the Vicomte de V——y," written in reality by Lamothe Langon, purport to be her correspondence when at La Salpêtrière. Their author claims that they contain the charms of fiction united with positive reality, of history more engaging than romance. He made her say:

> The tranquillity of the spot is insupportable. One might sleep through the whole day. The cannon of the Pont Neuf never thunders. There is no singing of the *Marseillaise* or the *Carmagnole* in the neighbouring streets. . . . The sovereign people, where are they?

Strange visions of crowds appeared to her in that quiet cell. She rarely knew she was alone.

> All our old friends become our enemies; follow one after the other. . . . If you could only see how they look at me; if you could only hear their plaints! . . . Danton, for example! . . . And Suleau—Suleau. He rarely leaves me. He speaks little; he stands apart; he places himself by the window, against the door. Sometimes he appears enveloped in the curtains of my bed, only his mutilated and bleeding head showing, . . . The rascal! He mocks at me, he offends my sight. . . . And I, sometimes I am frightened. Sometimes I charge at him, when he is not looking, and bury my finger-nails deep in his expressionless eyes.

Other ghostly visitors appear: Robespierre, his brother, Robespierre le Jeune, Egalité, and Mirabeau.

> The count chuckles, the prince grinds his teeth together, the lawyer plays foolish tricks. They say that their suffering is great.

They are experiencing terrible pains and penalties below. They await me.

And they vanish. Another chronicler gives a still more lurid glimpse of her madness.

She was seized with a fever, during which she raved of nothing but bloody heads and of devils demanding her as their prey. 'Do you not see,' she would exclaim, 'hell open under my feet, ready to swallow me up! Do you not see Suleau, with his head on, though bleeding, calling out to me, "Théroigne, you are my assassin! the furies of hell are waiting for you, to torment you through all eternity!"!'

But enough of such sensationalism.

Towards 1808 Théroigne had periods of greater lucidity, and recognised among the visitors at the Salpêtrière an official personage who had played a part in the Revolution. She heaped insults on his head, reproaching him for having betrayed the cause of the people. Several names have been suggested for this individual, among them those of Siéyès and of Regnaud de Saint-Jean d'Angély. At this time the latter was busying himself on her behalf, being anxious to improve her condition if possible.

On March 21st, 1808, he addressed a letter to the *Prefect* of the Department of Ourthe:

Monsieur, I beg you to make every inquiry possible at Méricourt, near to Liège, concerning the family of Mlle Théroigne. She has some money of her own, yet her relatives have left her in the hospital without resources and in a most deplorable condition.

I beg you will obtain all possible information as quickly as you can concerning the goods possessed and still in the possession of Mlle Théroigne,

It is believed that this unfortunate being has been robbed.

The *Prefect* of Ourthe put the matter into the hands of a subordinate, the *sous-Prefect* of Huy, on March 26th, 1808; but it was not until May 1809 that a reply came to this appeal. It was written to the *sous-Prefect* of Huy on April 28th, 1809, by Sieur N. Biron, the Mayor of Filat, as follows:

When I received the letter which you did me the honour to

write me on the 19th of this month, I hastened, sir, to make every inquiry possible concerning the supposed village of Méricourt, where the family of Mlle Théroigne were said to have resided.

However, no village of this name exists in the district of Xhoris, nor in the canton of Ferrières. But in seeking more deeply into the object of your inquiry, I have obtained some information concerning a lady who was known by this name, and who may have been a native of Méricourt in the department of Sambre and Meuse.

At the rise of the Revolution there arrived at Xhoris an adventuress, dressed in a riding-habit and known as Théroigne de Méricourt, who was visiting some of her relatives of the name of Terwagne in this district.

This lady spent some months in this country, and I believe I saw her myself sometimes in masculine clothes flirting with the *coquettes* of the neighbourhood, and sometimes in clothes more befitting her sex and in the company of certain frivolous young men. She suddenly disappeared, and they said that she went back to Paris, from which city she apparently had come thither.

Then he went on to say that the name of the family was Terwagne, but at that distance it was impossible for him to obtain better information concerning her relatives, although at Xhoris she might have distant connections who were living a simple and regular life on small but definite means.

During the interval which had occurred since his inquiry and the answer to it, Regnaud de Saint-Jean d'Angély had become Minister of State and might no doubt have used his authority to ameliorate the conditions in which Théroigne was living. Perhaps he had forgotten her existence by then, or, which is quite as probable, the authorities assured him that the manner in which she lived was more that of her own choice than of necessity. No change was made in her surroundings.

The last account of her is a medical one written by Esquirol in his work on *Insanity*, but it gives an exaggerated picture of her actions in the Revolution.

Téroenne or Théroigne de Méricourt, was a celebrated courtesan, born in the city of Luxemburg. She was of medium height, had chestnut-coloured hair, large blue eyes, a changeful physiognomy, and a sprightly, free, and even elegant carriage. The girl, in the opinion of some of honourable birth, and in that of others springing from the rank of courtesans, acted a truly deplorable part during the first years of the Revolution.

She was then from twenty-eight to thirty years of age. She devoted herself to the various chiefs of the popular party, to whom she was of service in most of the riotous disturbances, and attempted, especially on the 5th and 6th of October, 1789, to corrupt the Regiment of Flanders, by leading into its ranks women of ill-fame, and by distributing money among the soldiers. In 1790 she was sent into the city of Liège to arouse the people. She there took a military rank. She made herself remarkable among this unbridled populace, which was sent to Versailles on the 5th and 6th of October, 1790.

The Austrians arrested her in the month of January 1791. She was conducted to Vienna and confined in a fortress. The Emperor Leopold saw her, conversed with her, and caused her to be set at liberty in December of the same year. She returned to Paris, and once more appeared upon the stage during the period of the Revolution. She then made herself conspicuous upon the terraces of the Tuileries, and on the rostrum, haranguing the people with boldness, in order to bring them back to *moderation* and the Constitution.

This course cannot suit her long. The Jacobins shortly repair to Téroenne, and we immediately see her appear, a red bonnet upon her head, a sword by her side, and a pike in her hand, commanding an army of women. She took an active part in the events of September 1792. Although it may not be proved that she participated in the massacres, it is said, nevertheless, that she entered the court of the abbey and with her sword cut off the head of an unfortunate man whom they were conducting to the tribunal of this prison. We are assured that it was a former lover.

When the Directory was established and popular associations ceased, Théroigne lost her reason. She was taken to a house in the Suburb St. Marceau. They found among the papers of Saint-Just a letter from her, dated July 26th, 1794, in which signs of a wandering intellect are shown. In November 1800 she was sent to the Salpêtrière, and in the following month was transferred to the Petites Maisons, where she remained seven years. When the Administration of Hospitals caused the insane to be removed from the Petites Maisons, Théroigne returned to the Salpêtrière, September 1807. She was then about forty-seven years of age.

At the time of her admission she was very much agitated, reviling and threatening everybody, speaking only of liberty, of committees, of public safety, revolutionary committees, and accusing all who approached her of being moderates and royalists.

In 1808 a distinguished personage, who had figured as chief of a party, visited the Salpêtrière. Théroigne recognised him, raised herself from the bed of straw upon which she was lying, and overwhelmed the visitor with abusive language; accusing him of having abandoned the popular party, and of being a Moderate, *to whom a decree of the Committee of Public Safety would soon do justice.*

In 1810 she becomes more composed, and falls into a state of dementia, which enables us to observe traces of her early prevailing ideas. Théroigne was unwilling to wear any clothing. Every day, both morning and evening, and many times a day, she waters her bed, or rather the straw of it, with several buckets of water, lies down, and covers herself with her sheet only in summer, and with both sheet and coverlid in winter. She amuses herself in walking with naked feet in her cell, which was flagged with stone, and inundated with water. Severe cold causes her to change this regimen in no respect.

Never have they succeeded in inducing her to sleep in a night garment, nor to employ a second covering. During the last 21 three years of her life she was provided with a very large morning gown, which, however, she rarely put on. When it froze, and she had not water in abundance, she was accustomed to break the ice, and take the water which she obtained from it and wet her body, particularly her feet.

Although in a small and gloomy cell, very damp and without furniture, she enjoys good health, and pretends to be occupied with very important matters. She smiles at persons who accost her, and sometimes replies hastily, 'I don't know you,' and conceals herself under her covering. It is rare that she replies correctly. She often says, 'I do not know; I have forgotten.' If they insist, she becomes impatient, and talks to herself in a low voice. She articulates phrases, interspersed with the words for-

tune, liberty, committee, Revolution, rascal, warrant, decree, etc.
She applies many of them to the Moderates. She is angry and
transported with passion when opposed, especially when they
desire to prevent her from taking water. She once bit a companion with so much fury as to take out a piece of flesh.

The disposition of this woman had therefore outlived her
understanding. She rarely leaves her cell, generally remaining
there in bed. . . She takes but few steps, most frequently proceeding upon all fours, and extends herself upon the ground. . .
I have seen her devour straw, feathers, dried leaves, and morsels
of meat lying in the dirt. She drinks cistern water whilst they
wash the courts, although it may be dirty, preferring this drink
to every other.

I endeavoured to induce her to write. She traced a few words,
but was never able to complete a sentence. She never gave any
indication of hysteria. When we wished to obtain her portrait
in 1816, she willingly sat for it, but appeared to attach no importance to the work of the painter. . . .

This was the extraordinary representation of Théroigne by Gabriel.

On May 1st, 1817, her physical health gave way. She was taken to
the infirmary, where she died on June 9th, at the age of fifty-seven,
without for a moment being restored to reason. An autopsy showed
the abnormal condition of her brain.

Thus, at the hour when the great Napoleon was wearing out his
life in distant Saint Helena, the career of Théroigne de Méricourt
came to its sad close. It was difficult to see again, in the blotched, livid,
and fleshless creature she had become, the heroic charm, the clear
flaming eyes of the woman of the people, whose great love had not
been lavished upon a man or upon men, but upon an ideal, the passion
for justice, for liberty—for the Revolution.

Appendix

Théroigne and the Royalist Press

Reference has been made in the text to the treatment of Théroigne by the Royalist Press. Among the many journals which caricatured her, the *Actes des Apôtres* was perhaps the worst offender. The skit entitled "*Club de la Revolution*" appeared in No. 23. No. 32 contains a letter dated February 2nd, 1790, written from the Hôtel de Grenoble, in which Théroigne is supposed to say:

Your journal, *monsieur*, being consecrated to the purpose of spreading throughout the universe the new principles intended to ensure the happiness of France and of all other nations, I beg you to insert in one of your first demagogic works the beginning of a poem I wish to dedicate to one of the most illustrious sovereigns who has filled the chair of the nation with capability and weight. My righteous impatience to sing the praises of this great genius does not allow me to wait for the conclusion of the work which I have the honour of addressing you, if the public will deign to accept this feeble attempt by a feminine national muse. She dare not flatter herself that she will score a success with it, unless on account of the important topic she handles, a topic which should render her poem interesting to all posterity.

I am, with admiration of your demagogy, *monsieur*, your very humble and obedient servant, equal in rights and in knowledge of man,

Théroigne de Méricourt,
Wife of the Modern Sovereign.

Then follows a so-called "*herio-natio-epi-constitutiono-politicocomic*" poem entitled "*La Targetade*," beginning:

Je chante ce lourdaud, président de la France,
Et par droit de manège et par droit d'importance.

The first part of the Populus play referred to in chapter 3 appears in No. 38. Populus, Mirabeau, and Barnave are represented as her lovers. The Abbé Siéyès also plays a part.

In one act she is made to say:

O destins fortunés, triomphe glorieux!
Vingt sénateurs par jour remplissant tous nies voeux
Accourent à mes pieds, d'une flamme immortelle
Présenter à l'amour une offrande nouvelle.

She swears to Populus that she loves no one but him. Nevertheless, Populus has been told that Mirabeau is his rival. He offers to fight him; an offer that Mirabeau refuses on principle, for he never fights. The farce continues. Two more lovers appear, Barnave and Anon, under which guise Camille Desmoulins was indicated. At length the Secretary of the Assembly arrives and tells Théroigne that before the end of the day she must privately choose between her lovers. In doubt, Théroigne soliloquises:

O ciel, dans quel incertitude
Flottent mes sens et mes esprits!

She appeals to Mirabeau, regretting that she is not permitted to divide her affections amongst several, and asks him to remain at her feet at least till Populus comes. But he flees from her crying, "*Que le diable t'emporte.*"

In the end she makes it up with Populus.

Théroigne
Tu me verras, malgré ce soupçon trop injuste,
Fidèle à mes serments comma la diète auguste.

Populus
Dans cet heureux espoir, sans doute, il m'est bien doux
De mettre, avec men coeur, un trône à tes genoux.

Théroigne
Protège ces noeuds saints, ô dieu de la patrie!
Et que les Populus qui nous devront la vie,
De l'aristocratie ardens persécuteurs,
Deviennent potentats et régénerateurs;
Puisse le tendre amour sur leur jeune visage

231

Imprimer d'un époux la séduisante image;
Et que régulateurs des destins de l'état,
Chacun d'eux, soit un jour president du senat.

And so, the play closes. The following appears in No. 47 of the same journal.

This morning the beautiful Méricourt, displeased with her maid, spoke harshly to her. The servant, making a mistaken application of the first article of the Declaration of the Rights of Men and Women, dared to use her hands against our incomparable friend, and knocked her down in a manner quite new to Mlle Théroigne. The neighbours say she fell backwards and appeared to go into convulsions. Then she remained quiet for a time as though she were dead.

A bulletin as to her condition appeared in No. 49.

This divine maiden, restored by heaven . . . was within an ace of death.

Doctors, surgeons, and apothecaries were called in to relieve her, and the treatment which brought about a cure was by applications of discourses by M. de Gouay d'Arcy on her left temple, perorations by Target, and a harangue by Mirabeau steeped in salts of ammonia.

For a few numbers she was left in peace, and then followed coarse jokes in which Target and Mme de Stael figured.

In No. 94 Robespierre is supposed to refer to her in a letter to one Mlle Suzanne Forber.

You know Mlle Théroigne? We often speak of you. She is going to be married.

And he proceeds to ask his correspondent to look up certain records at Arras, her home, in order that she may trace Théroigne's descent from the noble family of the Comte de Térouenne. Some numbers later the reply to this letter comes, in which there is given a remarkable genealogical tree from which the "Semiramis of the Revolution," as Suzanne Forber names her, is supposed to have sprung.

In the interval another letter from Théroigne appears to her virtuous friends the Apostles, in which she signs herself "fraternally as demagogically, your sincere and faithful friend."

In No. 98 a marriage has been arranged between Quichotte-Hudibras-Rodomant-Gavachin, hitherto known as the Marquis de Saint-

Huruge, and Demoiselle Madelon-Friquet-Dulcinée-Théroigne de Méricourt, *majeure d'ans et mineure de coutume*, a widow by her first marriage with Cromwell-Honoré-Mirabeau; and this affords great distress to Populus.

Some numbers later she is affianced to Populus again, and a grand account of the national marriage celebrated at Surenne, near Paris, between M. Populus and Dlle Théroigne de Mere-y-court, is given.

The marriage day of Dona Térouenne was announced by a discharge of 60 guns in honour of the 60 districts of Paris, and 60 presidents were invited to the ceremony. The priest who pronounced the nuptial blessing called her the *rosière générale* of the French Empire, the star of the nation three times, the star of 39 provinces of the kingdom, the torch of 83 departments, and the people cried three times "*Vive Térouenne, vive Populus, vive Robespierre!*" There was a dinner, opera, ballet, and altogether a brilliant *fête*, after which Lady Térouenne, mounting her good steed, rides off to quell an insurrection and leaved Populus re-pining. At the close of twenty-eight printed pages he is con-soled and all ends well with the verse:

J'aimais Térouenne et j'ai perdu son coeur,
Pendant trois jours, men âme en fut émue;
Mais, à la fin, jugeant mieux mon malheur,
Je vis que ce n'était qu'une fille perdue.

The Apocalypse was a short way behind the *Actes des Apôtres* in profuseness of ridicule, but not at all in coarseness. In its pages Mme de Staël becomes a joint victim with Théroigne. In No. 3 the follow-ing appears:

Carried away by her patriotism, Théroigne made a speech at the Jacobins. She spoke with that victorious eloquence which mas-ters minds and obtains votes. Suddenly her voice grew weak, and in the middle of a phrase she went off into a dead faint. General consternation ensued. Barnave, Mirabeau, Le Chapeli-er, and Robespierre rushed towards the daughter of the Revo-lution and made her inhale aromatic vinegar. Dr. Guillotin was unfortunately absent, and Populus, distracted, ran to find him.

No. 4 contains a letter to the authors of the Apocalypse purporting to be from Mirabeau's head jockey. He has had the pleasure of reading the pages of their journal in Mlle Théroigne's *boudoir* when he went there to deliver his master's love-letters. He describes a banquet followed by a picnic to Longchamp, at which Théroigne, dressed in her favourite riding-habit, led the way mounted on a superb English bay. Mirabeau followed in a gorgeous "*wiski.*" Then came a number of others, and in the rear Mme de Stael and Talleyrand in a *berline.* When the cavalcade reached the *Bois de Boulogne,* the wheels of the *wiski* became entangled in the trees and it overturned, precipitating its occupant upon mother earth. Unfortunately, Le Chapelier's horses rushed upon the debris of the *wiski* and his *cabriolet* was upset, whilst the *berline* came down upon the rest. The resulting jumble must be read in the original to be appreciated.

In No. 7 there is a rechristening of many of the Paris streets. The Rue des Boucheries was to be renamed Rue Barnave; the Rue du Brave, Mirabeau; the Rue Tire-Boudin, Rue de Staël, and so on; while the Rue des Sept-Voies was to be known in future as Rue Théroigne.

Coarse jests run likewise through Nos. 10, 12, 14, 16, 18, and 19.

The *Journal de Pie* of February 11th, 1792, remarks that Théroigne was received well by the Jacobins, and that she had reversed her principles. A few days later the following appears in its pages:

> Mme D., having said aloud some days ago when she saw Mlle Théroigne de Méricourt that she wore a Jacobin air, was accosted in the Rue S. Martin, near the Café de l'Estrade, by four *sansculottes* who struck her a violent blow on the chest which knocked her down. She was saved from the hands of these brigands by an honest gentleman of her acquaintance who put them to flight. Someone cried out, 'We must complain to M. Pétion.' One of the brigands turned round and shouted back, 'He won't hurt us.' We leave it to honest folk to make their comments on this expression, clear as it is to us.

On February 27th, 1792, there is an account of a duel between Théroigne and a lady aristocrat. They did not catch hold of each other by the hair, as the spectators half expected they would, but they arranged a meeting in the *Bois de Boulogne.* Instead of using gunpowder, their seconds loaded the pistols with powder for the hair, and all the shots missed fire. This joke displeased the principals so deeply that they avenged themselves upon the perpetrators for the affront offered to their courage.

The *Martyrologe National,* the *Chronique du Manège,* and the *Feuille du Jour* were amongst the papers that amused themselves at Théroigne's expense. A quotation from the pages of *Le Rodeur* will serve to complete this short account of her claims to be regarded as a never-failing target for the shafts of wit let loose by aristocrat pamphleteers:

'*Le Rodeur' Réuni au Chroniqueur Secret de la Révolution*
Mlle Théroigne, who continually appears as the object of the good and bad pleasantries of MM. the *soi-disant* forty-five directors of the National Company of the *Ades des Apôtres*, is not an imaginary being, as many ignorant people have believed. She is an amiable young lady of two-and-twenty, born in the Luxemburg. She was at Rome when M. Bailli sounded at Versailles the destruction of all the orders, and hastened to return to the banks of the Seine to protect the dawning liberty of the French. Her enthusiasm for the rights of man soon made itself felt, and, as she took up the cause of the people with great warmth, the forty-five apostles imagined an intrigue between her and M. Populus.

This admirable girl has neither father nor mother; but she enjoys an income of ten thousand *livres*, which she shares with the honourable architects of the French Constitution, The *honorables* to whom she gives dinner have praised her; she has become noticeable in the *Salle du Manège*, assisting regularly at all the meetings, at all the debates, and encouraging by gesture and voice the honourable members. Revolutionary committees have been held at her house. They have driven many nails into the machinery of the Constitution; they have so exalted the rights of man that the forty-five apostles, seized by utter aristocratic impotence, have permitted themselves every form of ridicule and detraction that jealous rage could devise. Into what gall have they not dipped their pens of base alloy in the process of besmirching so vast a reputation as that of our heroine!

How correct was Voltaire when he called envy the eighth human sin! But that which will astonish our descendants and the centuries which are still in the embryo in the abyss of time, is that among the friends of Mlle Théroigne there is not one who has dared publicly to take up the cause of this adorable nymph and to prove her inviolable in the eyes of the forty-five apostles. The *honorables* have maintained a far too modest silence in this matter, and have contented themselves with meriting the superb device of Louis IV.:

Regna Assignata
Page terra marique parta.

Note on Some Portraits of Théroigne de Méricourt

1. A painting at the Musée Carnavalet attributed to Vestier. Théroigne is wearing a ribbon in her fair hair and a fichu over a yellow bodice. Frontispiece.

2. A painting at the Musée Carnavalet. Artist unknown.

3. A painting attributed to Greuze, exhibited at the Trocadero in 1878. Described by Henry Jouin in *Notices des Portraits Nationaux* (1879). "*En buste, la tête tournée vers l'épaule gauche; robe bleue, ouverte, fichu croisé; ceinture blanche; grand bonnet sur les cheveux.*"

4. Portrait at the *Bibliothèque Nationale*, wearing a cap of linen over her hair, which falls over her shoulders in ringlets. One breast uncovered. Reproduced by Dayot.

5. A drawing by Danlou; wearing an Amazon hat with tricoloured ribbons. In the possession of the Vicomte de Reiset. and reproduced in the *Carnet*.

6. An engraving by Devritz of No. 4.

7. Portrait appearing as a frontispiece to M. Marcellin Pellet's *Life of Théroigne*, and discovered by him.

8. A sketch by Raffet reproduced in Lamartine's *Histoire des Girondins*," inspired probably by the portrait in the Bibliothèque Nationale.

9. The profile drawing by Gabriel, made at the La Salpêtrière in 1816 when Théroigne was mad. This is the only authentic portrait.

9 781782 828938